Literature for Change

'*This compelling volume shows why literature matters, why literature in other languages matters, and – above all – why research into literature in other languages matters. Ten case studies, from Arabic to German, from medieval to contemporary, reveal the multilayered, multilingual power of literature to change lives and societies – including in the troubled present.*'
— **Neil Kenny, Senior Research Fellow and Professor of French, University of Oxford, UK**

'Literature for Change *is an ambitious, important and timely intervention which makes a compelling case for the ways in which studying literature through a foreign language develops citizens able to navigate the unprecedented challenges of climate change, increasingly isolationist governance, global capitalism and artificial intelligence. A seminal text.*'
— **Elizabeth Wren-Owens, Reader in Italian and Translation Studies, University of Cardiff, UK**

'Literature for Change *dives headlong into the gaping holes of contemporary cultural crises, and bounces back as an impassioned series of manifestoes bridging art and life. The thoughtful sequence of essays democratizes literature's transformative qualities. Running the gamut from major to minor and even ultra-minor modes of writing, the book's worldliness induces readers into the uncharted waters of an intellectual trance. Literature unlocks multitudes of empathy, carrying us through and across languages, nations, and genres that are ever expansive and mind-altering.*'
— **Yasser Elhariry, Associate Professor, Dartmouth College, USA**

Understanding Languages, Cultures and Societies

Understanding Languages, Cultures and Societies is an open access book series that supports and advances the integrated study of languages, cultures, and societies. Published in association with the Institute of Languages, Cultures and Societies (ILCS), one of the principal goals of the series is to demonstrate the subject area's significant contribution to addressing questions of current global concern. Proposals are welcomed for the series that focus on any geographical area or time period and engage with one or more of the following interrelated aims:

1. To explore issues of cultural and/or societal importance;
2. To foster and promote cross-language and cross-cultural study;
3. To chart new directions in the broadly-defined disciplinary field of Languages, Cultures and Societies.

Emphasising the interconnected nature of linguistic, cultural and social inquiry, the series encourages work that crosses disciplinary boundaries, engages with other areas of the educational and research landscape, and connects with creative practice. *Understanding Languages, Cultures and Societies* tackles issues that are at the core of the subject area's knowledge production, serving both as a means for disseminating new, original research and as a catalyst for developing innovative research agendas.

Series Editors

Editorial Advisory Board

ILCS INSTITUTE OF LANGUAGES CULTURES AND SOCIETIES | SCHOOL OF ADVANCED STUDY UNIVERSITY OF LONDON

Literature for Change

The Case for Literary Research Across Languages and Cultures

Edited by Charles Burdett, Joseph Ford, Godela Weiss-Sussex and Naomi Wells

UNIVERSITY OF LONDON PRESS

Available to purchase in print or download
for free at https://uolpress.co.uk

First published 2026 by
University of London Press
Senate House, Malet St, London WC1E 7HU

A CIP catalogue record for this book is available from The British Library.

ISBN 978-1-911507-78-9 (hardback)
ISBN 978-1-911507-79-6 (paperback)
ISBN 978-1-911507-82-6 (.epub)
ISBN 978-1-911507-81-9 (.pdf)
ISBN 978-1-911507-80-2 (.html)

DOI https://doi.org/10.63674/uwth6019

Cover credit: Photo by Eduardo Goody on Unsplash.

Cover design for University of London Press by Nicky Borowiec.
Book design by Nigel French.
Text set by Westchester Publishing Services UK in Source Sans Pro,
designed by Paul D. Hunt.

Contents

Notes on contributors

Heike Bartel is Professor of Health Humanities and German Studies at the University of Nottingham. Her research background is in literary and gender studies. She is working at the interface of literature, art and health and leads interdisciplinary projects with individuals affected by mental health problems, clinicians, artists, and arts and humanities scholars. She is Nottingham's lead for the 'Lived Experience Workstream' of the EDIFY consortium (Eating disorders: Delineating illness and recovery trajectories to inform personalised prevention and early intervention in young people; MR/W002418/1).

Emma Bond is Professor of Italian and Comparative Studies at the University of Oxford. Her research explores the legacies of colonialism and empire in visual and material cultures. Recent publications include *Scotland's Transnational Heritage: Legacies of Empire and Slavery* (2022) and *Curating Worlds: Museum Practices in Contemporary Literature* (2024). She is Project Lead on the UKRI-funded project 'Reassessing (Hi)stories of Early Italian Colonialism: The Afterlives of Luigi Robecchi Bricchetti's African Collections in Italy and Beyond' (2025–8).

Sarah Bowden is Professor of German and Medieval Studies at King's College London, where she is also Head of the Department of Languages, Literatures and Cultures. She is the author of *Bridal-Quest Epics: A Revisionary Approach* (2012) and *Writing Sin in the German Lands, 1050–1215: Confession, Penance, and Textuality* (2025).

Charles Burdett is Professor of Italian and Director of the Institute of Languages, Cultures and Societies (School of Advanced Study (SAS), University of London). The principal areas of his research are literary culture under Fascism; travel writing; the Italian colonial presence in Libya and East Africa and its legacies; theories of inter-cultural contact; and the representation of Islam and the Islamic world in recent Italian literature and culture. He was the Principal Investigator of the Arts and Humanities Research Council (AHRC) large grant, 'Transnationalizing Modern Languages: Mobility, Identity, and Translation in Modern Italian Cultures' (2014–18).

Joseph Ford is Senior Lecturer in French Studies at the Institute of Languages, Cultures and Societies (ILCS), based in the University of London's School of Advanced Study, where he specialises in contemporary French and Francophone Literature and Culture, with specific interests in North Africa. He has written on theories and discourses of world and comparative literature in relation to the wider Francosphere, on memory and responsibility in Europe, and on multilingualism and education in the UK. Together with Emanuelle Santos, he is the co-convenor of the Decolonising Languages Network.

Abir Hamdar is Professor in the School of Modern Languages and Cultures at Durham University and a practising playwright. She works on the medical humanities, cultural disability studies and cultural representations of death. Her publications include *The Female Suffering Body: Illness and Disability in Modern Arabic Literature* (2014) and the co-edited volume *Islamism and Cultural Expression in the Arab World* (2015).

Reham Hosny is Professor of Digital Literary and Cultural Criticism at Minia University and a Gates Scholar at Cambridge Digital Humanities. She is a member of King's College, Cambridge, and an Associate Fellow at the Leverhulme Centre for the Future of Intelligence at the University of Cambridge. Her research, supported by the British Academy and the Gates Cambridge Trust, among others, examines how AI and digital technologies reshape cultural expression, power relations and knowledge production, with a particular focus on Global South contexts.

Anja Rekeszus completed her PhD at King's College London, working with Ben Schofield and Catherine Smale. With a background in Romanticism and transnational fairy tales, her recent research has taken her in new directions, such as her participatory research project 'Re-telling the Urban Fox', which she undertook as an Inclusion, Participation and Engagement Fellow at SAS. She is especially interested in how storytelling in the broadest sense acts as an interface between humans and the more-than-human environment, in particular, how we view and identify with landscapes and animals. Anja is currently a Departmental Lecturer in German at the University of Oxford.

Emanuelle Santos is Associate Professor in Modern Languages at the University of Birmingham. Her research focuses on the intersections between the cultures of the Portuguese-speaking world, postcolonial studies and theories of world literature, drawing attention to the global–local dialectics in epistemology and literary and critical theory. She is the author of *The Late Postcolonial Condition: Twenty-first-century Reconfigurations in the Literatures of Portuguese-speaking Africa* (2025). Her work also addresses representations of race, gender and sexuality, memory studies, world-systems theory and decolonial critique, especially with regards to structures of inequality, oppression and hegemony.

Rachel Scott is Associate Professor in World and Hispanic Literatures at Royal Holloway, University of London, where she specialises in medieval and early modern Iberian literatures. Her research explores cross-cultural exchange and translation, focusing recently on the European reception of fables from the Arabo-Islamic world. Her publications include *Celestina and the Human Condition in Early Modern Spain and Italy* (Tamesis, 2017) and *Al-Andalus in Motion: Travelling Concepts and Cross-Cultural Contexts* (Boydell & Brewer, 2021).

Nicola Thomas is Lecturer in German Studies at Lancaster University. Her research explores cultural ways of knowing space, time and the environment across languages. Her first monograph, *Space, Place and Poetry in English and German, 1960–1975* (Palgrave, 2018), looked at engagements with place and landscape in the work of a range of writers working in the twentieth century. She is currently co-leading, with Dr Blake Ewing, a British Academy Knowledge Frontiers interdisciplinary research project on 'Wetland Times', comparing time, language and concepts across three global wetland landscapes.

Carol Tully is Professor Emerita of German at Bangor University. She studied German and Spanish at Strathclyde and completed her doctorate at Queen Mary London. She has since established an international reputation as a scholar in the area of European cultural exchange in the nineteenth century with a primary focus on Germany and Spain, and was the principal investigator on the AHRC-funded projects 'European Travellers to Wales 1750–2010' (http://etw.bangor.ac.uk) and 'Travellers to Wales' (http://footsteps.bangor.ac.uk).

Godela Weiss-Sussex is Emerita Professor of Modern German Literature at the Institute of Languages, Cultures and Societies at SAS, University of London, Co-Director of the Centre for the Study of Contemporary Women's Writing and Emeritus Fellow at King's College, Cambridge. Her main research interests lie in the culture and literature of the twentieth and twenty-first centuries in the following areas: women's writing, the works of German-Jewish writers produced in Germany and in exile, multi- and translingualism and postmigrant imaginaries of belonging.

Naomi Wells is Senior Lecturer in Italian and Spanish with Digital Humanities at the Institute of Languages, Cultures and Societies and the Digital Humanities Research Hub at the School of Advanced Study, University of London. Her recent research focuses on multilingualism on the internet and social media, and sits at the intersection of digital humanities, sociolinguistics, migration studies, and translation and cultural studies. She has a wider interest in supporting cross-languages digital research in her role as joint editor of the Digital Modern Languages section of the *Modern Languages Open* journal.

Introduction: making the case for literary research across languages and cultures

Charles Burdett, Joseph Ford, Godela Weiss-Sussex and Naomi Wells

In her 2010 publication *Not for Profit: Why Democracy Needs the Humanities*, the US philosopher Martha Nussbaum starts her analysis of the crucial educational importance of the humanities with the sobering recognition that '[w]e are in the midst of a crisis of massive proportions and grave global significance [. . .]: a world-wide crisis in education'.[1] Writing fifteen years on, in 2025, we recognise that this crisis has not passed, as the impact of isolationist governance, unbridled global capitalism, artificial intelligence and accelerated climate change continues to rise. The need for the humanities to equip citizens with the capacity to engage with these challenges is, thus, more urgent than ever, as it is the humanities that foster the abilities we need for the 'creation of a world culture capable of constructively addressing the world's most pressing problems' and to educate 'complete citizens who can think for themselves, criticize tradition, and understand the significance of another person's sufferings and achievements'.[2]

Of course, honing these skills is the task and the domain of all the humanities subjects. But the study of literature has unique and crucial aspects to offer in this regard, as we will argue and exemplify through selected case studies in this volume – each of which makes the case for the value of engaging with literature in the curricula of schools and universities and in the academic research agenda, in particular in the disciplinary field of modern languages, or languages, cultures and societies as it is increasingly known. This is not to defend a tradition of philological endeavour for the sake of it, but to expound and emphasise the acute importance of literary studies in the world we live in.

Literature – by which we mean imaginative writing in prose, poetry or dramatic form that transports ideas, emotions and aesthetic values – is one of the profoundest expressions of the human; in fact, it may be seen as an archive of human experience, shaped through language. By reading literary works, therefore, we can gain access to and relate to ways of thinking other than our own. George Eliot put this perfectly in 1856 when she described her art as 'the nearest thing to life; it is a mode of amplifying experience and extending our contact with our fellow men beyond the bounds of our personal lot'.[3] More recently, in 2024, the Israeli author David Grossman reminded us how far-reaching this contact with the experience of others can be: in an interview in *Die Zeit*, he explained that literature 'stärkt und erweitert [. . .] den Kontakt mit dem Leben, es dehnt die Oberfläche der Seele aus, die mit der Komplexität des Lebens in Berührung kommt' [strengthens and widens [. . .] our contact with life, it expands the surface of the soul as it encounters the complexity of life].[4]

Literature, thus, gives us access to other worlds, but it also enables us to experience the commonalities of being human across cultures. Literature enhances empathy; it gives us a vocabulary of emotional and psychological literacy. Of course, anthropology, geography, psychology and a range of other social sciences do this, too, but as Dorrit Cohn puts it, it is the 'principal privilege of the creative writer: to present the psyche of his subjects "omnisciently"'.[5] The epistemological uniqueness of the literary text allows the reader access to the interiority of its characters in a way that remains inaccessible to any other approach; it enables the experience of living in a certain world – rather than just diagnosing it from the outside.

No wonder, then, that this experiential subtlety develops the reader's capacity for empathy: Rick Rylance reports on psychological experiments showing not only that empathy grows with reading fiction,[6] but also that literary fiction that does not reaffirm convention and readers' expectations trains the mind in this way: 'social experiences [. . .] presented in literary fiction often disrupt our expectations. Readers of literary fiction must draw on more flexible interpretive resources to infer the feelings and thoughts of characters.'[7]

By eliciting empathy – and by so doing sowing the seeds of the will to action – literature has the power to promote change both on a global scale and in more localised ways. We could cite George Orwell's *Animal Farm* (1945) or Margaret Atwood's *The Handmaid's Tale* (1985), but pursuing literary studies in a languages and cultures setting allows us to see the power of literature across different scales and contexts. Taking the specific example of German literature, *Das Tränenhaus* [The House of Tears], a novel published by Gabriele Reuter in 1909, with its moving exploration of the plight of unmarried mothers in Wilhelmine Germany, illustrates this point. The book caused a minor scandal on its publication, but had a tangible impact on social policy, as it informed the campaign to improve state provision of maternity care for women giving birth out of wedlock.[8] There are many other examples of literary works across languages and cultures that have, in similar ways, highlighted social blind spots or deficiencies and have brought about change, through cognitive as well as affective engagement.

Once regarded as a central part of the curricula of Western democracies in the aftermath of the Second World War, books and the act of reading books are now increasingly seen as a threat to authoritarian and extreme right-wing agendas and social imaginaries in the United States and other parts of the world. Bans, which have very often involved removing books from schools and public libraries, target so-called 'anti-American' books that address themes of race, gender and LGBTQIA+ rights. It is notable that governments that divest from the importance of literary education – with the reasoning that studying books is less important than, say, STEM subjects – appear at the same time deeply threatened by the capacity of literature, and of those who study literature, to challenge authoritarianism and nefarious political agendas.[9] For as Reham Hosny highlights in this volume in relation to authoritarian regimes in the Middle East and North Africa (MENA) region, literature can function as both 'an archive and act of defiance' by voicing counter-narratives that challenge those of dominant power structures.

Combined with factual knowledge and a political will, it is 'narrative imagination' – to use Nussbaum's term – that can be the motor for change.[10] But narrative imagination does not only work towards eliciting empathy, and literature's potential for change does not only lie in its affective power. Literary fiction is also uniquely well placed to explore contingencies, to explore the 'what if'; in this sense, literary writing is nothing less than a laboratory of ideas that can act as beacons for transformation. Encapsulating this aspect of potentiality and futurity, Gabriele Reuter's contemporary, the activist and novelist Adele Schreiber, described works of fiction as 'die Spiegel [. . .], die uns die Strahlen kommender Zeiten zuwerfen' [the mirrors that show us the rays of times to come].[11]

To stay with the example of literature in German, some of the postmigrant writing we currently see emerging in German-language publications is exploring precisely this potentiality. Tomer Gardi's *broken german* (2016), for instance, ends with the hymnic celebration of a call shop in the centre of Berlin in which a multitude of languages mix with one another, 'wunderschön und lebendig' [incredibly beautifully and full of life].[12] This is an engaging image of vibrancy and conviviality, a hopeful encapsulation of the enrichment to be gained through cultural and linguistic plurality and, ultimately, it is an image of a society that embraces – rather than fears – heterogeneity. Gardi's book shows how the non-homogeneous, the hybrid and the fluid can be made narratable, and it is an exemplary model of an artistic endeavour that works towards 'undoing [. . .] modes of Othering'.[13] This is a literature that is generative and creative; it creates social imaginaries that, by transcending the boundaries of culture, can play a decisive part in societal transformation.

If all of this contributes to making the case for *reading* literature, it does not quite capture the particularity of *literary study*. For our argument, then, it is important to go further and draw attention to the fact that analysis of literary texts asks us to engage in a complex process of understanding that goes beyond gaining access to the mere content of any given text. Indeed, the study of literature engenders a way of thinking that equips us for an active and reflective engagement with the world. As Nicholas Harrison reminds us, '[a]ll writing, scientific/theoretical, "literary" or otherwise, demands interpretation', whether that is about unveiling hidden agendas or cultural assumptions in science, journalism or literary writing.[14] However, literary writing, in the way it can suspend reference and meaning in the world – in the way literary discourse operates as at once *rooted in* and *detached from* reality – might be seen to actively invite readers, as Harrison puts it, to think in creative and critical ways of making and remaking their worlds.[15]

Researching and teaching literary texts speaks precisely to this endeavour. Through academic engagement with literature, we uncover and make visible the discourses and ideologies that inform any given text; we foster the capacity for a way of reading that is attentive, critical and that discerns subtle detail; and we highlight how aesthetic form and content work together to construct or enhance the power of the text. Importantly, we do this in a way that does not negate the pure pleasure of reading. Avoiding a stance where 'a text is being diagnosed rather than heard', we aim to 'give equal weight to cognitive and affective aspects of aesthetic response',[16] to balance analysis and experience.

To explain and exemplify how this kind of literary research and teaching works, let us consider the definition of literature proposed by the scholar of German realism, Martin Swales, as 'an enriching reflection of and on being human in the world'.[17] The condensed brevity of this wording conceals the fact that there are four separate dimensions of analysis referenced here that need to be engaged with to comprehend literary texts fully: the condition of 'being human' requires psychological and affective understanding, and representations of 'being human in the world' can only be understood on the basis of a good knowledge of the society and culture that informs any given text. Furthermore, an understanding of literary writing as a reflection *of* a world (enabling the experience of it) and a reflection *on* the world (pointing to the text's inherent analytical quality), emphasises the multi-layered nature of literature. It is the task of literary research to clarify and lay bare the often-hidden entanglement and interaction of these layers. For, following Paul Ricoeur, we have to keep in mind that every mimetic act is a redescription, an interpretive, creative act.[18] Even the realism of Fontane, Dickens and Flaubert is not an unmediated record of the social world, but at the same time as depicting the real, it is also an interrogation of the conventions and assumptions of the real. Their novels show us the materiality and also the assumptions and values of the social world in which they are set – not as existentially unalterable entities, but as products of a particular culture and age. They present a world – and at the same time question it or allude to the intangible truths beyond the material and social manifestations. Theodor Fontane expressed this duality through reference to the 'tangible' and the 'true' in his essay *Unsere lyrische und epische Poesie seit 1848* [Our lyric and epic poetry since 1848] (1851): 'Der Realismus will nicht die bloße Sinnenwelt und nichts als diese; er will am allerwenigsten das bloß Handgreifliche, aber er will das Wahre.' [Realism does not want the mere world of the senses and nothing but this; least of all it wants the merely tangible, rather it wants what is *true*.][19]

Exposing this duality and uncovering the truth about social experience, which exceeds the fact of that experience, is one of the tasks of literary research. Or, to put it differently, the particular value of studying literature lies in the double reading, the 'aboutness' of literature. A reading of Thomas Mann's novel *Buddenbrooks* (1901), for instance, provides us with a wealth of detail, materiality and insights into the experience of a middle-class Hanse merchant family's life. At the same time, an analytical approach reveals how, through subtly changing leitmotifs, through symbolism of objects and locations, and through a gradual move from sturdy matter-of-fact realism to highly-strung aestheticism in the course of the novel, Mann provides us – without it needing to be said – with a study of social, moral and psychological decline.

Textual analysis thus leads to an understanding of the essential interpretability of the written word, but studying the literary text also leads to a grasp of the multi-valency, specifically of literary texts. It enables the experience of simultaneously holding different levels or even 'cross-currents of meaning'[20] at the same time. Students of literature learn to accept and cope with ambiguity and uncertainty, as they work on a complex text such as Goethe's *Faust*. Is *Faust* the study of a man's hubris as he vies with the gods? Is it the tragedy of the limitations of man? Is it a social tragedy about class and gender? Any attempt to provide a positive answer to these questions that doesn't also allow for the equal validity of the other possibilities is doomed to fail, as any attempt to reduce this text – or even the character of Faust himself – to a single interpretation does the text an injustice. Instead, what the study of the text reveals is that in order to understand the full complexity of Goethe's work, the need for clear-cut, single-strand simplification must be abandoned and an openness to a multiplicity of perspectives must be striven for.

Being able to do this multi-valent reading and this juggling of perspectives and interpretations in a language other than one's own is hugely empowering. Perhaps, we might say, it is a squaring of the possibilities afforded by language learning, as the bilingual or multilingual speaker's ability to engage with the world from several perspectives at once is equivalent to the literary analyst's ability to hold several meanings and perspectives at the same time. Taken together, the study of literature in another language not only means more voices, more contingencies, but also promises the deepening of experience, culturally framed. The starkness and psychological intensity of Hamsun's novels, the didacticism of

Brecht's texts and the social detail of Zola's works not only give us access to new worlds, but also to new ways of looking at the world. Building on Swales's definition of literature, then, we might propose to frame the study of literature in other languages as *the study of reflections of and on being human in the world through the lens of culture and language.*

Literary research in another language allows us a deeper understanding of the experience (in various positionalities) of living in a different culture – expressed in the framework of a language and aesthetic configurations that may be honed by specific traditions and influences. In her contribution to this volume, Sarah Bowden highlights the importance of studying texts from different eras to reveal the origins and the richness of such traditions. They may include untranslatable expressions of experience particular to this culture; take the idea of *Heimat* in German, for instance, a concept that is historically and ideologically enriched and only fully understandable with that knowledge of its tradition. And it may include literary conventions like the magical realism of Latin American writers, or embedded and nested narratives that emerge from Arabic storytelling and can be traced to early Sanskrit literature (see Rachel Scott, this volume), or Japanese *haiku*, all of which continue to influence authors from those and other parts of the world to this day.

Literary analysis enables transcultural and translingual perspectives and is a necessary background to any act of translation, whether linguistic or cultural. A recent study titled 'Interpreting communities: small, minority and minor literatures in Europe', for instance, set out to explore how being ascribed minority status provides a catalyst for literary writing, and privileges or forces particular forms of representation and aesthetic intervention. The study was set up as a cross-European comparative project, and thus a discerning analysis demanded deep cultural and linguistic understanding of individual cultures, conventions and languages, as well as great interpretative subtlety. Only on this basis was it possible to understand commonalities and (cultural and social) differences of literary strategies and contextualisations.[21]

The wider point is that no culture exists as a discrete formation but is the result of the complex interweaving of practices, lifeways and linguistic usages that are the inevitable result of histories of human mobility. A transnational approach to literature focuses on how texts written at different periods of time enable us to see the operation of the circulation of people, ideas and modes of behaviour. This is not to suggest that borders do not exist or that, in certain circumstances, they are not very tightly controlled. It is, however, to suggest that borders are contingent, porous and able only to obstruct – rather than impede – the effects of the movement of people and culture. By developing an approach that sees culture and territory as associated in ways that are fluid and constantly changing, we are far better equipped to address the social and psychological realities of mobility and migration and we are far better equipped to explore the legacies of centuries of European colonialism as they have been expressed through literary production. Over recent years, to take the example of literature in Italian,[22] the history of Italian colonialism and its legacies have been addressed by such writers as Gabriella Ghermandi and Igiaba Scego whose work has examined from a post- and de-colonial position how deeply the history of involvement in Africa is ingrained within Italy's transcultural past, its present and its likely future.[23] On the question of migration to Italy, texts like Amara Lakhous's *Divorzio all'islamica a viale Marconi* (2010) or Shirin Ramzanali Fazel's *Io e l'Islam* (2020), co-written with Simone Brioni, explore in detail both the nature of the transcultural present and the persistence of stereotypes with long antecedents.[24]

To highlight, as we do here, the unique contributions of literary research must not be understood as an effort to silo off the study of literature to an isolated or even elitist activity to be practised by the privileged few. While we might point to external forces that have sought to marginalise literary research to the sidelines of academia, there is an equal risk in highlighting the 'specialness' of literary research that we become overly defensive in demarcating the boundaries of the field.

To better understand such dangers, it is useful to take a longer view of the relationship between literature and other forms of knowledge. Literature had historically been understood to much more fluidly encompass different forms of knowledge, but from the seventeenth century onwards, the increasing 'scientification' of knowledge and associated consolidation of disciplinarity saw literature, and the humanities more broadly, increasingly placed in opposition to the natural sciences. Through this process, the sciences established the primacy of observation and facticity over imagination and fiction in ways that increasingly determined the evaluative criteria of research more widely.[25]

The consolidation of the social sciences, particularly sociology and anthropology, was also viewed as threatening what Vincent Debaene describes as 'the special prerogative of literature' in taking humankind as their object, leading, he argued, to an increasing marginalisation of literary study to an isolated focus on form.[26] Further disputes came to the fore in response to the emergence of cultural studies in the post-war years, which some literary researchers saw as a threat to both literature as a privileged object of study and to the study of literature in isolation from real-world concerns.[27]

These disciplinary territorial battles fought across the nineteenth and twentieth centuries have meant that literature and literary research have often suffered from being simultaneously dismissed as irrelevant to the serious business of 'research', while also being exalted to what Cary Nelson and Dilip Parameshwar Gaonkar describe as 'a timeless aesthetic realm outside history'.[28] In reality, as with many disciplinary disputes, such divisions served to obscure the ongoing interplay between literature, the sciences and the wider world throughout this period. For example, moving beyond the well-trodden 'two cultures' debate, Robert Craig and Ina Linge's volume on the language of science and literature around 1900 highlights the strong crosscurrents of epistemic and aesthetic exchange between literature and the biological sciences in and beyond this period.[29] In recent decades, the work of literary scholars has been crucial in pushing literary research to engage with broader social and political contexts, for instance that of postcoloniality (see Emanuelle Santos in this volume). Edward Said, in particular, called out the solipsism of literary theorists who refused to engage with the 'worldliness' of texts and the historical conditions in which they are created.[30] While, as Santos emphasises, postcolonial literary studies in more recent years has shown a tendency to withdraw from the political, decolonial literary research provides a renewed emphasis on the agency of the critic who is conscious of the aim and intentions of their 'worldly reading'. Cultural studies, equally, is arguably better understood not as an attempt to displace literary research but rather, as Stuart Hall emphasises, as an effort to impel such intellectual work to be reconfigured 'as a practice which always thinks about its intervention in a world in which it would make some difference'.[31]

Alongside such developments from within literary and cultural studies, there have been efforts in other disciplinary areas, particularly in the social sciences, to reconsider how literary work might more actively inform their own practices. The turn in areas such as anthropology to more critical perspectives on the purported 'objectivity' of research led to an increasing foregrounding of the complexities of human subjectivity in ways that were more closely aligned with literary perspectives. James Clifford and George Marcus's seminal volume on 'writing culture', in particular, sought to bring to the fore the poetics of ethnographic writing and the 'literary procedures [that] pervade any work of cultural representation'.[32]

Their work shines a light on the specific ways literature and literary research can contribute more broadly to knowledge production in terms of their ability to go beyond the limitations of scientific description of a purportedly objective reality. Such a perspective is captured in literary form in Jorge Luis Borges's short story *El etnógrafo*, in which the ethnographer of the title returns from a period of fieldwork unwilling to reveal 'the secret' he has learnt, declaring instead that 'Ahora que poseo el secreto, podría enunciarlo de cien modos distintos y aun contradictorios' [Now that I possess the secret, I could articulate in one hundred different and even contradictory ways].[33] The emphasis of literature and literary research on the unstable nature of meaning and the limitations of language to express a singular objective reality offers a vital contribution to understanding the complexities of our current time. Lisa Lowe, for example, argued that the global conditions of recent decades 'have pressed the empirical social sciences to its epistemological limits'.[34] Using the example of globalisation, she highlighted how its cultural mediations, including literary representations, provide the space and language for both critically interpreting global processes and, most importantly, for imagining the transformation and reorganisation of the current social order. In this volume, Anja Rekeszus further explores how processes of collaborative storytelling can provide communities with imaginative ways of engaging with complex social issues such as gentrification and of envisioning new forms of community action. As captured in the title of this volume, it is the capacity for literature and those who study it to imagine new realities beyond those captured by the scientific description of the world as it currently exists that arguably represents its greatest contribution to knowledge.

In order to fully realise this contribution, it is vital for literary researchers to look outwards and explore through collaborations with other disciplinary fields how such perspectives might be more directly brought to bear on other fields of knowledge. There is, nevertheless, the risk in interdisciplinary collaborations of literary researchers becoming marginal or subservient to more powerful and dominant fields. In particular, the value of interdisciplinary collaboration must be balanced with an acknowledgement of the real epistemological differences that exist, particularly between the more positivist tendencies of the sciences and the hermeneutic traditions of the humanities. The formation in recent decades of new interdisciplinary configurations within the humanities – such as the environmental humanities, the digital humanities and the medical humanities within which literary researchers play a central role – is vital for providing an institutional space where humanities researchers can engage with domains traditionally 'owned' by the medical, physical and computer sciences on their own terms.

To take the example of digital humanities, while they often borrow digital methods developed by computer and data scientists, their applications to humanities objects of study such as literary texts have been combined with critical reflection about the epistemological underpinnings of such tools. Most important here is the critical examination of the potential of such methods to obscure the complexities of human subjectivity and cultural expression. While there may be concerns that such methods are an effort to 'datafy' literature, bringing literary texts more actively into the broader realm of 'research data' has also provided an opportunity to highlight how the term 'data' itself must be reconceptualised not as neutral or objective categorisations of the world but rather as inevitably partial interpretations.

Bringing such complexities into the realms of computer and data sciences is proving of urgent importance in response to the rapid and often uncritical expansions of generative AI we are currently witnessing. As Lauren Klein and others highlight, the humanities have an underexplored potential to inform these developments with a more complex understanding of human culture and expression. Literary research has a particularly crucial role to play in bringing to the fore the complexities of meaning embedded in the 'training data' underpinning the development of generative AI tools and avoiding the reduction of 'the inventive and cultural capacities of culture to "content"'.[35] Researchers of literatures in languages other than English are particularly well placed to foreground the cultural contingency of meaning and the marginalised or silenced voices excluded from the flattening and universalising principles underpinning generative AI technologies.[36]

More generally, literary researchers embedded in highly interdisciplinary language schools or departments are uniquely positioned to further interdisciplinary dialogue and collaboration. In the UK context, such interdisciplinary configurations have been expanded through the move away from single-language departments to the consolidation of larger schools of languages that have increasingly collapsed the boundaries between the, traditionally, more literary European-language departments and the more social-sciences-oriented area studies departments. Tensions have, of course, arisen through such consolidations, driven at least partly by a fear that the primacy of literary scholarship within European-language departments might be under threat from a more applied vision of area studies. Certainly, the original political and instrumental drivers of establishing area studies after the Cold War are well known, but fields such as Latin American studies and Middle Eastern studies have undoubtedly evolved beyond such restrictions to encompass the study of a vast array of forms of cultural expression, including literature.

These new configurations could be seen to realise Gayatri Spivak's earlier call for a greater alignment between comparative literature and area studies by pushing area studies to view 'the language of the other not only as a "field" language' and pushing literary studies to acknowledge the limitations of 'the European outlines of its premise'.[37] In this respect, literary researchers from a more conventional modern languages tradition need not see these new configurations as a prompt to return to the old territorial wars fought between the sciences and the humanities, or between literary scholars and cultural studies researchers. Rather they present an opportunity for literary researchers to engage more closely with new collaborators and fields in ways that might further the potential of literary research to intervene more visibly in the world and its reimagination.

Such reimaginings of the world are at the heart of recent literary research that dialogues with other art forms, precisely as a way to understand the interpretative practices and structures that make our world. As exemplified by several contributions to this volume, the development of the field of comparative literature has led to critical engagements with written texts from across cultural and linguistic traditions. But the comparative lens also understands translation as a fundamentally human practice of understanding one another and our individual worlds. Thus, the 'comparison' in comparative literature is dynamic in that it spans the crossing of forms as well as cultures and times. Emma Bond's work in this volume, for instance, at the intersection of museums and literary studies, emphasises how post-fiction can help readers to challenge the object accumulation logics of the museum and usher in new ways of negotiating and reading the world through the imperative of 'letting go' of objects, practices and mnemonic frameworks.

Meanwhile, Rachel Scott's chapter addresses the intersection of the visual and the written word by focusing on a series of ancient tales and illustrations reimagined for contemporary audiences. Here, the literary exhibition, told in visual form, can be its own kind of 'epistemic method' reflective of a more holistic understanding of the material conditions of literature's production and circulation in the world, as well as its power to speak through new encounters with communities that might otherwise view literature as marginal to their interests or experiences.[38]

Similarly, in Abir Hamdar's chapter on the writing of an ethno-drama together with Arabic-speaking cancer patients, it becomes clear that otherwise silenced or taboo topics can become more acutely visible and alive in a literary space. Indeed, Hamdar's work encourages us to question the supposed boundary between the real and the imaginary as it is played out in the space of the theatre. Literature, in other words, is a kind of 'real life', just as the stories we tell ourselves create grounded and nuanced understandings of the challenges we face and help us overcome those challenges in the very process of telling and retelling them to others. Such acts of retelling in the chapters of Scott, Hamdar and also Rekeszus are further enhanced by the co-production methods they deploy in their respective projects.

The act of dialoguing across multiple forms and methodologies, while always returning to the literary as a mode of expression and critical interrogation, resonates with other chapters in the volume, engaged in interdisciplinary research that moves across languages and cultures, medical, environmental and digital humanities, as well as heritage studies. And much of this research also adopts modes of co-production that have become increasingly common across humanities and social science disciplines in recent years. At the heart of co-production is a desire to foster a reciprocal exchange of skills and knowledge, often deploying participatory methods that bring different communities into the world of research and vice versa. Here, so-called participants are increasingly brought in as 'co-researchers', as paid collaborators in research, challenging the idea that research is done only within the walls of the university, or by academics working alone with their 'source' texts.[39] Nicola Thomas's chapter, for instance, builds on the increasing prevalence of 'place-based' agendas that can incorporate the use of participatory methodologies alongside readings of literary texts, which can be used as a source of data for understanding how concepts of time have developed and changed in local languages and contexts. Carol Tully's contribution, similarly, highlights a mutually beneficial collaboration with the heritage industry in a joint endeavour to reveal historical depths, traditions and various travellers' perspectives on a particular region (here Wales). Heike Bartel, meanwhile, demonstrates the ways in which literary texts interrogate how place influences concepts of masculinity and practices of eating among men and boys with eating disorders. Bartel's work, both of drawing attention to existing literary texts from around the world about men with eating disorders and of facilitating readings of such texts by patients and health professionals, leads to new understandings of people's experiences of illness, particularly where common narratives around men's and boys' experiences benefit from being questioned.

Over many years, literary research, in particular, has involved a vision of researchers working alone, wrestling with meaning or positioned in the 'ivory tower' of the traditional university, professing knowledge out of their own work of close reading. And yet, for a long time, collaboration (whether through teaching or research) has been a core part of most researchers' experiences and brings about reciprocal insights and outcomes not available to the isolated academic researcher. Whether it is an exchange through teaching or one enabled through participatory research methods, literary study is, more often than not, a collaborative and socially engaged endeavour that enables spaces of cognitive and affective self-reflection not necessarily available through other forms of study. Our book provides yet another example of this kind of mutually beneficial collaboration.

If the myth of the lone academic belongs to a past of more static modes of literary criticism, the so-called 'creative critical' has recently emerged as an explicit challenge to the disciplinary ways of working that have become embedded particularly within literary studies. To quote Florian Mussgnug, Mathelinda Nabugodi and Thea Petrou's 'Prelude' to their 2021 volume, *Thinking Through Relation: Encounters in Creative Critical Writing*, the creative critical is not one thing, but rather 'stems from the artist or critic's ability to query the human from diverse angles, including the position of its least privileged and most vulnerable designations'.[40] In addition, they underline how the creative critical mode, through its interruptive practices, is well equipped to attenuate the risk of what Rita Felski calls 'antinormative normativity' which has arguably become a part of some more traditional literary critical practices.[41] Clearly, collaborative working has become a core part of doing this in recent literary studies research.

Across this volume we find explicit examples of collaborative, creative critical research that enact this challenge to 'antinormative normativity', by engaging through participatory methodologies with diverse communities of co-researchers in health, the arts and education on the question of why literature matters to wider society. Other approaches outside the scope of this book that deploy participatory and creative methodologies include the work of the theatre-maker and writer Neela Doležalová, who makes use of poetry in school-based workshops to encourage pupils to connect with the multiple languages they speak at home and in school. This work has led to the publication of *100 Poems for Belonging: An Anthology of Poems by Young Writers from Gearies Primary School* as well as the production of a podcast exploring the role of multilingualism in education, and is the outcome of collaboration across the education sector, linguistics and literary studies.[42] Poetry here is not simply a means of engaging young people's creativity when it comes to bringing otherwise hidden or forbidden languages into the often monolingual classroom space; it is about digging deep into the emotional resonances and allowing for the emergence of the emotional impact of working and living within systems that deny creativity and perpetuate monolingual forms of living that are contrary to people's everyday, affective existences.

Other examples of collaboration are evidenced in the UK's 2014 Research Excellence Framework (REF) assessment exercise, highlighted in Scott's chapter, where, for instance, literary scholar Anne Schwan's work has informed education practices of reading and writing in prisons or where Rehana Ahmed's work in postcolonial literature has informed wider understandings of Muslim culture and identities by British writers of Muslim heritage.[43] We could also cite Sam Durrant's research on bibliotherapy and the use of literature as a means of working through traumatic experiences relating to slavery, colonialism and racism with asylum seekers and refugees in the UK.[44] In the above examples, poetry and literary engagement are arguably about discovering connection, collective solidarities and new communities; they are about forming groups of people who think otherwise and wish to build alternative visions of the world together, and poetry and literature offer the imaginative space to deconstruct existing worlds and work towards building new ones.

While the above may represent more obvious examples of collaborative or participatory methods in practice, creative critical work offers a more implicit shift in literary criticism towards examining researcher positionality and disrupting formal conventions of academic writing.[45] For example, the work of Timothy Mathews, Mathelinda Nabugodi, Clare Lees and Gillian Overing is arguably much closer to what we might think of as the work of the literary critic, but it is also engaged in a level of personal and professional vulnerability that interrupts established ways of doing criticism.[46] Nabugodi uses marginalia of her text to, for instance, navigate practices of naming in Walter Benjamin's work, alongside that of her own personal experience:

> How I came by my patronymic is a family anecdote. Scene: my mother at the social services, registering my birth to make a Soviet citizen of me. Social worker: 'Given name?' 'Mathelinda.' 'Patronymic?' 'None.' 'What do you mean, "none"? Doesn't she have a father?'[47]

This more recent work sits at the border between what has become known as literary and creative criticism, and breaks that false division wide open. It does so in part by rehabilitating a tradition of twentieth-century cultural and literary criticism established in the work of bell hooks, Roland Barthes, Abdelkébir Khatibi, Helène Cixous, Walter Benjamin and others, but it is a practice, as Elina Mikkilä writes, that could be traced all the way back to Horace's *Ars poetica*.[48]

What is important here is not changing how we do literary criticism to demonstrate instances of impact that sit outside literary criticism, but rather to see that how we do criticism already contains within it a fundamentally creative mode of relating, or that there is always something else implied in critique that might not immediately be recognised. That might be, for many of us, a sort of psychosocial work on the self, on revealing or negotiating our own creative critical identities *as people* (as much as critics) – and, by implication, the identities of other readers – who come to encounter literary texts and who, of course, are no less capable critics than those employed in universities.

Such a practice is captured in a refrain in Mathews's 2022 book, *There and Not Here*, where he appears to ask whether critics are really 'trying to say something by writing about something else'.[49] This seems to be about the power of writing to engender forms of self-recognition, even (perhaps particularly?) when the writer-critic does not set out to consciously reflect on themselves. Or perhaps 'trying to say something by writing about something else' is a reflection of the fundamental work of interpretation in that the implications of one text are very often only more fully realised by reading that text filtered through another. A good example of this might be, say, reading Freud through W. H. Auden's powerful poem, *In Memory of Sigmund Freud*, where the poet reduces Freud's psychoanalysis to a repetitive practice of '[telling] the unhappy Present to recite the Past [. . .] till sooner / or later it falter[s] at the line where / long ago the accusations had begun, / and suddenly knew by whom it had been judged'.[50] In any case, it is reflective of that now-common idea that to think, write and engage with others is a particularly good way of coming to a deeper understanding of one's self. It resonates with the notion of 'the stranger's gaze' that has long permeated all aspects of a languages and cultures education,[51] but it is revealed perhaps most acutely in the deep imaginative engagement that emerges from acts of close reading and creative critical (re)writing.

We began this introduction to *Literature for Change* by citing Nussbaum's words about a crisis in education – a crisis, we acknowledge, that has not passed, but rather that has mutated, morphed or given way to further instances of yet more intense crises. This sense of permanent crisis in the humanities, and among literary scholars in particular, has become a recurrent feature of criticism that seeks to address the future of the discipline in ways that often call for change while not taking account of the change that is already all around us.[52] In her 2013 book *Anti-Crisis*, Janet Roitman makes the salient point that by always returning to the language of 'crisis', critics often fail to ask other important questions about how and why we might neglect to take account of the specificity of the realities we actually face.[53]

In literary studies, and languages, cultures and societies specifically, there is no doubt that there are increasingly recurrent material crises of survival. Yet, in reading the chapters that make up this volume, there is a sense in which change is embraced as a fundamental part of what literature does. That is to say, literature and literary studies are rarely held up as the answer to any given 'crisis' we might face. Rather, literature forces us humans to reckon with the idea that crises are a narrative production of the societies we inhabit; that events are at once mediated by and reckoned with through reading and studying literature; and that life itself cannot be comprehended without the real and imaginative encounters stories bring.

In other words, change is not always sudden or immediate, or demanding of an urgent response; change is perhaps most often part of extended, longer-term processes of collaboration, relationship building, co-creation and storytelling that make up the examples advanced in this volume. This is literature for change, but recognising that change is made at each instant and cumulatively across time in ways into which literature, and its study, gives us unique insights.

Notes

1 Martha Nussbaum, *Not for Profit: Why Democracy Needs the Humanities* (Princeton University Press, 2010), p. 1.

2 Nussbaum, *Not for Profit*, pp. 1–2.

3 George Eliot, 'The Natural History of German Life', *Westminster Review*, vol. LXVI, July 1856, pp. 51–79 (p. 54). http://georgeeliotarchive.org/files/original/8d91925f9de380897bfe2ade4667f243.txt [accessed 17 June 2026].

4 Jan Ross, 'Feindschaft ist ermüdend' [interview with David Grossman], *Die Zeit*, 5 December 2024, p. 6.

5 Dorrit Cohn, *The Distinction of Fiction* (Johns Hopkins University Press, 1999), p. 48.

6 See Rick Rylance, *Literature and the Public Good* (Oxford University Press, 2016).

7 David Comer Kidd and Emanuele Castano, 'Reading Literary Fiction Improves Theory of Mind', *Science*, 342 (18 October 2013), p. 378. Quoted after Rylance, p. 191.

8 See Charlotte Woodford, *Women, Emancipation and the German Novel, 1871–1910: Protest Fiction in its Cultural Context* (Legenda, 2014), p. 139.

9 PEN America maintains a list of banned books in the United States from 2025: https://pen.org/banned-books-list-2025/ [accessed 28 April 2026].

10 Nussbaum, *Not for Profit*, p. 95.

11 Adele Schreiber, 'Die Ansätze neuer Sittlichkeitsbegriffe im Hinblick auf die Mutterschaft', in *Mutterschaft. Ein Sammelwerk für die Probleme des Weibes als Mutter*, ed. by Adele Schreiber (Albert Langen, 1912), pp. 163–85 (p. 185).

12 Tomer Gardi, *broken german* (Droschl, 2016), p. 140.

13 Markus Hallensleben, 'Towards an Aesthetics of Postmigrant Narratives. Moving Beyond the Politics of Territorial Belonging in Ilija Trojanow's *Nach der Flucht* (2017)', in *Postmigration Art, Culture, and Politics in Contemporary Europe*, ed. by Anna Meera, and others (transcript, 2021), pp. 197–219 (p. 202).

14 Nicholas Harrison, *Postcolonial Criticism: History, Theory and the Work of Fiction* (Polity Press, 2003), p. 162.

15 See Nicholas Harrison, 'Who Needs an Idea of the Literary?', *Paragraph*, 28.2 (2005), p. 12.

16 Rita Felski, *Uses of Literature* (Blackwell, 2008), p. 6 and p. 16.

17 Martin Swales, 'Symbolism and Realism in Germany', in *The Cambridge History of Literary Criticism*, vol. 6: *The Nineteenth Century*, ed. by M. A. R. Habib (Cambridge University Press, 2013), pp. 313–24 (p. 314).

18 See Paul Ricoeur, *Time and Narrative*, vol. 1 (The University of Chicago Press, 1984), p. 57.

19 Theodor Fontane, 'Unsere lyrische und epische Poesie seit 1848', in *Sämtliche Werke*, vol. 21: *Literarische Essays und Studien*, part 1, edited by Kurt Schreinert (Nymphenburger Verlagshandlung, 1963), pp. 7–33 (p. 13).

20 Rylance, *Literature and the Public Good*, p. 164.

21 See *Contested Communities: Minor, Minority and Small Literatures in Europe*, ed. by Kate Averis, Margaret Littler, and Godela Weiss-Sussex (Legenda, 2023).

22 For a longer discussion of Italian literature in transnational perspective, see Charles Burdett and Loredana Polezzi, 'Beyond the National Paradigm: Transnational and Translational Approaches to Italian Literature', in *The Oxford Handbook of Italian Literature*, ed. by Stefano Jossa (Oxford University Press, 2026), pp. 101–112.

23 See for example Gabriella Ghermandi, *Regina di fiori e di perle* (Donzelli Editore, 2007); Igiaba Scego, *Adua* (Giunti, 2015).

24 Amara Lakhous, *Divorzio all'islamica a viale Marconi* (Edizioni e/o, 2010); Shirin Ramzanali Fazel, and Simone Brioni, *Io e l'Islam* (Edizioni Ca' Foscari, 2020).

25 James Clifford, 'Introduction: Partial Truths', in *Writing Culture: The Poetics and Politics of Ethnography*, ed. by James Clifford and George E. Marcus (University of California Press, 1986), pp. 1–26; Vincent Debaene, *Far Afield: French Anthropology between Science and Literature*, trans. by Justin Izzo (University of Chicago Press, 2014); Joe Parker and Ranu Samantrai, 'Interdisciplinarity and Social Justice: An Introduction', in *Interdisciplinarity and Social Justice: Revisioning Academic Accountability*, ed. by Joe Parker, Mary Romero, and Ranu Samantrai (SUNY Press, 2010).

26 Debaene, *Far Afield*, p. 21.

27 Cary Nelson and Dilip Parameshwar Gaonkar, 'Cultural Studies and the Politics of Disciplinarity: An Introduction', in *Disciplinarity and Dissent in Cultural Studies*, ed. by Cary Nelson and Dilip Parameshwar Gaonkar (Routledge, 1996), pp. 1–22.

28 Nelson and Gaonkar, 'Cultural Studies', p. 17.

29 See *Biological Discourses: The Language of Science and Literature Around 1900*, ed. by Robert Craig and Ina Linge (Peter Lang Ltd, 2017).

30 Edward W. Said, *The World, the Text, and the Critic* (Harvard University Press, 1983).

31 Stuart Hall, 'Cultural Studies and Its Theoretical Legacies', in *Cultural Studies*, ed. by Lawrence Grossberg, Cary Nelson, and Paula Treichler (Routledge, 1992), pp. 277–94 (p. 287).

32 Clifford, 'Introduction: Partial Truths', p. 4.

33 Jorge Luis Borges, *Elogio de La Sombra* (Emecé, 1969).

34 Lisa Lowe, 'Metaphors of Globalization', in *Interdisciplinarity and Social Justice: Revisioning Academic Accountability*, ed. by Joe Parker, Mary Romero, and Ranu Samantrai (SUNY Press, 2010), pp. 37–62 (p. 52).

35 Lauren Klein and others, 'Provocations from the Humanities for Generative AI Research' (arXiv, 2025), doi:10.48550/ARXIV.2502.19190, p. 13.

36 For more on this, see also Reham Hosny's chapter in this volume.

37 Gayatri Chakravorty Spivak, *Death of a Discipline* (Columbia University Press, 2003), p. 12.

38 Thomas Thiemeyer, 'The Literary Exhibition as Epistemic Method: How the Museum of Modern Literature in Marbach Reinterprets Literary Archives', *Word & Image*, 33.4, pp. 362–75, doi:10.1080/02666286.2017.1326787. See also Scott, this volume.

39 On the idea of the 'co-researcher', see Caroline Lenette, *Participatory Action Research: Ethics and Decolonization* (Oxford University Press, 2022).

40 Florian Mussgnug, Mathelinda Nabugodi, and Thea Petrou, 'Prelude', in *Thinking Through Relation: Encounters in Creative Critical Writing* (Peter Lang, 2021), p. 3.

41 Rita Felski, *The Limits of Critique* (University of Chicago Press, 2015), p. 9.

42 Neela Doležalová and others, *100 Poems for Belonging: An Anthology of Poems by Young Writers from Gearies Primary School* (2024), https://www.the-space-between.org/100-poems-for-belonging; see also: https://www.the-space-between.org/1000wordspodcast [accessed 28 April 2026].

43 https://impact.ref.ac.uk/casestudies/CaseStudy.aspx?Id=43947 [accessed 28 April 2026]; https://impact.ref.ac.uk/casestudies/CaseStudy.aspx?Id=30192 [accessed 28 April 2026].

44 https://impact.ref.ac.uk/casestudies/CaseStudy.aspx?Id=6382 [accessed 28 April 2026].

45 Various collectives exist, with web presences at: https://creativecritical.net/; https://creativecriticalwriting.wordpress.com/; https://ies.sas.ac.uk/news-events/seminars/out-practice-seminar. Elina Mikkilä writes of '*creat*-ical' research to capture a practice that 'generate[s] embodied, theoretical, metatexual, poetological and plurilingual insights'. See Elina Mikkilä, 'The Art of "Creatical Writing": Unlocking Insights Through Creative-Critical Fusion', *Life Writing*, 21.3 (2024), pp. 535–48.

46 Timothy Mathews, *There and Not Here: Chronicles of Art and Loss* (Ma Bibliothèque, 2022); Mathelinda Nabugodi, *Shelley with Benjamin: A Critical*

Mosaic (UCL Press, 2023); Clare Lees and Gillian Overing, *The Contemporary Medieval in Practice* (UCL Press, 2019).

47 Nabugodi, *Shelley with Benjamin*, p. 15.

48 Mikkilä, 'The Art of "Creatical Writing"', p. 535.

49 Mathews, *There and Not Here*, p. 15.

50 W. H. Auden, 'In Memory of Sigmund Freud', https://poets.org/poem/memory-sigmund-freud [accessed 17 June 2026].

51 See Michael Kelly, 'The Stranger's Gaze: The Emergence of French Cultural Studies', in *The Future of Cultural Studies: Essays in Honour of Joris Vlasselars*, ed. by Jan Baetens and José Lambert (Leuven University Press), pp. 107–21.

52 On the question of 'crisis' and literary studies, see Paul Jay, *The Humanities 'Crisis' and the Future of Literary Studies* (Palgrave, 2014).

53 Janet Roitman, *Anti-Crisis* (Duke University Press, 2013), p. 5.

References

Ahmed, Rehana, 'Muslims Writing Britain', https://impact.ref.ac.uk/casestudies/CaseStudy.aspx?Id=30192 [accessed 28 April 2026]

Auden, W. H., 'In Memory of Sigmund Freud', https://poets.org/poem/memory-sigmund-freud [accessed 17 June 2026]

Averis, Kate, Margaret Littler, and Godela Weiss-Sussex (eds), *Contested Communities: Minor, Minority and Small Literatures in Europe* (Legenda, 2023)

Burdett, Charles, and Loredana Polezzi, 'Beyond the National Paradigm: Transnational and Translational Approaches to Italian Literature', in *The Oxford Handbook of Italian Literature*, ed. by Stefano Jossa (Oxford University Press, 2026), pp. 101–112

Clifford, James, 'Introduction: Partial Truths', in *Writing Culture: The Poetics and Politics of Ethnography*, ed. by James Clifford and George E. Marcus (University of California Press, 1986), pp. 1–26

Cohn, Dorrit, *The Distinction of Fiction* (Johns Hopkins University Press, 1999)

Craig, Robert, and Ina Linge, *Biological Discourses: The Language of Science and Literature Around 1900* (Peter Lang Ltd, 2017)

Debaene, Vincent, *Far Afield: French Anthropology between Science and Literature*, trans. by Justin Izzo (University of Chicago Press, 2014)

Doležalová, Neela, and others, *100 Poems for Belonging: An Anthology of Poems by Young Writers from Gearies Primary School* (2024), https://www.the-space-between.org/100-poems-for-belonging [accessed 28 April 2026]

Durrant, Sam, 'Applying a New Model of Bibliotherapy to Improve the Mental Well-being of Asylum Seekers and Refugees', https://impact.ref.ac.uk/casestudies/CaseStudy.aspx?Id=6382 [accessed 28 April 2026]

Eliot, George, 'The Natural History of German Life', *Westminster Review*, vol. LXVI, July 1856, pp. 51–79, http://georgeeliotarchive.org/files/original/8d91925f9de380897bfe2ade4667f243.txt [accessed 28 April 2026]

Felski, Rita, *The Limits of Critique* (University of Chicago Press, 2015)

Felski, Rita, *Uses of Literature* (Blackwell, 2008)

Fontane, Theodor, 'Unsere lyrische und epische Poesie seit 1848', in *Sämtliche Werke, vol. 21: Literarische Essays und Studien*, part 1, ed. by Kurt Schreinert (Nymphenburger Verlagshandlung, 1963), pp. 7–33

Gardi, Tomer, *broken german* (Droschl, 2016)

Ghermandi, Gabriella, *Regina di fiori e di perle* (Donzelli Editore, 2007)

Hall, Stuart, 'Cultural Studies and its Theoretical Legacies', in *Cultural Studies*, ed. by Lawrence Grossberg, Cary Nelson, and Paula Treichler (Routledge, 1992), pp. 277–94

Hallensleben, Markus, 'Towards an Aesthetics of Postmigrant Narratives. Moving Beyond the Politics of Territorial Belonging in Ilija Trojanow's *Nach der Flucht* (2017)', in *Postmigration Art, Culture, and Politics in Contemporary Europe*, ed. by Anna Meera, and others (transcript, 2021), pp. 197–219

Harrison, Nicholas, *Postcolonial Criticism: History, Theory and the Work of Fiction* (Polity Press, 2003)

Harrison, Nicholas, 'Who Needs an Idea of the Literary?', *Paragraph*, 28.2 (2005), pp. 1–17

Jay, Paul, *The Humanities 'Crisis' and the Future of Literary Studies* (Palgrave, 2014)

Kelly, Michael, 'The Stranger's Gaze: The Emergence of French Cultural Studies', in *The Future of Cultural Studies: Essays in Honour of Joris Vlasselars*, ed. by Jan Baetens and José Lambert (Leuven University Press, 2000), pp. 107–21

Klein, Lauren, and others, 'Provocations from the Humanities for Generative AI Research' (arXiv, 2025), doi:10.48550/ARXIV.2502.19190

Lakhous, Amara, *Divorzio all'islamica a viale Marconi* (Edizioni e/o, 2010)
Lees, Clare, and Gillian Overing, *The Contemporary Medieval in Practice* (UCL Press, 2019)
Lenette, Caroline, *Participatory Action Research: Ethics and Decolonization* (Oxford University Press, 2022)
Lowe, Lisa, 'Metaphors of Globalization', in *Interdisciplinarity and Social Justice: Revisioning Academic Accountability*, ed. by Joe Parker, Mary Romero, and Ranu Samantrai (SUNY Press, 2010), pp. 37–62
Mathews, Timothy, *There and Not Here: Chronicles of Art and Loss* (Ma Bibliothèque, 2022)
Mikkilä, Elina, 'The Art of "Creatical Writing": Unlocking Insights Through Creative-Critical Fusion', *Life Writing*, 21.3 (2024), pp. 535–48.
Mussgnug, Florian, Mathelinda Nabugodi, and Thea Petrou, 'Prelude', in *Thinking Through Relation: Encounters in Creative Critical Writing* (Peter Lang, 2021)
Nabugodi, Mathelinda, *Shelley with Benjamin: A Critical Mosaic* (UCL Press, 2023)
Nelson, Cary, and Dilip Parameshwar Gaonkar, 'Cultural Studies and the Politics of Disciplinarity: An Introduction', in *Disciplinarity and Dissent in Cultural Studies*, ed. by Cary Nelson and Dilip Parameshwar Gaonkar (Routledge, 1996), pp. 1–22
Nussbaum, Martha, *Not for Profit: Why Democracy Needs the Humanities* (Princeton University Press, 2010)
Parker, Joe, and Ranu Samantrai, 'Interdisciplinarity and Social Justice: An Introduction', in *Interdisciplinarity and Social Justice: Revisioning Academic Accountability*, ed. by Joe Parker, Mary Romero, and Ranu Samantrai (SUNY Press, 2010)
PEN America, 'Banned Books List 2025', https://pen.org/banned-books-list-2025/ [accessed 28 April 2026]
Ramzanali Fazel, Shirin and Simone Brioni, *Io e l'Islam* (Edizioni Ca' Foscari, 2020)
Ricoeur, Paul, *Time and Narrative*, vol. 1 (The University of Chicago Press, 1984)
Roitman, Janet, *Anti-Crisis* (Duke University Press, 2013)
Ross, Jan, 'Feindschaft ist ermüdend' [interview with David Grossman], *Die Zeit*, 5 December 2024, p. 6
Rylance, Rick, *Literature and the Public Good* (Oxford University Press, 2016)

Said, Edward W., *The World, the Text, and the Critic* (Harvard University Press, 1983)

Scego, Igiaba, *Adua* (Giunti, 2015)

Schreiber, Adele, 'Die Ansätze neuer Sittlichkeitsbegriffe im Hinblick auf die Mutterschaft', in *Mutterschaft. Ein Sammelwerk für die Probleme des Weibes als Mutter*, ed. by Adele Schreiber (Albert Langen, 1912), pp. 163–85

Schwan, Anne, 'Promoting Literacy and Creative Writing Skills at HMP Edinburgh', https://impact.ref.ac.uk/casestudies/CaseStudy.aspx?Id=43947 [accessed 28 April 2026]

Spivak, Gayatri Chakravorty, *Death of a Discipline* (Columbia University Press, 2003)

Swales, Martin, 'Symbolism and Realism in Germany', in *The Cambridge History of Literary Criticism*, vol. 6: *The Nineteenth Century*, ed. by M. A. R. Habib (Cambridge University Press, 2013), pp. 313–24

Thiemeyer, Thomas, 'The Literary Exhibition as Epistemic Method: How the Museum of Modern Literature in Marbach Reinterprets Literary Archives', *Word & Image*, 33.4 (2017), pp. 362–75, doi:10.1080/02666286.2017.1326787

Woodford, Charlotte, *Women, Emancipation and the German Novel, 1871–1910: Protest Fiction in its Cultural Context* (Legenda, 2014)

Chapter 1

Modern medieval languages: reading in and out of time

Sarah Bowden

I'm going to start with a confession: I often lie about my job. When people I meet ask me what I do for a living, I tend to tell them blandly that I'm 'an academic'. If they question further and ask about my field, I either say 'German' (the resulting safe assumption being that I teach the German language) or 'I'm a medievalist' (I then respond to 'ah! Chaucer!' with a non-committal grunt). Very rarely do I put the two together and explain that I work on the literature and culture of the medieval German-speaking world.

Why do I act like this? I know perfectly well that I shouldn't, and that I'm a coward trying to avoid a difficult conversation. Partly, I'm fed up with years of furrowed brows, of people quickly changing the subject or saying 'how difficult!' (or worse, 'how boring!'). More seriously, my behaviour is a symptom of the place of modern languages research in the public understanding. All of us who work in languages departments are used to justifying ourselves and explaining exactly what it is we do to others, both within and outside the university, and this constant self-justification is exhausting.

It is not my aim in this chapter to tackle the (mis)conceptualisation of the subject more broadly, nor to explore the many and complex reasons behind it (which are the responsibility of many parties, not least ourselves). But the discourses of 'value', however measured, and 'relevance' within contemporary academic experience have inevitably contributed to the current shape of the discipline, to trends in research and teaching, and to how we present ourselves to the wider public. In an essay written nearly fifteen years ago, Simon Gaunt and Nicholas Harrison drew attention to a tendency in modern languages departments to move away from literature, particularly of the past, and towards present-day politics and cultural studies; a move they argued was driven by a misunderstanding of what might seem attractive and relevant to the student body.[1] Since then a number of crisis points and funding opportunities have forced a more positively critical reappraisal of the discipline, resulting in more thoughtful and holistic ways of demonstrating its vitality in contemporary society.[2]

One of the reasons why it is so difficult to describe – or understand – (modern) languages is the sheer diversity of the discipline, which can sometimes (wonderfully, but not unproblematically) resemble the entirety of the humanities rolled into one, with a bit of social science sprinkled on top. Even the name 'modern languages' is a challenge, and one from which dissatisfied departments and organisations are increasingly moving away.[3] As a term it is deceptively narrow and unrepresentative, and its very 'modernity' – originally adopted to distinguish itself from the then more established disciplines of classical languages – is confusing and problematic in more ways than one. In this chapter, I would like to tackle the issue of modernity to address one, often neglected, component of this diverse and fragmented discipline: the study of medieval literature as part of a modern languages degree. This chapter is not about justifying the existence of a threatened corner of a threatened discipline, but rather intends to show how thinking about the place of medieval literature contributes positively to existing work on the self-definition of modern languages teaching and research, and helps to emphasise the political urgency of the subject. In many respects, what I write is very personal, drawing on my own experiences and expertise, as well as current discourses within German studies, but it should also, I hope, be more widely applicable across the discipline. This chapter's arguments are not confined to medieval studies, but resonate with broader concerns about historicisation, periodisation and pastness. Ultimately, my aim is to argue that encounters with linguistic and cultural difference are profoundly enriched when approached from a perspective of historical depth.

In the first section of this chapter, I draw a connection between the relatively recent focus on the transnational in modern languages and scholarship on the politics of time, arguing that a fuller consideration of periodisation (especially the constructs of 'medieval' and 'modern') can – and should – play a significant role in cross-cultural thinking. I then turn more explicitly to the study of medieval literature within a languages degree in order to explore its positive contribution to the creative exploration of cultural difference.

Transnational modern languages and the politics of periodisation

In recent years, there has been a 'transnational turn' within modern languages teaching and research. Increasingly aware of the dangers of 'exclusivist, nationalist, and territorial thinking' in language-specific disciplines, and that 'German', 'French', 'Spanish', 'Italian' (etc.) run the risk of sounding like monolithic national concepts they have never been, scholars have sought ways of exposing the interconnectedness and fluidity of perceived linguistic, geographic and national boundaries.[4] Modern languages disciplines emerged in the nineteenth century, in a time of what Braun and Schofield, citing Ulrich Beck, refer to as 'methodological nationalism', and the specific contexts that shaped their foundation still persist today, particularly in terms of canon and genre formation.[5] There has been widespread dissatisfaction with what we might term the 'traditional' curriculum for some time now, but the growth of nationalist populism in contemporary politics has made a rethinking of the subject all the more urgent, and has led to approaches that both explore nation-formation and rejoice in its inadequacies, as well as in the multiplicity and diversity inherent in the languages and cultures we study. As Hodkinson and Schofield put it in the introduction to their volume *German in the World*, for instance, the aim of a transnational German studies is 'to grasp that while German-language culture can always be historically, linguistically, and geographically contextualized, its value, legacy and impact can never be entirely constrained by those temporal, linguistic, and geographic borders.'[6]

The transnational turn is fundamentally connected to projects that aim to 'decolonise' or 'expand' the curriculum and also stands in close relation to 'worlding' projects within English and comparative literature, in all their critical complexity. Its political stance is different, however, because of its direct connection to both nationhood and to the discipline of modern languages. The very essence of modern languages is working with difference: it is about crossing the divide between languages and cultures, and exploring critically the forms of connection and dislocation this crossing brings about.[7] This interconnected, messy discipline of studying language(s) and cultures (which, itself, can mean literature, film, history, politics and so on) is always one that involves radical destabilisation through the removal or marginalisation of the mother tongue, as well as through the process of cultural translation that unsettles us and forces us to think anew about the web of references that make up the way we understand the world and our place within it.

The transnational is often read as a contemporary phenomenon: it is a product of (and response to) globalisation, as well as to the related re-emergence of nationalist, populist political movements.[8] Yet the transnational cannot only be understood in the now.[9] Braun and Schofield draw attention to the intricate connection between the transnational and the transperiod, stressing the 'crucial awareness that the transnational is both the precursor as well as the result of the nation' and reminding us that critical reflection on nationhood has to draw into consideration historical situations before the emergence of the nation-state.[10] This connection they identify, amplified by the use of the prefix 'trans', draws attention to the fact that 'period' is just as much of a construct as 'nation', and is a term that is just as politically and historically loaded – and worthy of deconstruction.

Despite such recognition of the connection between the transnational and the transperiod, this is not a connection that has been sufficiently explored. While geographical broadness and cross-cultural thinking are key to the conceptualisation of modern languages teaching and research today, historical depth is not, and is rarely an element of our degree programmes that is marketed by our universities or expected by undergraduate students.[11] I would like to suggest, however, that historical depth is a vital component of thinking across languages and cultures, and that a truly transnational study of modern languages has to take seriously the politics of time. The fear of (ir)relevance is perhaps one of the reasons for the dogged contemporaneity in so much of the self-presentation of our subject. Yet a greater consideration of the politics of periodisation, as well as the way in which it interacts with nation-making (and breaking), would contribute in a very real way to the politics of relevance and offer new perspectives on contemporary social constructs and problems.

Periodisation is, in itself, a political act, not a neutral depiction of the course of history. Period units are constructs created to write narratives of ostensibly 'universal' concepts and, as scholars such as Dipesh Chakrabarty have shown, can result in the normalisation of problematic (Euro)chronologies that render particularly non-European forms of historical experience insignificant or less 'progressive'.[12] Modernity, so often treated as an apparently universal concept, is, Chakrabarty argues, in fact always already conditioned by particular histories. Political modernity is deeply contingent, yet it tends to be disguised as universal, which results in a tendency to think in terms of some nations 'catching up' while others are shown to be more normatively progressive.[13]

Chakrabarty writes from the perspective of subaltern studies, advocating for new ways of writing histories that take into account the politics of periodisation and their intersection with other constructed models of (Western) 'progress'. Yet he gestures in his writing towards a connection with the study of the Middle Ages, and, in fact, medieval studies can make a powerful and complementary contribution to this discussion.[14] The medieval plays a significant, if often unrecognised, part in contemporary conceptualisations of modernity; it is commonplace, for example, to use the term 'medieval' in a derogatory fashion to describe social practices that are excessively violent or that seem in some way to be unsophisticatedly primitive or barbaric. Not unconnected is the ahistorical and highly problematic appropriation of conceptualisations of the medieval and medievalism by contemporary far-right groups across the West in order to promote the politics of nationalism and white supremacy.[15] A recent – and frequently cited – instance is the adoption of crusading insignia and 'Viking' dress at the Capitol riots in January 2021.[16] It is not the purpose of this chapter (although it should go without saying) to promote a deeper and more nuanced historical education in contemporary society; the point I rather want to make here is to stress the fact that the 'medieval' is a construct that, in itself, helps us to grasp the shape of the equally constructed modernity.

The most sophisticated discussion of the role of the constructed 'medieval' in the politics of time is Kathleen Davis's *Periodization and Sovereignty*.[17] Focusing on feudalism and secularisation, Davis shows that the conceptualisation of modernity is governed by a period divide from the monolith of the medieval – in essence, that the 'formation of some of our most basic historical and political assumptions' (in other words, the emergence of secularism and sovereignty) is shaped by a relationship with the 'defining attributes' of the medieval.[18] The 'medieval' or the 'Middle Ages', that is, stands as an oppositional monolith to modernity and acts as a construct or idea characterised by sacrality and feudalism from which the modern can distinguish itself. For some time now, medievalists have from various angles been complicating the assumptions of this monolithic idea of the Middle Ages, arguing forcefully for a more nuanced understanding of the medieval for both our own consumption and that of a wider public.[19] Yet Davis's argument deconstructs the medieval from a different perspective, in other words, from that of modernity. If we want to understand modernity, she argues, then we need to consider the historicity of fundamental concepts such as religion, secularism or democracy that shape the logic of the 'now' in often unthinking ways. In order to achieve this, we need to understand how these concepts are determined by the construction of an oppositional Middle Ages.

The creation of a divide between a medieval and a modern period, originally a European invention, has thus transformed into a 'global category of time', which 'intensively assumes world-historical implications for categories such as the sovereign state and secular politics'.[20] The medieval has, Davis shows, become a 'mobile category, applicable at any time to any society that has not "yet" achieved modernity or, worse, has become retrograde';[21] equally, modernity, however implicitly, is dependent on this monolith of a sacred, feudal, retrograde medieval for its own self-understanding.

Davis's work is closely related to postcolonial approaches to historiography, as exemplified by Chakrabarty: as she shows, the medieval/modern divide is a European invention, a political act of periodisation that must be understood together with colonialism and nationalism in the creation of a white, Eurocentric idealisation of modernity.[22] Indeed, the dialogue between medieval and postcolonial studies is an extraordinarily productive one that has enriched both disciplines considerably, offering new temporal depth to the postcolonial and a vital conceptual and geographical diversity to the medieval.[23] It is also helpful for clarifying the real value of the kind of argument Davis makes for the disciplinary identity of modern languages.

The point I want to make here is not, of course, to try to make a case for the marginalised medieval in practices of expanding and decolonising the curriculum; this could quickly turn out to be rather crass and, of course, medieval studies can (and should) be made more diverse in its own right.[24] Rather, the point is to stress the vital interconnection between thinking across space and thinking across time. Davis's work is primarily a theoretical reflection on the politics of time, that argues for a greater and more careful consideration of how many of the assumptions of modernity are better understood with recourse to the historical shaping of the medieval. And she is, of course, not the only person who has discussed the vital political work of medieval studies, and how it can make a powerful contribution to understanding the contemporary world.[25]

This argument, I suggest, is peculiarly relevant to the discipline of modern languages: because how can we think across cultures and languages without considering how vital the politics of time and periodisation are for the establishment and persistence of Eurocentric thinking, and how they continue to shape conceptualisations of modernity and the nation? As Emily Apter states, 'the politics of periodization defines how "globalization" is mapped onto the humanities, often producing institutional and disciplinary configurations that reproduce economic inequality'.[26] Her conclusion that 'literary history needs to open up to radical re-sequencing, through anachronic timelines, non-Eurochronic descriptions of duration, and a proliferation of new names for periods as yet unnamed' is not an easy task, but one that all literary historians should take seriously.[27] It is also one to which modern linguists are peculiarly well-suited to respond.

Much of the work that explores the complicated relationship of the medieval to contemporary literature and culture, exposing collapsing, layered temporalities, focuses primarily on the anglophone world.[28] From within medieval studies there have been powerful statements about the importance of transnational approaches, particularly Simon Gaunt's exploration of the postcolonial Middle Ages, which he argues must not be confined within the anglophone or anglo-centric context.[29] Yet the important connection between the politics of time and the politics of space is one that is rarely made, and this is where a powerful opportunity lies for modern languages.[30] If modern languages is about crossing borders – linguistically, culturally, geographically – then it must contend seriously with the historical mechanisms behind the formation of these borders, and articulate its value in comprehending and analysing the world through cultural differences that are inflected through time as well as through language, culture and nationhood. If modern languages can tackle contemporary global challenges, then it needs to contend with time, and it needs to contend with the past – and this is both a challenge and an opportunity.

Medieval literature in the modern languages classroom

Apter makes a plea for the rewriting of literary history, but what about the teaching of medieval literature in the modern languages classroom? Following on from the arguments made in the previous section, I would like to suggest that reading medieval literature (or, by extension, any literature of the past) can – and should – function as a fundamental part of the practice of modern languages of looking askance at the familiar and performing acts of critical destabilisation. Much like learning new languages, the study of literature is always destabilising, an activity that challenges and promotes an imaginative response. Medieval literature complements this practice through the added dimension of pastness, and thus through a temporal destabilisation that refocuses the familiar and the unfamiliar, showing how the 'now' is shaped by the past and how the past is always present.

Medieval literature tends to make this way of thinking obvious in itself. Medieval theories of time are diverse, yet rarely linear, and often manifest in cyclical or layered conceptualisations of temporality that attempt to grapple with creation, salvation, worldly history and eternity.[31] Perhaps the two most widely received theories of time throughout the Middle Ages – those of Augustine and Boethius – make this abundantly clear. For Augustine, as expressed most famously in Book 11 of his late-fourth-century *Confessions*, time is something we experience in our minds, not something that actually exists: the past is gone, the future yet to arrive and the present so fleeting that it is impossible to grasp. When we talk about past and future, therefore, what we really describe is a kind of recollection or extension of the mind (*distentio animi*). In his work *The Consolation of Philosophy*, written in 523, Boethius offers a different perspective: for God, the future and past are just as 'present' as the present moment, rendering temporal reality tenseless.[32]

These and other complex ways of thinking about time are, of course, made manifest in art. Medieval saints' lives and visionary narratives, for instance, tend to be constructed around an insistence on both the historical past of the narrative and its continued presence through the active reception of the audience; this reception then shapes the future but contributes to the possibility of salvation.[33] From a broader perspective, Alexander Nagel and Christopher S. Wood describe what they term the 'anachronicity' of the premodern work of art.[34] Focusing primarily on the visual arts and on the Renaissance, but in an argument that can easily be (and has been) stretched back to the Middle Ages, they explore how premodern artworks 'fold' time through the ways in which they shift between temporal anchoring and a rejection of linearity. The result is a complication (or folding) of pasts, presents and futures, and a temporal instability on which artworks often reflect explicitly. The anachronic work, they argue, can summon or create pasts and futures, and 'hold incompatible models in suspension without deciding'.[35]

It is not, of course, necessary to deal with this kind of theoretical complexity in the classroom (although there is no reason why one couldn't). In a more general sense, though, it is helpful to recognise and reflect on the fact that works of art always outlive those who make them and take on new forms of meaning with new audiences: they always *become different* through time, shaped by the experiences and contexts of their recipients. The extreme difference of medieval literature, which on first read can feel bizarre, freakish and wild, rams home just how far away modern readers are from conditions of reception. The difference is partly thematic – from the frankly mad plots of romance, to casual encounters with dragons, shapeshifting, accidental incest, etc. – and partly formal (versification, manuscript transmission, anonymity, textual instability). This strangeness of medieval literature is often described, following Hans Robert Jauss, in terms of 'alterity'. For Jauss, medieval alterity is primarily understood with respect to aesthetic pleasure; readers may need to shift their horizons of expectation to access this pleasure, but an acceptance of the aesthetics of difference and surprise allows, he argues, a recognition of the modernity of medieval literature.[36] Jauss does not refer here to the constructed idea of modernity I discussed above (he is more interested in aesthetics), but his exploration of alterity is a reminder to think differently and to reset expectations when approaching medieval literature – not to judge it on the same terms as forms of contemporary cultural production. I am more interested here in how that difference forces us to think about ourselves and to recognise the context in which we read; how it fosters, if you will, a heightened awareness of our own positionality and of the critical assumptions of the society in which we live. Medieval literature, through its very strangeness, is an excellent tool for encouraging self-reflection and for thinking critically about the social structures we might otherwise take for granted; for understanding the contingency of our own status as moderns and, as discussed above, of modernity itself.

Like all of the cross-cultural work in modern languages, the sideways perspectives offered by medieval literature act as forms of destabilisation that lead us to question radically our norms and assumptions. Medieval literary texts resonate strikingly with many of the concerns that shape our lives in the modern West: from race and gender to ecology and subjectivity. And, of course, their very status as literary texts – creative forms rather than historical sources – doubles down on their potential for experimental (re)thinking. Let us just take two examples to explore these possibilities further: Hartmann von Aue's early-thirteenth-century *Iwein*, a story of a knight that is one of the most famous German Arthurian romances and a reworking of Chrétien de Troyes's Old French *Yvain*; and the twelfth-century narrative *Herzog Ernst*, which tells of the adventures of an exiled duke in a fabulous East inhabited by hybrid and monstrous beings.[37]

Iwein, set in the Arthurian court where knights must constantly state and restate their own prowess, plays out in a context of competitive (and highly fragile) hypermasculinity, where honour can be lost and regained in seconds. This hypermasculine environment is interspersed with the appearance of female figures who exert their own specific, often unusual, forms of power: one has a ring that makes its wearer invisible, another has access to a miraculous healing salve, and most possess an ability for strategic thinking seemingly unknown to male characters. As well as reading the text through a specific context of medieval ethics of 'courtliness' (much of which is a later scholarly invention), it can be productive to use *Iwein* as a relatively straightforward way into thinking about the nature of gender as performance, as well as the slipperiness and interchangeability of gender roles, in both medieval and modern contexts. Iwein is married to a powerful, rather uncanny woman, Laudine, whose feelings for him are perhaps more transactional than his for her. After he is dismissed by her for breaking his promise to return to her within an allotted period of time, he undergoes a kind of total breakdown, often referred to as 'madness', in which he loses all sense of self and lives in the forest in a primitive and animalistic state. This scene can lead to productive classroom discussions around the socially determined construction of subjectivity and identity, and how this intersects with public understandings of mental health; together with Iwein's later 'befriending' of a lion (Is it a 'real' lion? Is it a component of Iwein's reforming selfhood?), it helps us to conceptualise the blurred boundaries between the human and the animal – and, accordingly, the constructedness of both categories.

Herzog Ernst tells a different kind of story. Here, the protagonist becomes embroiled in a political conspiracy (largely not of his own making), that results in him having to leave his lands, ostensibly to join the Crusades. His ships are quickly blown off course and the majority of the narrative consists of a journey through distant, 'wondrous' lands, which enables reflection on medieval geographies, both real and imagined, as well as worldmaking, colonisation and the postcolonial. The inhabitants of these lands – from hybrid crane-men who inhabit an astonishingly civilised and beautiful city (with hot and cold running water!) yet peck a (Christian) princess to death, to giants, pygmies and beings with enormous feet to shade them from the sun or enormous ears to wrap themselves in – lead us to think about processes of racialisation through imagined physical difference, as well as the construction of humanity, animality and normativity. This text, which exists in multiple forms, in German and Latin, from the twelfth century to the twentieth century, also invites reflection on acts of reception, rewriting, recontextualisation and translation across languages and media. Much like *Iwein*, there is also the potential to introduce dialogue with contemporary critical theory. I have found that *Herzog Ernst* offers a good opportunity to introduce students to postcolonial and critical race theory; *Iwein*, with its highly performative gender roles, provides a helpful way in to the work of Judith Butler.

Neither of these examples is a particularly radical choice – many more creative options are available, from a variety of different genres. But I have chosen these because they highlight peculiarly strongly what we might want to term the productive strangeness of medieval literature: the way in which its content seems radically strange to the modern world yet nonetheless resonates sharply with many of its central concerns. My own experience in the classroom is that distance from the present moment can allow for more openness and critical reflection in discussion, leading to a broadening of perspectives and opportunities for creative rethinking of urgent contemporary topics. These opportunities can be brought into sharper relief through comparative or transperiod teaching or through dialogue with other forms of cultural production. *Herzog Ernst*, for instance, could be read comparatively with texts from multiple periods that explore and (de-)construct forms of racial and physical difference. From a broader perspective, reading in dialogue medieval and modern texts that deal with similar themes (but are not otherwise related) can push the productive practice of destabilisation even further and encourage new, imaginative ways of thinking.[38]

Another reason I chose the two examples above is because they both have published translations that are of good quality and are highly accessible; online editions can be acquired easily by institutions via JSTOR. Yet language is clearly the elephant in the room here: how do we overcome the simple linguistic obstacle of medieval (or any premodern) literature? Strange plotlines are one thing, but strange words pose a different challenge altogether. Linguistic difficulty is not only an issue for teaching medieval literature in the modern languages classroom, but for teaching any kind of challenging, authentic material in a context of increasing predominance of ab initio learners. This is partly beyond the remit of this chapter, but the interconnection between language learning and what is often (unfortunately) termed 'content' is becoming an increasingly urgent subject of discussion, especially given that long-held assumptions of the language level of new students no longer stand. In my mind, the answer is not to avoid challenging material (from any period) until an adequate language aptitude has been reached, but rather to compromise; it is possible to work creatively *with* and *in* translation and to build in language learning slowly, moving away from the assumption that students will (and must) read complex literary material in the original language right from the start of their degree. In an ideal world, students would have the opportunity to take specific classes aimed at reading Middle High German, but I am not so naïve as to think that this could be possible other than in a very few institutions; at my own university it would be impossible, and, in fact, teaching in translation is an essential way of meeting module floors and allowing material to be taught at all.[39] Compromises must therefore be sought: there are ways of scaffolding language-learning while teaching in translation, increasing expectations throughout the course of the degree, and of introducing (optional, unassessed) reading groups and seminars that focus more on linguistic challenges. There are some excellent resources, such as *An Introduction to Middle High German* by Howard Jones and Martin H. Jones.[40] And we should all get translating to allow a wider diversity of texts to become accessible to a wider range of students; there are rich opportunities, for instance (if we can find time and money) for collaborative translation activities with students, both undergraduate and postgraduate, and across institutions.[41]

Conclusion

One of the dangers of the argument I have been making is that I might be perceived to be suggesting that languages degrees should *teach everything*. Of course, this is impossible – there will always be an element of compromise, of contingency, of practicality. But what I am asking us to question is the assumption behind what is left out automatically; to question why we implicitly (because it is almost always implicit) prioritise certain areas over others. And to those of us who are pre-modernists, I ask us to think about what we teach, and how we teach it.

One of the greatest values of modern languages – or whatever we want to call it, now and in the future – is the fact that it forces critical engagement with other ways of looking at the world, usually through the lens of linguistic and cultural difference. 'Difference' in this sense is never about simple comparison, nor is it ever straightforwardly 'other'; rather, it destabilises, unsettles, forces a rethink of assumptions and perspectives. The medieval world was just as complicatedly transnational and multilingual as the modern one. In a present day in which it is all too easy to get caught up in the urgency (and ease) of the immediate, the now, the quick fix, a moment that is obsessed with itself and its own currency, modern languages has a vital opportunity that it must seize: an opportunity to promote a truly transnational way of thinking and working that has serious historical as well as geographical depth.

Notes

1 Simon Gaunt and Nicholas Harrison, 'Integrated Learning: Teaching Literature in French', in *French Studies in and for the 21st Century*, ed. by Philippe Lane and Michael Worton (Liverpool University Press, 2011), pp. 107–17 (pp. 107–8).

2 I am thinking particularly of the Arts and Humanities Research Council (AHRC) Open World Research Initiatives projects, or the AHRC Future of Languages Fellowships, as well as the works of, for example, the British Academy and the University Council for Languages (UCFL). The UCFL website is a vital source of information on new projects and their outcomes: https://university-council-for-languages.org [accessed 25 April 2025].

3 See, for instance, the recent name changes of the Institute of Modern Languages Research (to the Institute of Languages, Cultures and Societies) and the University Council of Modern Languages (to the University Council for Languages).

4 James Hodkinson and Benedict Schofield, 'Introduction: German in its Worlds', in *German in the World: The Transnational and Global Contexts of*

German Studies, ed. by James Hodkinson and Benedict Schofield (Camden House, 2020), pp. 1–14 (p. 2).

5 Rebecca Braun and Benedict Schofield, 'Introduction: Transnationalizing German Studies', in *Transnational German Studies*, ed. by Rebecca Braun and Benedict Schofield (Liverpool University Press, 2020), pp. 1–14 (pp. 5–6).

6 Hodkinson and Schofield, 'Introduction', p. 8.

7 See Jennifer Burns and Derek Duncan, 'An Introduction', in *Transnational Modern Languages: A Handbook*, ed. by Jennifer Burns and Derek Duncan (Liverpool University Press, 2022), pp. 1–8 (pp. 5–6): 'The possibilities opened up by strangeness and discomfort, as well as awareness of the pain and exclusion that they may bring, are what there is to be explored and gained through the conjoined study of languages and cultures'.

8 See Hodkinson and Schofield, 'Introduction', p. 6 for useful examples of the contemporaneity of the transnational. Their own conclusion that German studies can learn productively from world literature, where Goethe features widely, in order to 'broaden our temporal range of enquiry' (p. 7) as far back as the early nineteenth century comes as something of a disappointment.

9 Burns and Duncan's recent *Transnational Modern Languages: A Handbook* is exemplary in this regard, ranging widely and (vitally) without distinction between historical moments, and including a chapter by Sharon Kinoshita on 'Premodernity' – which reminds us, if we needed reminding, of the fact that the premodern world was just as multilingual and interconnected as the world today, and just as complicatedly.

10 Braun and Schofield, 'Introduction', p. 12.

11 Such expectations are, inevitably, at least partly connected to languages curricula in secondary education, the vast majority of which focus on contemporary life; if cultural topics have a historical dimension, this tends to be restricted to the twentieth century. Challenges of marketing in higher education are a different matter and one beyond the subject of this chapter, but it suffices to say that I have been told in my own institution by a colleague in marketing that medieval languages 'look bad' and that our degree programmes, both undergraduate and postgraduate, would be 'more attractive' if I had never been employed.

12 See Dipesh Chakrabarty, *Provincializing Europe: Postcolonial Thought and Historical Difference* (Princeton University Press, 2000).

13 This argument is stated forcefully in the preface to the 2007 edition of *Provincializing Europe*, pp. xi–xxi.

14 Chakrabarty, *Provincializing Europe*, pp. 109–11.

15 See Andrew B. R. Elliott, *Medievalism, Politics and Mass Media: Appropriating the Middle Ages in the Twenty-First Century* (Brewer, 2017).

16 For an overview, see Matthew Gabriele, 'Vikings, Crusaders, Confederates', https://www.historians.org/perspectives-article/vikings-crusaders

-confederates-misunderstood-historical-imagery-at-the-january-6-capitol-insurrection-january-2021/ [accessed 23 April 2025].

17 Kathleen Davis, *Periodization and Sovereignty: How Ideas of Feudalism and Secularization Govern the Politics of Time* (University of Pennsylvania Press, 2008).

18 Davis, *Periodization and Sovereignty*, p. 6.

19 On feudalism, see fundamentally Susan Reynolds, *Fiefs and Vassals: The Medieval Evidence Reinterpreted* (Oxford University Press, 1994). The complexities of medieval secularism and religious belief are widely discussed; for a recent important intervention see Barbara Newman, *Medieval Crossover: Reading the Secular against the Sacred* (Notre Dame University Press, 2015).

20 Davis, *Periodization and Sovereignty*, p. 5.

21 Davis, *Periodization and Sovereignty*, p. 5.

22 As Chakrabarty states, 'Can the designation of something or some group as *non-* or *premodern* ever be anything but a gesture of the powerful?'. Dipesh Chakrabarty, *Habitations of Modernity: Essays in the Wake of Subaltern Studies* (University of Chicago Press, 2002), p. xix.

23 For a good summary, see Kathleen Davis and Nadia Altschul, 'The Idea of "the Middle Ages" Outside Europe', in *Medievalisms in the Postcolonial World: The Idea of 'the Middle Ages' Outside Europe*, ed. by Kathleen Davis and Nadia Altschul (Johns Hopkins Medieval Press, 2009), pp. 1–24.

24 This is not to say that the parallel is entirely without validity – yet a comparison between the 'othering' of the Middle Ages and of (post)colonial spaces is always going to be a highly problematic one. See Simon Gaunt, 'Can the Middle Ages Be Postcolonial?', *Comparative Literature*, 61.2 (2009), pp. 160–76 (pp. 161–2).

25 See, for instance, Carolyn Dinshaw's classic *Getting Medieval: Sexualities and Communities, Pre- and Postmodern* (Duke University Press, 1999), which exposes the queerness of the medieval in narrations of modernity and the vital role it has to play in contemporary cultural and queer theory.

26 Emily Apter, 'Rethinking Periodization for the "Now-Time"', in *Being Contemporary: French Literature, Culture and Politics Today*, ed. by Lia Brozgal and Sara Kippur (Liverpool University Press, 2016), pp. 29–42 (p. 30).

27 Apter, 'Rethinking Periodization', p. 35.

28 Some important recent interventions include Joshua Davies, *Visions and Ruins: Cultural Memory and the Untimely Middle Ages* (Manchester University Press, 2018); Robert Mills, *Derek Jarman's Medieval Modern* (Brewer, 2018); Alexander Nagel, *Medieval Modern: Art Out of Time* (Thames and Hudson, 2012).

29 Gaunt, 'Can the Middle Ages'. For a recent example of the productive possibilities of transnational work within medieval studies and postcolonial studies, see Doriane Zerka, *Imagining Iberia in Medieval German Literature* (Legenda, 2023).

30 Davis's edited volume with Nadia Altschul draws explicit connection between the idea of the Middle Ages and the idea of Europe; see Davis and Altschul, 'The Idea', p. 1: '"the Middle Ages," like "Europe," is an idea rather than an internally unified entity and [. . .] to an important extent the histories of the Middle Ages and Europe *as ideas* have over the course of centuries been mutually constitutive'. The volume as a whole is an interesting provocation, exploring the construction of the Middle Ages from non-European perspectives.

31 For an excellent and accessible new introduction, see Gillian Adler and Paul Strohm, *Alle Thyng Hath Tyme: Time and Medieval Life* (Reaktion, 2023).

32 See Almut Suerbaum and Annie Sutherland, 'Introduction', in *Medieval Temporalities: The Experience of Time in Medieval Europe*, ed. by Almut Suerbaum and Annie Sutherland (Brewer, 2021), pp. 1–13; Sarah Bowden, Lea Braun, and George Younge, 'Time in the Twelfth Century', *Interfaces: A Journal of Medieval European Literatures*, 10 (2023), pp. 1–16.

33 *Anfang und Ende: Formen narrativer Zeitmodellierung in der Vormoderne*, ed. by Udo Friedrich, Andreas Hammer, and Christiane Witthöft (Akademie, 2014); Sarah Bowden, 'Time and Textuality in Visionary Writing: Narrating the Afterlife in Alber's *Tnugdalus*', *Interfaces: A Journal of Medieval European Literatures*, 10 (2023), pp. 38–58.

34 Alexander Nagel and Christopher S. Wood, *Anachronic Renaissance* (Zone Books, 2010).

35 Nagel and Wood, *Anachronic Renaissance*, p. 18. The authors argue that the Renaissance is a particularly vital time for encapsulating this temporal characteristic of art: it is, they argue, the time when authorial presence becomes institutionalised, which leads to a heightened self-awareness of temporal complexity and a tension between the pre-Renaissance 'substitutional' and the new 'authorial' model of production. One could easily think about twelfth-century Europe in the same light, however.

36 Hans Robert Jauss, 'The Alterity and Modernity of Medieval Literature', trans. by Timothy Bahti, *New Literary History*, 10.2 (1979), pp. 181–229.

37 Hartmann von Aue, *Gregorius. Armer Heinrich. Iwein*, ed. and trans. by Volker Mertens (Deutscher Klassiker, 2008). English translation: *German Romance Volume III: Iwein or The Knight with the Lion*, ed. and trans. by Cyril Edwards (Brewer, 2007). *Herzog Ernst*, ed. and trans. by Mathias Herweg (Reclam, 2019); English translation in *Three Political Tales from Medieval Germany: Duke Ernst, Henry of Kempten, and Reynard the Fox*, trans. by Brian Murdoch (Camden House, 2024).

38 Asking students to write comparatively across periods is challenging, but highly productive. New comparative perspectives can result in entirely new readings of individual works, bolstering student confidence and allowing them to demonstrate their capabilities as independent and original researchers.

39 With a current module floor of fifteen (and it's not going to go down), it is essential for me to offer modules with translated material so that they can be taken without German; these courses often attract highly motivated students studying (for example) English or Liberal Arts, adding to the diversity of the seminar room. It also means it is possible to teach together with colleagues working in other language areas.

40 Howard Jones and Martin H. Jones, *An Introduction to Middle High German* (Oxford University Press, 2024). This is a dedicated student edition of their earlier *The Oxford Guide to Middle High German* (Oxford University Press, 2019).

41 A good example is the *Global Medieval Sourcebook*, based at Stanford University, https://sourcebook.stanford.edu [accessed 23 April 2025].

References

Adler, Gillian, and Paul Strohm, *Alle Thyng Hath Tyme: Time and Medieval Life* (Reaktion, 2023)

Apter, Emily, 'Rethinking Periodization for the "Now-Time"', in *Being Contemporary: French Literature, Culture and Politics Today*, ed. by Lia Brozgal and Sara Kippur (Liverpool University Press, 2016), pp. 29–42

Bowden, Sarah, 'Time and Textuality in Visionary Writing: Narrating the Afterlife in Alber's *Tnugdalus*', *Interfaces: A Journal of Medieval European Literatures*, 10 (2023), pp. 38–58

Bowden, Sarah, Lea Braun, and George Younge, 'Time in the Twelfth Century', *Interfaces: A Journal of Medieval European Literatures*, 10 (2023), pp. 1–16

Braun, Rebecca, and Benedict Schofield (eds), *Transnational German Studies* (Liverpool University Press, 2020)

Burns, Jennifer, and Derek Duncan (eds), *Transnational Modern Languages: A Handbook* (Liverpool University Press, 2022)

Chakrabarty, Dipesh, *Habitations of Modernity: Essays in the Wake of Subaltern Studies* (University of Chicago Press, 2002)

Chakrabarty, Dipesh, *Provincializing Europe: Postcolonial Thought and Historical Difference* (Princeton University Press, 2000)

Davies, Joshua, *Visions and Ruins: Cultural Memory and the Untimely Middle Ages* (Manchester University Press, 2018)

Davis, Kathleen, *Periodization and Sovereignty: How Ideas of Feudalism and Secularization Govern the Politics of Time* (University of Pennsylvania Press, 2008)

Davis, Kathleen, and Nadia Altschul (eds), *Medievalisms in the Postcolonial World: The Idea of 'the Middle Ages' Outside Europe* (Johns Hopkins Medieval Press, 2009)

Dinshaw, Carolyn, *Getting Medieval: Sexualities and Communities, Pre- and Postmodern* (Duke University Press, 1999)
Edwards, Cyril (ed. and trans.), *German Romance Volume III: Iwein or The Knight with the Lion* (Brewer, 2007)
Elliott, Andrew B. R., *Medievalism, Politics and Mass Media: Appropriating the Middle Ages in the Twenty-First Century* (Brewer, 2017)
Friedrich, Udo, Andreas Hammer, and Christiane Witthöft (eds), *Anfang und Ende: Formen narrativer Zeitmodellierung in der Vormoderne* (Akademie, 2014)
Gabriele, Matthew, 'Vikings, Crusaders, Confederates', https://www.historians.org/perspectives-article/vikings-crusaders-confederates-misunderstood-historical-imagery-at-the-january-6-capitol-insurrection-january-2021/ [accessed 23 April 2025]
Gaunt, Simon, 'Can the Middle Ages Be Postcolonial?', *Comparative Literature*, 61.2 (2009), pp. 160–76
Gaunt, Simon, and Nicholas Harrison, 'Integrated Learning: Teaching Literature in French', in *French Studies in and for the 21st Century*, ed. by Philippe Lane and Michael Worton (Liverpool University Press, 2011), pp. 107–17
Global Medieval Sourcebook, https://sourcebook.stanford.edu [accessed 23 April 2025]
Herweg, Mathias (ed. and trans.), *Herzog Ernst* (Reclam, 2019)
Hodkinson, James, and Benedict Schofield (eds), *German in the World: The Transnational and Global Contexts of German Studies* (Camden House, 2020)
Jauss, Hans Robert, 'The Alterity and Modernity of Medieval Literature', trans. by Timothy Bahti, *New Literary History*, 10.2 (1979), pp. 181–229
Jones, Howard, and Martin H. Jones, *An Introduction to Middle High German* (Oxford University Press, 2024)
Jones, Howard, and Martin H. Jones, *The Oxford Guide to Middle High German* (Oxford University Press, 2019)
Mills, Robert, *Derek Jarman's Medieval Modern* (Brewer, 2018)
Murdoch, Brian (trans.), *Three Political Tales from Medieval Germany: Duke Ernst, Henry of Kempten, and Reynard the Fox* (Camden House, 2024)
Nagel, Alexander, *Medieval Modern: Art Out of Time* (Thames and Hudson, 2012)

Nagel, Alexander, and Christopher S. Wood, *Anachronic Renaissance* (Zone Books, 2010)

Newman, Barbara, *Medieval Crossover: Reading the Secular against the Sacred* (Notre Dame University Press, 2015)

Reynolds, Susan, *Fiefs and Vassals: The Medieval Evidence Reinterpreted* (Oxford University Press, 1994)

Suerbaum, Almut, and Annie Sutherland (eds), *Medieval Temporalities: The Experience of Time in Medieval Europe* (Brewer, 2021)

von Aue, Hartmann, *Gregorius. Armer Heinrich. Iwein*, ed. and trans. by Volker Mertens (Deutscher Klassiker, 2008)

Zerka, Doriane, *Imagining Iberia in Medieval German Literature* (Legenda, 2023)

Chapter 2

Literary research after the decolonial turn: towards new *praxis*

Emanuelle Santos

Literature conjugates language and storytelling into aesthetic forms rich in multiplicity of meaning. Encased in its home discipline of literary studies, literary research, as it is known in Western academia, resorts largely to qualitative methods to understand this artistic craft of human cognitive and social faculties. Through the continuous carving of analytical techniques to unveil literature's plethora of meanings in its work with language, literary studies illuminate important questions related not only to the cultures and societies within which literature is produced but also to the contexts wherein literature is received across space and time. In its inherent connection with literature's multiplicity of interpretative possibilities, enabled by the generative intersection of aesthetic historicity and its resignification in reception through time, literary studies is bound to be a dynamic field. Always attuned to the interplay of past and present concerns surrounding its many contexts of reading, literary studies' intrinsic capacity for change has ensured literary research's long tradition as a privileged medium to understand cultures and societies.

Literature's privilege is my point of departure to argue for the advantages that a decolonial praxis has as a specific decolonial approach capable of harbouring societal change. Its status as one of the most visible battlegrounds for movements seeking to decolonise the curriculum in UK Higher Education (UKHE) evidences literature's pivotal role in society. It indicates the relevance of a structured decolonial approach in equipping literary studies to continue serving as a nodal discipline, driving the kind of change needed to promote epistemic justice, build cultural, political and social bridges, and feed other disciplines in the humanities. Yet, for a candid appreciation of literary studies' privileges as a mode of inquiry, it is important to admit that literary research has never really been very inclusive. By that, I mean not that issues pertaining to the inclusion/exclusion paradigm are irrelevant to literary studies; instead, I propose that we face how they are historically at the field's very core. As the development of literary theory testifies, to speak of literature is to separate the literary from the non-literary based on a judgement of literariness, itself grounded on critics' benchmarks based on the literary theory of the day. In fact, I would go as far as arguing that the inclusion/exclusion paradigm is intrinsic both to literary studies' *object* and to its *structure* as a discipline and *method* of enquiry. After all, can we really dissociate the lack of diversity in mainstream literary syllabi from the exclusivist structure of higher education and the Cartesian legacy of the scientific method? My hypothesis is that this dissociation is not just impossible but rather a reality in the field and a main reason why curricular diversification, as important as it is, falls short of living up to any significant decolonial transformative potential.

The shockwaves of the decolonial boom in the academia of the Global North this century have exposed mainstream literary studies' continued focus on canonicity and written language, especially that selected to be published in former colonial metropoles, as a major obstacle to the realisation of the field's potential as a mode of knowing, experiencing and connecting with diverse cultures in their diversity. However, the move past the excitement of the changes brought by challenges to curricular coloniality has given rise to robust debates on the limitations of diversification, if that is to be regarded as the main job of decolonial thought in literary studies. Whereas these developments constitute a welcomed intervention, keeping us from diversity-washing cultural structures deeply rooted in coloniality, they inadvertently give way to unhelpful scepticism that can be quick to dismiss the decolonial paradigm before matters of structure and methods have received due attention. Before we give up on what the decolonial aim can do in, to and through our discipline, we ought to have a more substantial debate on the fundamental issue of methodology in literary research if we are to overcome the obstacles preventing us from delivering the impactful work that the decolonial paradigm can be conducive to doing.

In this chapter, I sketch a novel methodological framework for a decolonial critique in literary studies inspired by Freirean praxis. Defined as an action-driven dialectics that is aware of its *aim* and its *processes*,[1] a praxis-based framework is capable of reconnecting decolonial criticism, at a methodological level, with its aim to expose and eliminate coloniality from its practice through a conscious approach to process, which I conceive as the field's *structure* and *method*. In what follows, I start by looking into the relevance of structures in literary studies by reflecting on fundamental aspects underpinning the emergence of our discipline, such as its late-modern professionalisation and institutionalisation. Focusing on the rise of vernacular literary studies connected to the institutionalisation of English as a discipline in the UKHE, I assess the impact of these structures in the development of fields designed to address inequality, such as postcolonial and decolonial studies. Next, I turn to the intimate relationship between institutionalisation and research methods, recovering forgotten histories that reveal the arbitrariness of lines dividing the subjectivity of the critic and the objectivity of method at the foundations of literary studies, which I regard as evidence of our field's built-in fitness for a decolonial criticism capable of promoting the kind of cognitive transformation that supports societal change. I conclude by reflecting on the effectiveness of praxis-based decolonial readings of the book *As Telefones* [The Telephones] (2020) by Angolan-Portuguese writer and academic Djaimilia Pereira de Almeida.[2]

On structures: institutionalisation and the paradox of diversity

It is not an understatement to say that diversity – or the lack thereof – is a concept intrinsically connected to all aspects of literary research; yet it feels like one of its most elusive aspects to tackle. The discipline's inception as the 'poor man's Classic',[3] in tandem with the debut of English in UKHE curricula, speaks of a class divide from its get-go. Class, religion, race and gender are only a few indicators of the lack of diversity at the basis of literary studies. In what follows, I trace this phenomenon through the field's history and assess its processes with the view to informing a praxis-based decolonial critique.

The institutionalisation of literary studies through the rise of English cannot be overlooked if we are to examine the disciplinary development of the field. Mainstream narratives, such as Terry Eagleton's *Literary Theory: An Introduction*,[4] privilege the development of literary approaches to the concrete aspects of field institutionalisation, which certainly accompanies it.

This kind of approach sets up a departure point for literary studies in England, with Matthew Arnold, who occupied the position of Professor of Poetry at the University of Oxford between 1857 and 1867, and his social criticism registered in *Culture and Anarchy*.[5] From there, attention shifts to Cambridge and the practical criticism of I. A. Richards, in post between 1922 and 1939, followed by the close reading of F. R. Leavis, appointed as an academic in the institution between 1927 and 1964. Other renditions remain in Cambridge a little longer and offer accounts of the cultural Marxism of Raymond Williams, appointed between 1961 and 1983 and, should one's scope on literary studies be wide enough to encompass cultural studies, I would hope for a mention of Stuart Hall in Birmingham between 1964 and 1979.

Disregarding the institutional dimensions of these narratives risks obscuring how literary research found a foothold in the university. Though often associated with the origins of English studies, Matthew Arnold's tenure at Oxford does not mark their beginning, as the discipline only emerged there in 1882, after his departure from the institution.[6] Arnold's role as Professor of Poetry was largely honorary and unrelated to English as a formal academic field. Instead, the roots of vernacular literary studies are more accurately traced to London, where a utilitarian ethos supported educating working men. England's first professorships in English literature were established at University College in 1828 (today's University College London, UCL) and King's College in 1831 – with both positions initially held by the same man as he changed jobs – and gained particular popularity among female students. Yet, even this narrative omits crucial developments, such as the rise of English literary studies in colonial India during the 1820s,[7] or earlier efforts by dissenters of the Anglican establishment across England, Scotland and the American colonies in the late seventeenth century.[8] Most telling in what they leave out, standard narratives on the history of the field paint a familiar picture for the contemporary reader as religious minorities, colonised peoples and workers, not to mention women, are excluded.

Different takes on the panorama of literary studies in English, using the UK as a case study, will, irremediably and rightfully, be capable of pointing to many more historical omissions than this brief panorama. They could also point to the different ideologies, missions and means taken by each of these beginnings of literary studies, especially on the grounds of how English was conceptualised (rhetoric, philology, literature, history, etc.) or whether we are speaking of *belles lettres*, criticism or research. All these considered, the point remains. To open literary research to a decolonial critique committed to transformation, literary approaches must be considered alongside historically informed appreciations of the concrete conditions enabling them. In the UK context, literary research's canonical poiesis gives prominence to developments carried out by its elite – and so-called ancient – universities; situates its beginning between the late-nineteenth and early-twentieth centuries; and excludes the agency of those at odds with state ideology and an elite way of life.

The reckoning with literary studies' legacy of elitism, imperialism and racism – its coloniality – may be a fresh memory to readers contemporary to this piece. The last decade has seen a concrete push for change in terms of inclusivity taking place in the Global North driven by student-led movements across the North/South divide seeking to decolonise the academic curriculum at the higher education level. While what may have stayed in collective memory are polemics around universities' curricular reviews fuelled by waves of protests and activism in the context of the Black Lives Matter movement – often framed by media in sensationalistic terms like 'replacing Jane Austen by Toni Morrison' and 'removing Chaucer's white Western sonnet from the university curriculum',[9] or headlines such as 'Has "wokeness" killed the English literature degree?' – the debate went well beyond that.[10] If the depth and breadth of the discussion in the public domain were hindered by media misinformation,[11] they still managed to move the issue beyond the point of tokenistic inclusion, not replacement, of what has been termed non-DWM (Dead White Male) authors in literary syllabi. In the words of Sandeep Bakshi, 'the move to decolonise literary syllabi considers the veritable question of *how* a work of literature is produced and *how* we consider it as partaking in a specific reading list. In other words, it pivots on decolonising *our* methodology of relating to and teaching literature.'[12] Yet, as much as this definition is in keeping with the work left to do to open literary studies to the unlimited possibilities of articulation of human experience through language, it feels like this work is pretty much what literary studies has been doing, at least since the advent of colonial discourse analysis in the late 1970s, evolving later into the postcolonial approach to literatures and cultures. Why not just make the case to continue doing that?

Postcolonial studies has undeniably transformed literary scholarship. Robert Young went as far as saying that its influence now extends across nearly all disciplines in the humanities and social sciences, becoming 'part of the consciousness of our era'.[13] Emerging from colonial discourse analysis, most notably Edward Said's work exposing the colonial logic embedded in cultural artefacts shaped by material structures of empire,[14] postcolonial theory evolved a diverse body of theories that not only identify and critique cultural oppression but also trace aesthetic forms of agency, empowerment and resistance rooted in the imagi-*nations* of anticolonial movements. Transnational from its inception, reflecting both the global reach of colonialism and the internationalism of its opposition, postcolonial studies challenged the boundaries of Western nationalisms underpinning canon formation in mainstream literary studies. It enriched the field with aesthetics and theories capable of calling hegemonic metropolitan frameworks by their name and created interpretative models now canonical in their own right. Bringing metropolitan traditions into dialogue with literatures from Africa, the Americas, the Middle East, Asia and Oceania reshaped the institutional structure of literary studies, increasingly dissolving boundaries between English departments and those of comparative literature and modern languages.[15]

Despite the seismic shift that postcolonial studies brought to literary studies, the debate that decolonial thought has raised is evidence that this subfield of literary studies has enough blind spots to raise the question of whether it has reached its point of stagnation. This question, however, is not new. To some, like Ella Shohat, postcolonial studies was born past its time. In an essay published as early as 1992, she questions the field's 'ahistorical and universalizing deployments, and its potentially depoliticizing implications' and speaks of the contradiction of thinking in terms of 'post' when economic and political practices supporting the reincarnation of colonialism into neocolonialism in the *longue durée* of capitalism were (and are) still present in what was then called the Third and the Fourth Worlds.[16] While this kind of criticism of the field subsided with time and through the cutting-edge work of many scholars who put the postcolonial lens to the service of the causes of the oppressed,[17] the matter never really went away. In her 2004 text 'The Institutionalisation of Postcolonial Studies', Benita Parry refined that critique by defining the validity of the postcolonial as critical theory in its commitment to historicisation and political engagement.[18] For Parry, the postcolonial aspect of a literary work lies precisely in its aesthetic registration of life in the context of colonial oppression anchored in the need to maintain exploitative and extractivist production, which historically lay in localised, internationalist activism that was explicitly anticolonial, hence political.[19] By that logic, the postcolonial approach to literary studies will only work as a mode of critique, a set of theories or even a field if it sees culture *in relation to*, and *not separated from*, the political and economic realities that define the postcolonial condition.

Tracing what happened to the commitment to material history in the course of the establishment of postcolonial studies in Anglo-American academia in the 1980s, Parry locates the failure to fulfil its transformative potential at the societal level to its institutionalisation that 'took place at a time when the linguistic turn was in the ascendant within philosophy and literary theory, and at the moment when cultural studies was in the process of turning its back on its materialist beginnings, operating increasingly with "an essentially textualist account of culture"'.[20] Looking at the state of affairs in the field almost a decade later, in a piece titled 'What is Left in Postcolonial Studies', Parry responds to Young's article of the same year, referred to earlier in this piece. She deepens her critique of postcolonial studies' loss of rigour due to abandoning its commitment to articulate concrete historical and political tensions. At this point, for Parry, 'postcolonialism effectively became a reconciliatory rather than a critical, anti-colonialist category'.[21] Her view of Young's proposition of postcolonialism permeability in the fields of humanities and social sciences is seen as an exaggerated praise lacking fundament as it 'ignore[s] the meticulous work produced by scholars on the very issues they address—globalisation, Islam, [I]ndigenous peoples, migration'.[22] Young's view of racism and discrimination as the othering foundation of modernity is seen as a refusal to acknowledge the single-modernity paradigm of chiefly economic rather than culturalist drive connecting the peoples of Europe, Africa, Asia and the Americas. Parry recognises postcolonial criticism's tendency to focus on European agency and self-consciousness to which its (post)colonial other would only serve as a countermodern reference point, 'which interrupts, interrogates, and displaces its truth claims'.[23]

Parry does not disavow postcolonial studies altogether, despite the vehemence of her positions, as in both pieces she recognises that much quality work has been done, including her own. As well as Shohat who later admitted being her own case,[24] Parry critiques from within, even though she paints a panorama where approaches embedded in historical materialism like hers are now marginal in the field. Despite its many layers, what this debate shows in the context of my intervention is that the hegemonic postcolonial approach in literary research, popularised by highly cited critics and theorists in the Anglo-American academic circuit, has demonstrated a tangible withdrawal from the political contexts surrounding the literary work in its concrete, historical, worldly existence. This apolitical stance takes root at the same time the field is institutionalised, which makes the time when the aesthetic of the subaltern other gains a seat at the table of hegemonic knowledge the time when their plea for political change effaces from critical view: '[t]he postcolonialist shift away from historical processes has meant that discursive or "epistemic" violence has tended to take precedence in analysis over the *institutional* practices of the violent social system of colonialism'.[25]

The rise of vernacular literary studies in Britain through the institutionalisation of English was tied to efforts aimed at educating politically marginalised groups: dissenters, colonial subjects and the working class. While these initiatives were far from egalitarian, often serving ideological domination and enacting violence,[26] acknowledging the role played by these minoritised groups is crucial for exposing how dominant historical narratives of literary studies marginalise their contributions in favour of developments at elite institutions like Oxford and Cambridge. This erasure is even more pronounced in postcolonial studies, where the incorporation of postcolonial and postimperial literary aesthetics into hegemonic frameworks often obscures their foundational ties to political movements seeking material transformation. The disconnection between mainstream postcolonial criticism and its anticolonial roots has created a critical void that decolonial approaches now seek to address.

The fact that one of the most visible trenches of decolonial epistemic activism is the curriculum of literary studies, attests to the field's concrete relevance to society at large, moving beyond the isolating metaphor of the academic ivory tower. Not only a result of the discipline's historic role in building ideological projects of master narratives of nations and empires, the decolonial battle for the curriculum in literary studies speaks of the discipline's power, as well as its historic role, in deconstructing these very same narratives of nation and empire as has already been shown by postcolonial studies. The anticolonial verve animating literature in the former colonial world crystallised in much of the innovation marking the inauguration of their future national literary systems, captivating scholars and critics across the colonial divide. Literary studies' privilege is at stake again as a nodal point of aesthetic rendition of empire, liberation and culture – the latter in its broad sense of a way of life – in history, turning it into a battleground for a decolonial activism seeking concrete action.

Despite its commitment to expose, explain and work towards ending coloniality in the aftermath of classic forms of European colonialism, decolonial studies itself is far from an even playing field. The unevenness sustaining the hegemonic mode of capitalist organisation today inevitably taints the production and circulation of these ideas as they rely on space made through their very institutionalisation via the creation of programmes of study, academic positions, journals, conferences and research grants, a process of which this piece is not exempt. As a result, any responsible attempts to pin down the field's beginnings in terms of time, place and intellectual tradition would require a multilingual, transnational and multimodal effort that far exceeds the constraints of this piece and the skills of this academic. My view of decolonial studies understands it as a pluricentric field rooted in localised concrete activism in terms of political, economic and epistemic rights and whose relation with institutionalised academic discourse can be troublesome.

Take, for example, the scathing criticism that Bolivian sociologist, historian and lifelong activist Silvia Rivera Cusicanqui makes of this '"political economy" of knowledge' in relation to the decolonial epistemology developed by the Argentinean cultural theorist Walter Mignolo and his collaborators: 'Walter Mignolo and company have built a small empire within an empire, strategically appropriating the contributions of the subaltern studies school of India and the various Latin American variants of critical reflection on colonization and decolonization'.[27] For Cusicanqui, the institutionalisation of these efforts creates '[n]eologisms such as *decolonial*, *transmodernity*, and *eco-si-mía* [. . .], and such language entangles and paralyzes their objects of study: the [I]ndigenous and African-descended people with whom these academics believe they are in dialogue'.[28] Her assertion warns of decolonial institutionalisation's danger of alienating knowledge born from contexts of political, economic and cultural struggles from its material political horizon of realisation and explains how it can eclipse the very minoritarian forms of knowledge that it purportedly advocates for: '[t]hrough the game of who cites whom, hierarchies are structured, and we end up having to consume, in a regurgitated form, the very ideas regarding decolonization that we [I]ndigenous people and intellectuals of Bolivia, Peru, and Ecuador have produced independently'.[29]

The consequences of the institutionalisation of decolonial studies assessed by Cusicanqui is just one of the many readings of the decolonial which will, invariably, be rooted in the sociohistoric conditions marking the worldliness of each intervention, including the hegemonic ones. This inscribes the decolonial – be it in *decoloniality* as theorised by Mignolo's Latin American prism, *decolonisation* as seen by Cusicanqui via her experience with Bolivian Indigenous struggles or *decolonisation* as seen by Nigerian philosopher Olúfẹ́mi Táíwò when looking at the African continent[30] – in the fruitful realm of inherent incompleteness of 'travelling theory' proposed by Edward Said.[31] Yet, one fundamental commonality among serious formulations in decolonial thought is a twofold commitment to exposing the continuation of practices that can be traced back to colonialism – or coloniality – and a pledge towards transformative action at the societal level that goes against these legacies. Wide enough to encompass the whole array of experiences of colonialism – direct, indirect, political, economic, cultural, social, biological, etc. – across time and space, the focus on situated forms of coloniality in tandem with a commitment to transformative action in the horizon of a realisable degree of change constitutes a matrix ideally configured to be potentialised by the worldliness of the critic.

Towards a *praxis* for the literary research method

The institutionalisation of literary, postcolonial and decolonial studies discussed attests to the fundamental relation between our kind of epistemic endeavour and the conditions of production framing academic labour, which constitutes the very reason why literary curricula are an important arena for decolonial action. When the decolonial activist disputes a given curricular choice, they are not necessarily advocating for the abandonment of aesthetics or the very idea of literariness. What they question is the intersection of the principles underlying that choice and coloniality. By doing so, they put in check two major aspects at the root of Western epistemology: the sanctity of the scientific method and the objectivity of the researcher.

Just as was the case with the matter of diversity, it turns out that issues of method and objectivity were also at the heart of the constitution of the field as an academic discipline in the Western model of the university. In a 2018 article titled 'The Debate with Method in the History of Literary

Studies', literary scholar Mark Hewson argues that '[t]he decisive problem for literary studies [. . .] was programmed from the outset, with its entry into the university, and its conception of itself as a research discipline' whose methodological standardisation clashed with established forms of practical criticism, anchored in aesthetic value and centred on the figure of the critic.[32] This chapter of disciplinary history is now effaced from view with the subsiding of the argument into the sublative victory of the research paradigm, due – in great part – to the critic's devising of methods such as close reading to 'show that seriousness and rigor are not the exclusive possession of scholarship'.[33] Hewson's recovery of the debate does a great job of exposing the tension between objectivity and subjectivity that lies at the intersection between the premise of methodologically rigorous, hence reproducible and systematic, quest for knowledge and the very relational nature between literature and the subjectivity of the critic. As he explains, '[t]he diverse critiques of method-based research in literary studies converge toward the claim that the literary work depends for its existence on the reading: as such, it does not have the status of an object, available for a progressive work of knowledge and verification' given that 'literature itself has no objective reality; it is only real when there is a critical discourse that gives it existence; without such a discourse, there can be texts or fictions, novels, poems or plays, but no literature'.[34] As such, the decolonial pressure affects literary studies because of our discipline's role in the realm of ontology. Given that the literary object is not initially given prior to the ontological gesture of a critical tradition that establishes the literariness giving rise to literature as an object of inquiry,[35] the processes encapsulated in our work make it into a pivotal frontier of coloniality: a place where it can be both enacted and opposed.

Hewson's focus on the importance of method in the poiesis of literary studies restores the relevance of the critic in the field, echoing the 1983 work of Edward Said in *The World, the Text and the Critic*. Said's experience in a North American academia speaks of the professionalisation of the literary critic through a high degree of specialisation entailing a 'very precise division of labour' that saw critical work divorced from the reality of the world,[36] retreating into disembodied notions of textuality. Conceived as 'the somewhat mystical and disinfected subject matter of literary theory',[37] Said saw textuality as 'the exact antithesis and displacement of what might be called history'.[38] Despite writing at one of the highest points for theory in the history of literary studies, it was the critic that Said saw as the main historical agent in the process of reconnecting 'texts and the existential actualities of human life, politics, societies, and events' and of making theory travel across cultures.[39] In its capacity of grounding theory, critics' critical consciousness works as a 'sort of spatial sense, a sort of measuring faculty for locating or situating theory' and whose job is 'to open it [theory] up toward historical reality, towards society'.[40]

The agency of the critic is, thus, one of the most significant loci for a decolonial praxis capable of further unlocking the potential for transformative change in literary studies. The battle over the objectivity of method at the genesis of the field's institutionalisation, professionalisation and specialisation of culture studies attests to our discipline's unique position in the coloniality frontier, as a broker capable of both promoting and countering it. In our ontological gesture of creating literature through reading cultural artefacts as literature, we critics, aware of the worldliness of our own views and values, act upon the world by validating as culture the aesthetic formations of stories where those at the margins of society can recognise themselves as subjects in their historical agency. Elevated to the same subjective positions as those occupying hegemonic positions in society, those relegated to the other side of the colonial difference can better oppose processes of dehumanisation subjacent to their commodification in capitalist modes of production. In this context, the critic's action can transcend the type of critical consciousness conceived by Said, as a binding agent between text and/in history, to achieve the liberatory potential of critical consciousness conceived in Paulo Freire, whose objective is to liberate from oppression. In a context marked by the maintenance of coloniality, a decolonial literary praxis is one centred on the agency of the critic, whose worldly reading is aware of its processes. In our field, this implies localising the worldviews underlying methods and material conditions shaping the structures within which we develop our labour.

From action to reflection, and from reflection upon action to a new action

A decolonial praxis in literary studies is not only dedicated to the worldling of literature but is also committed to transforming literary tradition when it comes to its own coloniality. This demands a critical reading equally capable of instating a text as literature and of tracing how the admission of that text interacts with the coloniality of a given literary tradition. It is by honouring a principle of praxis that is pledged to an action aware of its aim and process – understood in the literary context as a method and material structure – that the critic's ontological gesture can live up to the drive for change that distinguishes the decolonial literary research. Like what happens in the relationship between teacher and student described by Paulo Freire regarding the transformative potential of critical pedagogy in the process of adult literacy, the study of non-hegemonic literary aesthetics should be a dialogical process that transforms text in literature as much as it transforms the critics' attitudes towards their disciplines and their labour. Seen in these terms, the challenge involved in the decolonial critical endeavour becomes clearer, and any attempts to conceive ways forward for this praxis call for a candid appreciation of its extent.

In my research for a 2024 piece on *As Telefones* [The Telephones] by Angolan-Portuguese author Djaimilia Pereira de Almeida, I could appreciate some of the challenges for a decolonial critique. The novel explores a thirty-year telephone relationship between a mother and daughter separated by migration from Angola to Portugal. Narrated from the fragmented perspective of the daughter, sent as an infant to live with her aunt in Lisbon for improved living conditions, the story unfolds through a fractured coming-of-age shaped by sporadic connections with her mother and heritage. Critics widely interpret the novel as a poignant depiction of the Afro-diasporic experience in Portugal, emphasising its textual engagement with subjectivity disintegrated by migration and maternal separation, with the telephone serving as a prosthetic to bridge this divide. Others adopt a more explicitly decolonial lens, highlighting the narrative's challenge to the Portuguese postcolonial canon through its focus on marginalised historical memories. However, such interpretations often stop short of addressing the structural processes through which that canon is constituted.

While efforts to grant visibility to works like *As Telefones* are crucial for positioning them within hegemonic literary canons, they fall short of decolonising those canons when they ignore their structural entanglement with coloniality. As I argued in my piece on *As Telefones*, 'the decolonial potential of [Pereira de Almeida's] work is frequently cited in relation to the Portuguese literary canon, the Portuguese imperial legacy, or a very specific type of peripheral experience – that exclusive to Black people whose heritage is in former Portuguese African colonies – hence recentring the very coloniality such interpretations of her work intend to dislodge'.[41] In this instance, a genuinely decolonial reading must attend to how coloniality is produced within the canon itself. This entails recognising that the presence of minoritised structures of feeling is instrumental to coloniality, insofar as their aesthetic value lies precisely in their colonial difference. Such a reading must also transcend the binary of colonial difference embedded in canonical formation that perpetuates colonial structures. More challengingly, a decolonial reading that embraces a decolonial praxis must relinquish the liberal impulse for inclusion that remains complicit in coloniality's meritocratic illusion and its capacity for co-optation.

Curiously, my reading of the book went in a very different direction. What struck me was its refined aesthetic treatment of the telephone as a failed prosthetic for late-twentieth-century subjective disconnection within the context of the Black diaspora in Europe. The narrative's engagement with the history of the medium – particularly through diegetic references to Walter Benjamin's *Berlin Childhood Around 1900*,[42] written just before the catastrophic instrumentalisation of technology in the Second World War and his suicide – offered a powerful lens on the entanglement of Black diasporic experience and European modernity. My analysis thus focused on Pereira de Almeida's depiction of the failure of twentieth-century communication technologies to fulfil their liberatory promise of bridging distances. There, the Black experience worked as a powerful catalyst for the experience of migration and the shifting dynamics of the international division of labour in the *longue durée* of the capitalist world-system. The piece was never meant to be a decolonial reading of the work, but rather one that dialogued with the idea of hypercontemporaneity that guided the volume *The Hypercontemporary Novel in Portugal: Fictional Aesthetics and Memory after Postmodernism*, where it was inserted.[43]

Yet, the contradictions that I observed in the well-intentioned decolonial readings of the book prompted me to reassess the decolonial potential of my own critical approach. The focus on *As Telefones*' meticulous intertextuality with a wide European tradition to assess the failed liberatory promise of technology in the context of capitalist progress released the work from the confines of postcolonial Portuguese literature. Trapped there, where it can only live as an index of Portuguese imperialism and colonial difference, *As Telefones* has little by way of a chance to destabilise any hegemonic tradition – literary or otherwise. Seen in its connection with a European tradition of discourses of technological betrayal – usually centred on the voices of men to the North of the continent – the narrative serenely inscribes the necessity of the perspective of the African migrant in the *longue durée* of modernity. In the book's contemporary setting, the portrayal of the African woman severed from her heritage and of the African mother separated from her offspring both echoes the transgenerational trauma of objectification and commodification of the transatlantic trade of enslaved African people and reforges the wilfully forgotten ties between migration now and then. In doing so, the novel exposes the coloniality embedded in modernity's discourse without recentring it. Ultimately, the narrative's aesthetic exploration of intersubjective crisis mediated by technology transcends the specificity of Black experience, articulating a human condition – akin to Benjamin's – while remaining intersectionally grounded.

In the end, I recast my own reading of *As Telefones* as 'a decolonial approach'. The reasons, however, have only become clear to me in the process of developing the reflections that gave way to the present chapter. As I write this, I realise the Freirean praxis at work on my critical gesture, as the committed critical action that I took in my 2024 piece on Pereira de Almeida's work has generated a reflection aware of its aim and process that has taken the form of the present text, which is now ready to engender further – hopefully transformative – action. In this reflection of my path towards a decolonial literary praxis, I should not forget to consider the impact of worldliness in my approach to that narrative. Different from the critics who had produced decolonial appreciations of *As Telefones* at the time, I do not identify as Portuguese nor work within that academic sphere. Freer from the urge to transform that literary tradition whose excluding principles do not confront me on an everyday basis, my approach is perhaps imbued with a privileged weightlessness that releases my gaze to more easily find the potential of the work beyond the context of Black Portuguese identities. Perhaps the fact that I, too, am a Black woman living as an immigrant, away from home and in touch with my mother only through the use of technology, is part of a worldliness conducive to my connection to the narrative at a human level.

All this considered, while my positionality has probably had something to do with my take on the work, I do not believe that the potential for a decolonial praxis is tied to any specific coordinates in terms of a critic's positionality. Instead, my view is that any critic can produce a decolonial intervention so long as their critical action relies on the awareness of the decolonial aim and critical process bounded by its historicity and materiality.

This relates to Hewson's historicisation of literary studies' struggle at the intersection between the subjectivity of the critical ontological gesture and objectivity of the Cartesian method, whose rigour relies on a decontextualised, standardised and reproducible mode of knowing. Such historicisation evokes the work of Said on critical consciousness and worldliness that guide the ontological gesture of the critic who transforms texts into literature. Together, and as I hope this text has demonstrated, these aspects attest to the intrinsically fertile ground that literary studies are to grow the seeds of truly transformative change through literary praxis. All we need is the courage to embrace the power of our own agency and the responsibility for our choices.

Notes

1 Paulo Freire, *The Politics of Education: Culture, Power, and Liberation* (Bergin & Garvey, 1985), p. 44.

2 Djaimilia Pereira de Almeida, *As Telefones* (Relógio D'água, 2020).

3 D. J. Palmer, *The Rise of English Studies: An Account of the Study of English Language and Literature from its Origins to the Making of the Oxford English School* (Oxford University Press, 1965), pp. 10–11.

4 Terry Eagleton, *Literary Theory: An Introduction* (University of Minnesota Press, 2008).

5 Matthew Arnold, *Culture and Anarchy* (Oxford University Press, 2006).

6 D. J. Palmer, 'English', in *The History of the University of Oxford: Volume VII: Nineteenth-Century Oxford, Part 2* (Oxford University Press, 2000).

7 Gauri Viswanathan, *Masks of Conquest: Literary Study and British Rule in India* (Columbia University Press, 2015).

8 Palmer, *The Rise*, pp. 1–14; Miller, Thomas P., 'Where Did College English Studies Come From?', *Rhetoric Review*, 9.1 (1990), pp. 50–69.

9 Craig Simpson, 'Universities Drop Chaucer and Shakespeare as "Decolonisation" Takes Root', *Telegraph.co.uk*, 2022.

10 Claire Alfree, 'Has "Wokeness" Killed the English Literature Degree?: With Universities Starting to Axe the Course, the Subject That Helped Shape Britain's Sense of Itself is in Crisis', *Sunday Telegraph*, 1 December 2024, p. 13.

11 Leon Moosavi, '"Woked Up the Bum" and Other Moral Panics About Academic Decolonisation in the British News Media', *Comparative Education*, 61.3 (2025), pp. 1–17.

12 Sandeep Bakshi, 'Towards the Unmaking of Canons: Decolonising the Study of Literature', in *Doing Equity and Diversity for Success in Higher Education:*

Redressing Structural Inequalities in the Academy, ed. by Dave S. P. Thomas and Jason Arday (Springer International Publishing, 2021), pp. 117–26 (p. 124).

13 Robert J. C. Young, 'Postcolonial Remains', *New Literary History*, 43.1 (2012), pp. 19–42 (p. 22).

14 See both Edward Said's *Orientalism* (Pantheon Books, 1978) and *Culture and Imperialism* (Vintage, 1993).

15 Anna Bernard, *Decolonizing Literature: An Introduction* (Polity Press, 2023), p. 4.

16 Ella Shohat, 'Notes on the "Post-Colonial"', *Social Text*, 31–2 (1992), pp. 99–113 (p. 99).

17 Benita Parry, 'The Institutionalization of Postcolonial Studies', in *The Cambridge Companion to Postcolonial Literary Studies*, ed. by Neil Lazarus (Cambridge University Press, 2004), pp. 66–80 (pp. 71–3).

18 Parry, 'The Institutionalization', pp. 71–3.

19 Parry, 'The Institutionalization', pp. 71–3.

20 Parry, 'The Institutionalization', p. 74.

21 Benita Parry, 'What is Left in Postcolonial Studies?', *New Literary History*, 43.2 (2012), pp. 341–58 (p. 342).

22 Parry, 'What is Left', p. 343.

23 Parry, 'What is Left', p. 354.

24 Emanuelle Santos, Patricia Schor, Robert Stam and Ella Shohat, 'Interview with Ella Shohat and Robert Stam: "Brazil is Not Travelling Enough": On Postcolonial Theory and Analogous Counter-Currents', *Portuguese Cultural Studies*, 4.1 (2012), pp. 13–40.

25 Parry, 'The Institutionalization', p. 75; emphasis in the original.

26 Terry Eagleton, *Literary Theory: An Introduction* (University of Minnesota Press, 2008); Viswanathan, *Masks of Conquest*.

27 Silvia Rivera Cusicanqui, 'Ch'ixinakax Utxiwa: A Reflection on the Practices and Discourses of Decolonization', *The South Atlantic Quarterly*, 111.1 (2012), pp. 95–109 (pp. 98, 103).

28 Cusicanqui, 'Ch'ixinakax Utxiwa', p. 102; emphasis in the original.

29 Cusicanqui, 'Ch'ixinakax Utxiwa', p. 103.

30 Olúfẹ́mi Táíwò, *Against Decolonisation: Taking African Agency Seriously* (Hurst Publishers, 2022).

31 Edward W. Said, *The World, the Text, and the Critic* (Harvard University Press, 1983).

32 Mark Hewson, 'The Debate with Method in the History of Literary Studies', *Comparative Literature Studies*, 55.1 (2018), pp. 23–46 (p. 24).

33 Hewson, 'The Debate with Method', p. 38.

34 Hewson, 'The Debate with Method', p. 43.

35 Hewson, 'The Debate with Method', p. 39.

36 Said, *The World*, p. 2.

37 Said, *The World*, p. 3.

38 Said, *The World*, pp. 3–4.

39 Said, *The World*, p. 5.

40 Said, *The World*, pp. 241–2.

41 Emanuelle Santos, 'Of Technology and Lost Connections: A Decolonial Approach to *As Telefones* by Djaimilia Pereira de Almeida as a Hypercontemporary Novel', in *The Hypercontemporary Novel in Portugal: Fictional Aesthetics and Memory After Postmodernism*, ed. by Ana Paula Arnaut and Paulo de Medeiros (Bloomsbury, 2024), pp. 141–56 (p. 144).

42 Walter Benjamin, *Berlin Childhood Around 1900*, trans. by Howard Eiland (Harvard University Press, 2006).

43 Arnaut and de Medeiros, *The Hypercontemporary Novel*.

References

Alfree, Claire, 'Has "Wokeness" Killed the English Literature Degree?: With Universities Starting to Axe the Course, the Subject That Helped Shape Britain's Sense of Itself is in Crisis', *Sunday Telegraph*, 1 December 2024, p. 13

Bacon, Alan, 'English Literature Becomes a University Subject: King's College, London as Pioneer', *Victorian Studies*, 29.4 (1986), pp. 591–612

Bakshi, Sandeep, 'Towards the Unmaking of Canons: Decolonising the Study of Literature', in *Doing Equity and Diversity for Success in Higher Education: Redressing Structural Inequalities in the Academy*, ed. by Dave S. P. Thomas and Jason Arday (Springer International Publishing, 2021), pp. 117–26

Benjamin, Walter, *Berlin Childhood Around 1900*, trans. by Howard Eiland (Harvard University Press, 2006)

Bernard, Anna, *Decolonizing Literature: An Introduction* (Polity Press, 2023)

Court, Franklin E., 'The Social and Historical Significance of the First English Literature Professorship in England', *PMLA*, 103.5 (1988), pp. 796–807.

Cusicanqui, Silvia Rivera, 'Ch'ixinakax Utxiwa: A Reflection on the Practices and Discourses of Decolonization', *The South Atlantic Quarterly*, 111.1 (2012), pp. 95–109
Eagleton, Terry, *Literary Theory: An Introduction* (University of Minnesota Press, 2008)
Etherington, Ben, and Jarad Zimbler, 'Decolonize Practical Criticism?', *English: Journal of the English Association*, 70.270 (2021), pp. 227–36
Freire, Paulo, *The Politics of Education: Culture, Power, and Liberation* (Bergin & Garvey, 1985)
Hewson, Mark, 'The Debate with Method in the History of Literary Studies', *Comparative Literature Studies*, 55.1 (2018), pp. 23–46
Irvine, Robert, 'English Literary Studies Origins and Nature', in *The Edinburgh Introduction to Studying English Literature*, ed. by Dermot Cavanagh and others (Edinburgh University Press, 2014), pp. 16–24
Krishnaswamy, Revathi, and John C. Hawley, *The Postcolonial and the Global* (University of Minnesota Press, 2007)
Miller, Thomas P., 'Where Did College English Studies Come From?', *Rhetoric Review*, 9.1 (1990), pp. 50–69
Moosavi, Leon, '"Woked Up the Bum" and Other Moral Panics about Academic Decolonisation in the British News Media', *Comparative Education*, 61.3 (2025), pp. 1–17
Palmer, D. J., 'English', in *The History of the University of Oxford: Volume VII: Nineteenth-Century Oxford, Part 2* (Oxford University Press, 2000)
Palmer, D. J., *The Rise of English Studies: An Account of the Study of English Language and Literature from its Origins to the Making of the Oxford English School* (Oxford University Press, 1965)
Parry, Benita, 'The Institutionalization of Postcolonial Studies', in *The Cambridge Companion to Postcolonial Literary Studies*, ed. by Neil Lazarus (Cambridge University Press, 2004), pp. 66–80
Parry, Benita, 'What is Left in Postcolonial Studies?', *New Literary History*, 43.2 (2012), pp. 341–58
Pereira de Almeida, Djaimilia, *As Telefones* (Relógio D'água, 2020)
Said, Edward W., *Culture and Imperialism* (Vintage, 1993)
Said, Edward W., *Orientalism* (Pantheon Books, 1978)
Said, Edward W., *The World, the Text, and the Critic* (Harvard University Press, 1983)
Santos, Emanuelle, 'Of Technology and Lost Connections: A Decolonial Approach to *As Telefones* by Djaimilia Pereira de Almeida as a

Hypercontemporary Novel', in *The Hypercontemporary Novel in Portugal: Fictional Aesthetics and Memory after Postmodernism*, ed. by Ana Paula Arnaut and Paulo de Medeiros (Bloomsbury, 2024), pp. 141–56

Santos, Emanuelle, Patricia Schor, Robert Stam and Ella Shohat, 'Interview with Ella Shohat and Robert Stam: "Brazil is Not Travelling Enough": On Postcolonial Theory and Analogous Counter-Currents', *Portuguese Cultural Studies*, 4.1 (2012), pp. 13–40, doi:10.7275/R59Z92T0

Shohat, Ella, 'Notes on the "Post-Colonial"', *Social Text*, 31–2 (1992), pp. 99–113

Simpson, Craig, 'Universities Drop Chaucer and Shakespeare as "Decolonisation" Takes Root', *Telegraph.co.uk* (2022), https://www.telegraph.co.uk/news/2022/08/27/universities-drop-chaucer-shakespeare-decolonisation-takes-root/ [accessed 28 April 2026]

Táíwò, Olúfẹ́mi, *Against Decolonisation: Taking African Agency Seriously* (Hurst Publishers, 2022)

Viswanathan, Gauri, *Masks of Conquest: Literary Study and British Rule in India* (Columbia University Press, 2015)

Young, Robert J. C., 'Postcolonial Remains', *New Literary History*, 43.1 (2012), pp. 19–42

Chapter 3

The geopolitics of literary studies in a time of crisis

Reham Hosny

Introduction

The humanities, and in particular literary studies, are essential for making sense of the world's most urgent crises. Whether we are confronting climate change, navigating the ethical dilemmas of artificial intelligence or grappling with war, injustice and racism, it is the humanities that equip us with the tools to think critically, to imagine alternatives and to reflect on what it means to live together responsibly. Without these capacities, no technical solution or economic policy can hope to be truly sustainable. And yet, paradoxically, the very disciplines that cultivate these vital skills are being pushed to the margins of academia, dismissed as irrelevant in a system shaped by a complex web of forces – ranging from short-term economic priorities to shifting cultural values and institutional restructuring. While this chapter situates the discussion within the broader crisis of the humanities, its central concern is with literary studies, whose decline most sharply illustrates the wider marginalisation of humanistic inquiry.

The digital age introduces another layer to this crisis, one that is neither wholly detrimental nor entirely liberating for the humanities. On the one hand, the proliferation of online media has dramatically expanded access to knowledge, enabling broader participation in academic discourse and opening new modes of collaboration across borders. Online and hybrid learning models, in particular, have allowed students who might otherwise be excluded – whether for geographic, financial or personal reasons – to engage with higher education in meaningful ways. On the other hand, this transformation has also reshaped patterns of information consumption, often privileging speed, surface-level engagement and fragmented attention over the deep, reflective inquiry that the humanities cultivate. Scholars have raised concerns that such shifts, while democratising in form, may dilute the quality of education and erode the communal and dialogical dimensions of traditional academic life.[1] For literary studies especially, where close reading and sustained dialogue remain central practices, the challenge lies not in rejecting digital modes outright, but in critically reimagining how these tools can be aligned with the values of humanistic inquiry rather than undermining them.

This chapter expands on the causes behind the marginalisation of literary studies, arguing for greater attention to the geopolitical dimensions of this crisis in relation to both authoritarian and democratic regimes. The chapter explores why the world is more in need of humanities and literary studies than ever, given the disorder that prevails across the globe. Reflecting on my personal scholarship and experiences, two case studies focused on digital literary activism and lexical algorithmic disruption clarify the potential of literary studies to safeguard our shared humanity against the forces of authoritarianism and neoliberalism. The chapter concludes by proposing practices for navigating the current crisis in the humanities and literary studies.

Geopolitical dimensions of the crisis of the humanities

The suppression of humanistic inquiry is a global phenomenon shaped by both authoritarian and democratic regimes, albeit through distinct yet interconnected mechanisms. In authoritarian states, critical disciplines such as philosophy, history, political science and literature are often perceived as destabilising forces, leading to systematic control over academic institutions. As Hyslop-Margison and Leonard argue, the suppression of the humanities is not merely an economic consequence of post-neoliberal restructuring but a deliberate strategy employed by states to undermine democratic engagement and critical discourse.[2] Authoritarian governments recognise that these disciplines cultivate independent thought, challenge official narratives and foster civic participation – elements that contradict the need of these governments for ideological conformity. Hyslop-Margison and Leonard highlight that under repressive regimes, universities are no longer spaces of intellectual resistance but are instead transformed into instruments of state ideology, ensuring that curricula reinforce rather than critique dominant power structures. The elimination or defunding of humanities programmes, often justified through economic rationales, can be understood as a calculated move to erode democratic values. By limiting access to disciplines that encourage approaches such as historical analysis and ethical reasoning, authoritarian states weaken the public's capacity to question governance, resist misinformation and advocate for justice. Thus, as Hyslop-Margison and Leonard emphasise, the crisis of the humanities is not just an academic concern but a fundamental threat to democratic society itself, necessitating urgent resistance to policies that prioritise economic utility over intellectual freedom.[3]

Authoritarian regimes in the Middle East and North Africa (MENA) region, for example, have suppressed the humanities and academic freedom as potential sites of political dissent. Brand (2007) states that universities and scholars in the MENA area have faced systematic harassment, censorship and persecution as part of broader efforts to maintain regime control. Brand highlights how academics have been dismissed, imprisoned or even tortured due to their writings and activism. This suppression forms part of broader human rights violations crucial for regime maintenance[4] extending beyond individual persecution, as governments impose direct control over university curricula, censor classroom materials and restrict historical and political research. In Tunisia and the United Arab Emirates (UAE), academics have been summarily dismissed for their work; in Egypt, classroom materials have been subjected to censorship; and in countries like Iran, Saudi Arabia, Syria and Sudan, and under the Palestinian Authority, scholars and students have been imprisoned for their academic work or political views. Additionally, university campuses in Bahrain and Tunisia have experienced government infiltration and violent crackdowns.[5]

Furthermore, the repression of academic freedom intersects with geopolitical struggles, as authoritarian regimes use national security justifications to stifle critical inquiry. Brand notes that civil wars, insurgencies and foreign interventions have destroyed educational institutions and provided a pretext for heightened surveillance and restrictions on academic discourse. In Iraq, for example, the 2003 US invasion and subsequent instability have devastated the academic sector, leading to assassinations of scholars, the destruction of libraries and the mass displacement of faculty members. Similarly, in Palestine, Israeli occupation policies – such as movement restrictions, denial of entry to foreign scholars and the destruction of educational infrastructure – have severely hindered academic freedom and access to education.[6] A recent example is the reported 'assassination' of Palestinian academic, writer and poet Refaat Alareer, a professor of English literature at the Islamic University in Gaza, who was also widely known for his outspoken criticism of Israel through his literary work and public writings. Alareer was killed in an Israeli airstrike in northern Gaza in December 2023.[7] Reports from organisations such as the Euro-Mediterranean Human Rights Monitor indicate that his killing was 'apparently deliberate' after he received multiple death threats.[8]

These patterns of repression highlight how the humanities, with their emphasis on critical thinking and historical inquiry, pose a challenge to authoritarian and colonial power structures. To be clear, humanities research is not merely abstract theorising: it involves the recovery and interpretation of texts and archives and the critical reframing of cultural memory. These practices, often slow and dialogical, equip scholars to question dominant narratives and reveal forms of knowledge that authoritarian systems seek to erase. Thus, the crisis of the humanities in the MENA region cannot be seen in isolation from the larger framework of state control and global political interests.

Yet, the erosion of the humanities is not confined to authoritarian regimes alone. Across the world, fields that cultivate critical and historical inquiry are also marginalised alongside student movements challenging dominant power relations. The suppression of dissent is particularly evident in the treatment of pro-Palestinian student activists in American universities.[9] Here, the devaluation of humanities disciplines that promote historical analysis, ethical reasoning and political critique aligns with a broader pattern of silencing voices that contest prevailing geopolitical narratives. This systemic devaluation of the humanities is reinforced by neoliberal economic imperatives that shift educational priorities toward disciplines with direct market applications.

In the UK, for example, this economisation of education is exemplified by the Teaching Excellence and Student Outcomes Framework (TEF) that evaluates teaching quality through sector-wide indicators such as student retention, satisfaction and, most controversially, graduate employment and earnings data.[10] By equating the 'value' of degrees with post-graduation salaries, the TEF conflates educational worth with labour market outcomes, despite widespread criticism that income levels cannot serve as a valid proxy for teaching excellence.[11] Collectively, these pressures embed a market logic that diminishes the space for long-term critical and ethical inquiry, eroding the civic and democratic purposes of the humanities and constraining the capacity of higher education to foster informed, politically engaged citizens.

This corporatisation of universities has significantly weakened the humanities, as higher education institutions increasingly function as corporate entities where financial efficiency and market-driven priorities dictate academic decisions. Chau describes this transformation, noting that 'education is transformed into a commodity, students into consumers, faculty into entrepreneurs, and institutions of higher learning into storefronts'.[12] As Nussbaum warns, nations that prioritise economic output over intellectual independence risk producing 'generations of useful machines, rather than complete citizens who can think for themselves, criticize tradition, and understand the significance of another person's sufferings and achievements'.[13] This shift privileges profit-driven disciplines such as business, engineering and applied sciences while marginalising fields that do not directly contribute to economic growth. In the United States, public universities are eliminating humanities programmes, such as philosophy, history and English, citing declining enrolments, while prioritising career-oriented fields like computer science and finance.[14]

The erosion of the humanities is not merely an economic trend but a broader ideological shift that reconfigures universities as corporate enterprises, aligning them with state and military interests at the expense of their ethical and civic responsibilities. Giroux warns that in the absence of a democratic vision of education, universities have increasingly integrated themselves into military, intelligence and corporate networks, compromising their role as spaces for independent thought and social critique. He highlights Yale University's collaboration with the Department of Defense in establishing the US Special Operations Command Center of Excellence for Operational Neuroscience, which trained military personnel in intelligence-gathering techniques using immigrant populations – primarily poor Hispanics, Moroccans and Iraqis – as test subjects. This integration of military intelligence practices into academic spaces, Giroux argues, reflects a larger trend in which universities facilitate, rather than critique, state surveillance and authoritarian governance.[15]

As Giroux argues, the neoliberal restructuring of universities risks transforming faculty from scholars and public intellectuals into mere technicians and grant writers, stripping them of their authority and reducing education to a transactional service industry. The rise of artificial intelligence (AI) and automation further exacerbates this crisis by reinforcing the notion that humanities education is obsolete, a misconception echoed in recent policy decisions such as West Virginia University's 2023 preliminary recommendation to eliminate its world languages and other humanities programmes, justified in terms of budget shortfalls, declining enrolments and the need to invest in specialisations that are 'more relevant to today's student'.[16] As universities restructure themselves to cater to technological and economic imperatives, fields like philosophy, history and literature are increasingly dismissed as impractical, sidelining critical discussions about the ethical, philosophical and sociopolitical implications of AI and automation. Governments eager to dominate AI development channel vast resources into computational sciences while neglecting the humanistic inquiry necessary to guide the responsible and ethical uses of these emerging technologies. This shortsighted approach not only accelerates the marginalisation of the humanities but also risks creating technological infrastructures that serve authoritarian and corporate interests at the expense of democratic governance.

Nussbaum underscores the importance of humanistic education in resisting dehumanising trends, stating, 'Socratic thinking is important in any democracy. But it is particularly important in societies that need to come to grips with the presence of people who differ by ethnicity, caste, and religion'.[17] The absence of such thinking is demonstrated in the use of predictive policing systems that have been shown to disproportionately target communities of colour, or automated hiring platforms that replicate gender and racial biases embedded in their training data. Rather than addressing inequalities and biases, these systems reproduce them under the guise of efficiency and neutrality.[18] Together, these cases underscore the dangers of technological determinism – the belief that innovation alone guarantees social progress – while ignoring the political, ethical and cultural frameworks that shape how AI is deployed. With today's increasing automation and digital governance, the humanities provide essential tools for interrogating how technological systems shape power structures and social realities.

In this era defined by rapid technological shifts and political instability, literary research has a particularly crucial role to play in navigating these contemporary global challenges. Literature's capacity to foster empathy, historical awareness and ethical reasoning is particularly indispensable in an age where misinformation and algorithmic governance threaten democratic discourse. More specifically, the study of literature provides critical tools for understanding human agency and diverse cultural narratives – areas that become increasingly urgent as AI and authoritarianism reshape societies. While science, technology, engineering and mathematics (STEM) disciplines dominate discussions on technological progress, literary research offers a necessary counterbalance by interrogating the social, political, cultural and philosophical implications of these changes. Moreover, the resurgence of authoritarianism and populism underscores the role of literature in preserving democratic values. Levitsky and Ziblatt emphasise that democratic erosion often begins subtly, with shifts in rhetoric and policy that gradually undermine civil liberties.[19] Literary research can cultivate the historical awareness and political literacy necessary to recognise and resist these threats, as will be explored in the following two case studies that focus on digital literary activism and lexical algorithmic resistance. Similarly, by analysing dystopian fiction, political allegories and suppressed literary voices, scholars can reveal how language and storytelling shape public consciousness and influence political outcomes.

Arab women's digital literary activism

My recent research has investigated how Arab women's digital literary activism resists both patriarchal and neocolonial structures. Analysing digital literary works such as Nissmah Roshdy's *La'eb Al-Nard* [The Dice Player] (2013) – a visual–poetic animation based on Mahmoud Darwish's poem that brings together calligraphy, voice and motion in a web-based reflection on chance and identity – and Amira Hanafi's *Qamos al-Thawra* [A Dictionary of the Revolution] (2017) – a born-digital, multi-voiced lexicon built from interviews with nearly 200 Egyptians in the wake of the 2011 uprising – demonstrates how literature mediated through digital platforms becomes a powerful instrument of political resistance and cultural memory.[20]

Literary scholarship can reveal and counteract the mechanisms of oppression embedded in both local and global structures. The concept of *digital post/colonial feminism* provides a theoretical framework that captures the dual struggle faced by Arab women: resisting internal patriarchal forces while simultaneously challenging external colonial and imperialist narratives. This conceptual approach aligns with postcolonial feminist scholarship, which critiques how Western feminist discourse often co-opts and misrepresents the struggles of women from the Global South.[21]

Digital literary activism functions here as an evolving site of resistance, with digital media offering new modes of expression that traditional literary forms might not accommodate, particularly in repressive political environments.[22] For example, Roshdy's *La'eb Al-Nard* utilises animation, visual art and poetry to depict the Palestinian experience under occupation. Roshdy converts Darwish's paper-based poetry into a kinetic–digital form that blends text, animation and sound to create a multi-sensory experience that resists the reduction of Palestinian identity to mere statistics or news headlines. In so doing, this digital piece draws several aesthetic and artistic pictures based on a clever use of digital media. Thus, this work challenges the colonial erasure of Palestinian narratives, in addition to intervening in the very processes through which cultural memory is constructed and preserved in the digital age.

From a methodological perspective, this case study demonstrates that literary research can no longer be confined to textual exegesis alone. Digital literary activism necessitates an expanded critical lens that accounts for multimodality – animation, interactivity, soundscapes – as integral to meaning-making and resistance. By engaging with such works, research reveals how literature, when mediated through digital technologies, creates alternative spaces of resistance that traditional print-based forms may not sustain, particularly in repressive political contexts. The adaptability of this form of activism is crucial in the face of ever-evolving mechanisms of surveillance and censorship. While authoritarian regimes seek to silence dissent through control of publishing infrastructures or media channels, digital works like *La'eb Al-Nard* circumvent these barriers by inhabiting fluid, networked spaces that are more difficult to police. Multimodality here is not only an aesthetic choice but also a political strategy: it expands the reach and affective power of the text while destabilising the boundaries between literature, art and activism.

Similarly, Hanafi's *Qamos al-Thawra* exemplifies how digital literary forms can serve as archives of resistance, preserving alternative historical accounts that authoritarian regimes seek to erase. Through a collaborative storytelling process, Hanafi collects and organises oral testimonies about the Egyptian Revolution of 2011, creating an interactive digital dictionary that challenges state-sanctioned narratives. Therefore, by weaving together accounts that reflect the lived experiences and diverse linguistic registers of Egyptians from different regions, Hanafi disrupts the state's unified account of the 2011 revolution and brings forward the many realities witnessed by those who were directly involved.[23] Hanafi's piece is a significant example of how literature engages with history, memory and identity, resisting epistemic violence and ensuring that marginalised perspectives are preserved.

Literature here functions as a political act, particularly in contexts where free speech is restricted. The erasure of marginalised voices is not only a historical phenomenon but an ongoing reality in many regions of the world. In the Arab world, where governments frequently use censorship and digital surveillance to control dissent, literature – especially in its digital form – becomes a site of defiance. Unlike traditional print, which is bound by state-controlled publishing infrastructures, digital literary forms such as interactive narratives, multimedia poetry and hypertext fiction allow writers to experiment with modes of circulation that evade censorship. Their multimodality – integrating text, image, animation and sound – creates layered meanings that are harder to suppress or police, while the networked nature of digital platforms enables works to reach transnational audiences, amplifying voices that regimes attempt to silence.

This defiant potential of literature, as explained in the previous section, aligns with Edward Said's assertion that literature is deeply intertwined with power, serving not only as a reflection of political struggles but as an active force in shaping them. Said argues that while imperialism is fundamentally a struggle over land, literature serves as a powerful form of resistance by contesting ownership, settlement and the future of that land through narrative. Storytelling becomes a site of defiance, where literary texts challenge imperialist claims, disrupt hegemonic histories and reclaim erased voices. By offering counter-narratives, literature not only exposes the mechanisms of colonial domination but also asserts the agency of the oppressed, transforming political and historical battles over territory into acts of cultural resistance and survival.[24] In this way, literature transcends mere artistic expression; it becomes a tool of intellectual resistance, preserving histories that dominant powers seek to erase and giving voice to those silenced by political oppression.

These two literary and artistic pieces by Roshdy and Hanafi reinforce the argument that literature is not merely a mirror of power structures but an active site for contesting them. Whether through the reanimation of Palestinian resistance poetry or the archiving of revolutionary testimonies, such works function as counter-narratives that unsettle hegemonic control. Yet the role of literary research extends beyond recognising these acts of resistance. Scholarly analysis enables us to situate these works within broader socio-political histories, uncover the aesthetic and rhetorical strategies through which they intervene and trace the cultural networks that shape their production and circulation. By doing so, literary research amplifies the political force of the texts themselves, in addition to equipping us with the critical frameworks needed to understand how digital narratives challenge misinformation and state propaganda. It transforms individual creative acts into a wider map of resistance, illuminating how cultural expression operates as both testimony and tactic in the struggle over meaning and memory.

'Lexical algorithmic resistance' on Facebook

While the first case study highlighted the role of literary research in challenging power structures through cultural memory and narrative reclamation, this second case study broadens the scope to address how language acts as a vital tool of resistance. Together, these approaches demonstrate how literature and other forms of linguistic expression function as complementary sites of defiance: literature reclaims erased histories and voices, while linguistic strategies directly subvert mechanisms of control in everyday communication. This second case study examines how Arab users strategically manipulate language to evade Facebook's algorithmic censorship, particularly in relation to the suppression of pro-Palestinian voices. The research traces specific linguistic practices – including splitting words, using dotless letters or substituting letters – that users adopt to prevent automated systems from flagging or removing their posts. It also analyses patterns in platform moderation policies and user responses to highlight the constant negotiation between censorship mechanisms and grassroots strategies of visibility.[25] By foregrounding how linguistic ingenuity enables users to bypass digital surveillance, the research underscores that resistance in the digital age requires not only the preservation of cultural narratives but also the tactical adaptation of language itself against authoritarianism and the corporate domination of public discourse.

The strategic manipulation of language to deceive algorithms is part of a broader history of resistance through literary and linguistic subversion. Literature and language have long served as a battleground where narratives of oppression are contested using several techniques, such as symbolism and the coded language that defied totalitarian regimes and colonisation. For instance, among the Moriscos in Spain, *aljamiado* writing – Romance languages written in Arabic script – allowed them to navigate their dual identities while maintaining their Islamic heritage under the oppressive scrutiny of the Spanish Inquisition. This linguistic adaptation enabled them to resist cultural erasure and sustain their traditions despite systemic repression.[26]

Today, algorithmic governance represents a new frontier of control, where automated systems dictate the visibility and circulation of political discourse. My research situates this digital form of censorship within the framework of 'data colonialism',[27] which critiques how digital platforms appropriate human communication for profit and political control. Technology companies are thus complicit in reinforcing geopolitical power asymmetries. Facebook's biased moderation policies disproportionately target Arabic content, particularly expressions of solidarity with Palestine, while permitting violent rhetoric in other political contexts.[28] This selective enforcement mirrors historical state-sponsored censorship, where colonial and authoritarian regimes suppressed literary works that fostered national consciousness and anti-colonial sentiment. Nkrumah identified control over cultural expression as a central pillar of neo-colonial domination, a notion that remains relevant in the digital age, where algorithmic censorship operates as a form of linguistic imperialism.[29]

To counter this censorship, Arab users employ various lexical resistance techniques to evade content moderation algorithms that systematically suppress discussions in relation to Palestinian resistance.[30] This manipulation of Arabic script in digital resistance reflects an ongoing struggle against the erasure of Palestinian narratives by Western-dominated social media corporations. By deploying language as an instrument of resistance, Arab users engage in what James C. Scott terms 'hidden transcripts' – subversive discourses that challenge hegemonic power beneath the surface of public discourse.[31]

The implications of this research extend beyond digital resistance to broader debates on the role of literary and linguistic scholarship in political activism. By analysing how language is weaponised against marginalised communities, scholars can expose the ways in which discourse itself becomes a mechanism of control, reinforcing hierarchies and legitimising systems of exclusion. Literary research is thus not confined to the interpretation of texts in isolation, but rather engages with the lived realities of oppression, where language and narrative are central to struggles over visibility, legitimacy and rights. In this sense, literary and linguistic inquiry becomes a form of political praxis: it interprets and actively disrupts the discursive strategies used to silence subaltern voices. Such research affirms the humanities as indispensable in confronting contemporary crises of power and justice.

Additionally, this research contributes to debates on algorithmic justice and the ethical governance of digital platforms. As mentioned earlier, scholars such as Broussard and Noble have critiqued the biases embedded in AI, arguing that algorithmic systems reinforce existing social hierarchies rather than neutralise them. My research provides empirical evidence of these biases, demonstrating how Facebook's content moderation disproportionately impacts Arabic-speaking users, effectively silencing political dissent. By foregrounding how particular linguistic communities are marginalised through automated moderation, this work challenges universalist claims of algorithmic neutrality and exposes the unequal distribution of visibility and voice in digital spaces. In this sense, literary and linguistic research can push for digital policies that protect freedom of expression and recognise the legitimacy of politically sensitive narratives, marginalised voices and region-specific cultural contexts that are often sidelined in global platform governance.

Furthermore, the research highlights the resilience and adaptability of digital resistance movements. Despite Facebook's attempts to refine its content moderation algorithms, Arab users continuously develop new lexical strategies to circumvent censorship, reflecting what de Certeau describes as 'tactics' – improvised actions that challenge dominant structures from within.[32] This underscores the dynamic interplay between control and resistance, illustrating that language remains a potent tool for subverting authoritarianism, whether in traditional literary forms or other forms of digital activism.

In sum, these two case studies highlight the enduring relevance of literary studies in resisting the forces of authoritarianism. Digital literary activism among Arab women illustrates how literature functions as both an archive and an act of defiance, preserving counter-narratives that challenge dominant ideological formations. Meanwhile, research on lexical algorithmic resistance reveals how digital spaces, far from being neutral platforms, are shaped by political bias and systemic censorship. The suppression of pro-Palestinian discourse on social media echoes historical patterns of linguistic and literary repression, illustrating how power operates through control over language and representation.

Conclusion

This chapter exemplifies why literary studies remain indispensable in contemporary scholarship, particularly in resisting authoritarianism and structural oppression. Literature serves as an instrument of resistance, identity reclamation and political engagement. The adaptability of literary forms – whether in print, digital animation or interactive archives – demonstrates literature's continued relevance in addressing power dynamics and advocating for justice. As authoritarian regimes and corporate interests seek to monopolise narratives, literary research ensures that the distinct voices and perspectives of marginalised groups persist, challenging the erasure of histories, identities and struggles. In this context, literary studies reaffirm the humanities' indispensable role in analysing and challenging the structures of power that shape our digital and political realities. As authoritarianism and algorithmic governance converge, literary research remains a vital space for contesting oppression, fostering critical consciousness and envisioning alternative futures. By foregrounding the transformative potential of literature in both historical and contemporary struggles for justice, the research outlined in this chapter underscores the urgency of preserving and advancing the humanities as a means of resisting erasure and imagining more just and equitable societies.

The crisis facing literary studies, and the humanities in general, is consequently not simply a matter of declining enrolments or budget cuts; it is a symptom of broader struggles over power, knowledge and resistance. As this chapter has argued, the marginalisation of disciplines that cultivate critical thinking and historical awareness is not incidental but a deliberate restructuring of knowledge production. Authoritarian regimes seek to control intellectual inquiry by suppressing academic freedom, while democratic societies, driven by market imperatives, increasingly prioritise financial returns over intellectual and civic engagement. This transformation threatens not just higher education but democracy itself, reducing education to a tool of compliance rather than a space for questioning and resisting unjust structures.

Despite these challenges, the humanities remain a vital force for resistance and transformation. Their adaptability to technological and political shifts demonstrates their continued significance. Moving forward, scholars, educators and students must resist the instrumentalisation of education and reaffirm the humanities' role in fostering intellectual freedom and social responsibility. Institutional and grassroots efforts are needed to challenge funding structures that marginalise the humanities, resist corporate influence in academic decision-making and promote interdisciplinary collaborations that connect literary and linguistic studies to urgent global concerns such as digital ethics and human rights.

In conclusion, literary studies are not in crisis because they lack relevance but because they challenge structures of power that seek to curtail critical thought and suppress alternative narratives. This chapter reaffirms the necessity of literary research and the humanities more widely in resisting these forces and highlights the urgency of preserving these disciplines as a domain of resistance and intellectual liberation. Today, as global disorder intensifies, defending the humanities is not merely an academic obligation but a political imperative essential to the survival of democratic and just societies.

Notes

1 Caitlin Cassidy, '"Teaching to an Empty Hall": Is the Changing Face of Universities Eroding Standards of Learning?', *The Guardian*, 19 February 2025, https://www.theguardian.com/australia-news/2025/feb/19/teaching-to-an-empty-hall-is-the-changing-face-of-universities-eroding-standards-of-learning? [accessed 24 April 2026].

2 Emery J. Hyslop-Margison and Hugh A. Leonard, 'Post Neo-Liberalism and the Humanities: What the Repressive State Apparatus Means for Universities', *Canadian Journal of Higher Education*, 42, 2.1 (2012), pp. 1–12 (p. 8).

3 Hyslop-Margison and Leonard, 'Post Neo-Liberalism', p. 11.

4 Laurie A. Brand, 'Middle East Studies and Academic Freedom: Challenges at Home and Abroad', *International Studies Perspectives*, 8.4 (2007), pp. 384–95 (p. 384).

5 Brand, 'Middle East Studies', p. 385.

6 Brand, 'Middle East Studies', pp. 385–6.

7 Palestine Chronicle Staff, 'Refaat Alareer's Body Laid to Rest after 15 Months – His Words Endures', *The Palestine Chronicle*, 5 February 2025, https://www.palestinechronicle.com/refaat-alareersbody-laid-to-rest-after-15-months-his-words-endures/ [accessed 24 April 2026].

8 Euro-Mediterranean Human Rights Monitor, 'Israeli Strike on Refaat al-Areer Apparently Deliberate', 8 December 2023, https://euromedmonitor.org/en/article/6014/Israeli-Strike-on-Refaat-al-Areer-Apparently-Deliberate [accessed 24 April 2026].

9 Middle East Eye, 'US Universities Intensify Crackdown on Pro-Palestinian Activism', *Middle East Eye*, 25 October 2024, https://www.middleeasteye.net/news/us-universities-intensify-crackdown-pro-palestinian-activism [accessed 24 April 2026].

10 Aneta Hayes, 'The Teaching Excellence Framework in the United Kingdom: An Opportunity to Include International Students as "Equals"?', *Journal of Studies in International Education*, 2.5 (2017), pp. 483–97.

11 The British Academy, 'Response to the Independent Review of the Teaching Excellence and Student Outcomes Framework (TEF)', *The British Academy*, 28 February 2019, https://www.thebritishacademy.ac.uk/documents/1938/2019-The-British-Academy-TEF-independent-review-response.pdf [accessed 24 April 2026].

12 Paule Chau, 'Online Higher Education Commodity', *Journal of Computing in Higher Education*, 22 (2010), pp. 177–91 (p. 178).

13 Martha C. Nussbaum, *Not for Profit: Why Democracy Needs the Humanities* (Princeton University Press, 2010), p. 2.

14 Shannon Watkins, 'Protecting the Liberal Arts and Humanities in American Higher Education', *Manhattan Institute*, 5 December 2024, pp. 4–5, https://manhattan.institute/article/protecting-the-liberal-arts-and-humanities-in-american-higher-education [accessed 24 April 2026].

15 Henry A. Giroux, 'The Disappearing Intellectual in the Age of Economic Darwinism', *Policy Futures in Education*, 9.2 (2011), pp. 163–71.

16 'WVU Announces Preliminary Recommendations, Academic Transformation Next Steps', *WVU Today*, 11 August 2023, https://wvutoday.wvu.edu/stories/2023/08/11/wvu-announces-preliminary-recommendations-academic-transformation-next-steps [accessed 24 April 2026].

17 Nussbaum, *Not for Profit*, p. 54.

18 See Safiya Umoja Noble, *Algorithms of Oppression: How Search Engines Reinforce Racism* (New York University Press, 2018); Virginia Eubanks, *Automating Inequality: How High-Tech Tools Profile, Police, and Punish the Poor* (St Martin's Press, 2018); Meredith Broussard, *Artificial Unintelligence: How Computers Misunderstand the World* (MIT Press, 2018).

19 Steven Levitsky and Daniel Ziblatt, *How Democracies Die* (Crown, 2018), p. 10.

20 Reham Hosny, 'Digital Post/Colonial Feminism: Poetics and Politics of Digital Literary Activism by Arab Women', *Journal of Postcolonial Writing*, 21 (2024), pp. 1–15 (p. 1), doi: 10.1080/17449855.2024.2410344.

21 Audre Lorde 'The Master's Tools Will Never Dismantle the Master's House', in *This Bridge Called My Back: Writings by Radical Women of Color*, ed. by Gloria Anzaldúa and Cherríe Moraga (Kitchen Table Press, 1983), pp. 94–101; Chandra Talpade Mohanty, 'Under Western Eyes: Feminist Scholarship and Colonial Discourses', *Boundary*, 2, pp. 333–58.

22 Hosny, 'Digital Post/Colonial Feminism', p. 1.

23 Amira Hanafi, *Qamos Al-Thawra* [A Dictionary of the Revolution], http://qamosalthawra.com (2017), p. 10 [accessed 24 April 2026].

24 Edward W. Said, *Culture and Imperialism* (Vintage, 1993), pp. xii–xiii.

25 Reham Hosny and Mohamed A. Nasef, 'Lexical Algorithmic Resistance: Tactics of Deceiving Arabic Content Moderation Algorithms on Facebook', *Big Data & Society*, 12.2 (2025), doi:10.1177/20539517251318277.

26 Paige Milligan, 'After al-Andalus/Palestine: Resistance and Collaboration in Morisco and Palestinian Literatures' (unpublished doctoral thesis, University of Michigan, 2022), doi:10.7302/4646.

27 Nick Couldry and Ulises A. Mejias, *The Costs of Connection: How Data Is Colonizing Human Life and Appropriating it for Capitalism* (Stanford University Press, 2019).

28 Human Rights Watch, 'Meta's Broken Promises: Systemic Censorship of Palestine Content on Instagram and Facebook', 21 December 2023, https://www.hrw.org/report/2023/12/21/metas-broken-promises/systemic-censorship-palestine-content-instagram-and [accessed 24 April 2026].

29 Kwame Nkrumah, *Neo-Colonialism: The Last Stage of Imperialism* (Thomas Nelson & Sons, Ltd, 1965).

30 Hosny and Nasef, 'Lexical Algorithmic Resistance'.

31 James C. Scott, *Weapons of the Weak: Everyday Forms of Peasant Resistance* (Yale University Press, 1985).

32 Michel de Certeau, *The Practice of Everyday Life*, trans. by Steven Rendall (University of California Press, 1984).

References

Brand, Laurie A., 'Middle East Studies and Academic Freedom: Challenges at Home and Abroad', *International Studies Perspectives*, 8.4 (2007), pp. 384–95

The British Academy, 'Response to the Independent Review of the Teaching Excellence and Student Outcomes Framework (TEF)', *The British Academy*, 28 February 2019, https://www.thebritishacademy

.ac.uk/documents/1938/2019-The-British-Academy-TEF-independent-review-response.pdf [accessed 24 April 2026]

Broussard, Meredith, *Artificial Unintelligence: How Computers Misunderstand the World* (MIT Press, 2018)

Cassidy, Caitlin, '"Teaching to an Empty Hall": Is the Changing Face of Universities Eroding Standards of Learning?', *The Guardian*, 19 February 2025, https://www.theguardian.com/australia-news/2025/feb/19/teaching-to-an-empty-hall-is-the-changing-face-of-universities-eroding-standards-of-learning? [accessed 24 April 2026]

Chau, Paule, 'Online Higher Education Commodity', *Journal of Computing in Higher Education*, 22 (2010), pp. 177–91

Couldry, Nick, and Ulises A. Mejias, *The Costs of Connection: How Data is Colonizing Human Life and Appropriating it for Capitalism* (Stanford University Press, 2019)

de Certeau, Michel, *The Practice of Everyday Life*, trans. by Steven Rendall (University of California Press, 1984)

Eubanks, Virginia, *Automating Inequality: How High-Tech Tools Profile, Police, and Punish the Poor* (St Martin's Press, 2018)

Euro-Mediterranean Human Rights Monitor, 'Israeli Strike on Refaat al-Areer Apparently Deliberate', 8 December 2023, https://euromedmonitor.org/en/article/6014/Israeli-Strike-on-Refaat-al-Areer-Apparently-Deliberate [accessed 24 April 2026]

Giroux, Henry A., 'The Disappearing Intellectual in the Age of Economic Darwinism', *Policy Futures in Education*, 9.2 (2011), pp. 163–71

Hanafi, Amira, *Qamos Al-Thawra* [A Dictionary of the Revolution] (2017), http://qamosalthawra.com/ [accessed 24 April 2026]

Hayes, Aneta, 'The Teaching Excellence Framework in the United Kingdom: An Opportunity to Include International Students as "Equals"?', *Journal of Studies in International Education*, 2.5 (2017), pp. 483–97

Hosny, Reham, 'Digital Post/Colonial Feminism: Poetics and Politics of Digital Literary Activism by Arab Women', *Journal of Postcolonial Writing*, 21 (2024), pp. 1–15, doi:10.1080/17449855.2024.2410344

Hosny, Reham, and Mohamed A. Nasef, 'Lexical Algorithmic Resistance: Tactics of Deceiving Arabic Content Moderation Algorithms on Facebook', *Big Data & Society*, 12.2 (2025), doi:10.1177/20539517251318277

Human Rights Watch, 'Meta's Broken Promises: Systemic Censorship of Palestine Content on Instagram and Facebook', 21 December 2023, https://www.hrw.org/report/2023/12/21/metas-broken-promises/systemic-censorship-palestine-content-instagram-and [accessed 24 April 2026]

Hyslop-Margison, Emery J., and Hugh A. Leonard, 'Post Neo-Liberalism and the Humanities: What the Repressive State Apparatus Means for Universities', *Canadian Journal of Higher Education*, 42, 2.1 (2012), pp. 1–12

Levitsky, Steven, and Daniel Ziblatt, *How Democracies Die* (Crown, 2018)

Lorde, Audre, 'The Master's Tools Will Never Dismantle the Master's House', in *This Bridge Called My Back: Writings by Radical Women of Color*, ed. by Gloria Anzaldúa and Cherríe Moraga (Kitchen Table Press, 1983), pp. 94–101

Middle East Eye, 'US Universities Intensify Crackdown on Pro-Palestinian Activism', *Middle East Eye*, 25 October 2024, https://www.middleeasteye.net/news/us-universities-intensify-crackdown-pro-palestinian-activism [accessed 24 April 2026]

Milligan, Paige, 'After al-Andalus/Palestine: Resistance and Collaboration in Morisco and Palestinian Literatures' (unpublished doctoral thesis, University of Michigan, 2022), doi:10.7302/4646

Mohanty, Chandra Talpade, 'Under Western Eyes: Feminist Scholarship and Colonial Discourses', *Boundary*, 2 (1984), pp. 333–58

Nkrumah, Kwame, *Neo-Colonialism: The Last Stage of Imperialism* (Thomas Nelson & Sons, Ltd, 1965)

Noble, Safiya Umoja, *Algorithms of Oppression: How Search Engines Reinforce Racism* (New York University Press, 2018)

Nussbaum, Martha C., *Not for Profit: Why Democracy Needs the Humanities* (Princeton University Press, 2010)

Palestine Chronicle Staff, 'Refaat Alareer's Body Laid to Rest after 15 Months – His Words Endures', *The Palestine Chronicle*, 5 February 2025, https://www.palestinechronicle.com/refaat-alareersbody-laid-to-rest-after-15-months-his-words-endures/ [accessed 24 April 2026]

Said, Edward W., *Culture and Imperialism* (Vintage, 1993)

Scott, James C., *Weapons of the Weak: Everyday Forms of Peasant Resistance* (Yale University Press, 1985)

Watkins, Shannon, 'Protecting the Liberal Arts and Humanities in American Higher Education', *Manhattan Institute*, 5 December 2024, pp. 4–5, https://manhattan.institute/article/protecting-the-liberal-arts-and-humanities-in-american-higher-education [accessed 24 April 2026]

WVU Today, 'WVU Announces Preliminary Recommendations, Academic Transformation Next Steps', *WVU Today*, 11 August 2023, https://wvutoday.wvu.edu/stories/2023/08/11/wvu-announces-preliminary-recommendations-academic-transformation-next-steps [accessed 24 April 2026]

Chapter 4

Place and planet: comparative literary research in an age of 'global challenges'

Nicola Thomas

Introducing the 'place-based' research agenda

This chapter sets out how languages and cultures research in general, and literary research in particular, contribute to understanding the relationship between the local and the planetary in the context of place-based research. Recent years have seen a pronounced shift towards a 'place-based' agenda for UK research. As early as 2019, Philip McCann identified this as part of a broader move towards place-based thinking across national and international policy circles, connecting the development of place-based policymaking to productivity agendas centred around maximising the efficiency of local economies.[1] This thinking clearly informs the British Academy's 2021 report on place-based approaches to research funding in the social sciences, arts and humanities in the UK, which mentions 'productivity' seventeen times in sixteen pages, placing a strong emphasis on community knowledge exchange, the skills economy and the closing of the 'regional productivity gap'.[2] Place was also identified as a strategic priority for UK Research and Innovation (UKRI) in 2021.[3] Some of these developments are specific to the UK context, in which addressing the significant economic imbalances between regions, notably between London and elsewhere, has been a political ambition for successive governments not only in Westminster but also in the devolved nations and regions. Although comparable regional economic disparity clearly exists in other countries, including some of our closest European neighbours, the UK seems to have placed a unique emphasis on mobilising academic research and the higher education sector in order to bridge these productivity gaps.

It is possible to see the promotion of place-based research (via the strategic agenda set by UKRI and other funding bodies in dialogue with government) as a natural development of what has long been understood, in the British context, as the university's obligation to be a good local citizen and to make a positive contribution to civic life. Stefan Collini, adopting a rather traditional view of the function of academic knowledge, critiques the attempt to 'subordinate universities to the currently favoured form of economic policy' rather than allow them to 'concentrate on their principal task of extending and deepening human understanding'.[4] Regardless of whether or not one subscribes to this understanding of what universities are 'for', it is worth noting that the successful implementation of a place-based approach to research at the level of higher education institutions (HEIs) is far from straightforward: a recent report examined the evidence for the efficacy of place-based research and development (R&D) investment against the backdrop of the previous government's 'levelling up' agenda and found that there were risks as well as affordances in the encouragement of a place-based approach.[5] An emphasis on place and civic engagement required significant capacity within HEIs, and 'younger' HEIs, as well as those serving marginalised and 'left behind' places, were more likely to regard themselves as having a responsibility towards civic engagement which resulted in them being 'overburdened by local need' – all while HEIs in 'thriving' areas were free to focus on research excellence and internationalisation for their own sake.[6] These risks can be keenly felt in the context of arts and humanities research, where building in an emphasis on regional and place-based impact, let alone impact that results in increased local productivity or skills development, often feels at odds with the abstract 'task of extending and deepening human understanding' to which Collini asks researchers to aspire, and which many (though not all) active research academics in the humanities would recognise as their own.[7]

With all this in mind, what might intellectually meaningful and socially valuable placed-based research look like in the arts and humanities? The University of Glasgow's Arts and Humanities Research Council-funded place-based research hub makes a passionate case for place as a lens to human experience:

> Place is the foundation stone of individual and collective life, a geographic location and a repository of emotions, experiences, meanings, and memories. Places are where life courses are shaped, social networks are formed and the site of lived and felt experiences.[8]

This echoes Rebecca Madgin's view, writing for UKRI, that:

> Artworks, poems, novels, films, museums, and exhibitions each powerfully curate, tell and translate the stories of place. In addition, through research and creative practice the arts and humanities actively shape the everyday lived and felt experiences of people within places. [. . .] Together, the arts and humanities bring to life why places matter to people and help us to understand the past, present, and future of places.[9]

Through the lens of the arts and humanities, place becomes the site of lived experience and a vital force in shaping and enabling communities to grow and identities to develop. The findings of one project connected to the Glasgow hub, Feeling Towns, report the impact of creative methods in helping residents of a range of places articulate their feelings (of pride or otherwise) about their local area. Far from being 'subordinate [. . .] to the currently favoured form of economic policy', Feeling Towns explicitly aims to go '[b]eyond econometric approaches' in accounting for forms of value, and values of place, not oriented towards local productivity agendas.[10]

While 'Feeling Towns' and the Glasgow hub bring together a variety of localities and communities across the UK to share findings, it is often assumed or implied that 'place' is local to the institution in question (and, indeed, that the institution is situated in space in such a way as to render the idea of 'place' meaningful). Other projects funded in response to a 2021 call focus exclusively on heritage, culture and place in the UK and almost all are specifically local to the HEI in question: a project at the University of Nottingham examines the city's 'hidden heritage' in its cave network; Coventry University leads on 'securing the place legacy' of Coventry City of Culture 2021, and so on.[11] This feeds the assumption that place-based research is connected to responsible civic engagement on the part of the university.

In addition to the practical hazards of this approach, as set out by Kempton and others, there is an intellectual challenge here too. 'Place' means much more than 'regions or cities in the UK with a university, outside of London'. If the objective of place-based research is to understand the 'felt experiences of people within places' in a holistic and meaningful way, rather than merely to support regional economic development in the UK or enable HEIs to act as responsible citizens in a particular local context, then the sense of what constitutes a place ought to be properly defined as the embodied corollary to the abstract 'space' in the broadest possible sense. It must encompass places without significant connections to local HEIs, including 'centres' as well as margins and peripheries; and above all, it must consider those 'other' places beyond national borders in which felt and lived experience is every bit as rich and meaningful, and significant to local and global economies, as it is in Britain.

Global challenges

One counterweight to UKRI's place-based agenda that does, on paper, have the potential to enrich these local agendas is the emphasis on 'global challenges'. The UK government's Global Challenges Research Fund (GCRF) launched in 2016, funded by 0.7 per cent of the UK's overseas development aid (ODA) budget to a total of £1.5 billion, had the stated objective of contributing to the UK's aid strategy by ensuring 'that the UK's development spending will meet our moral obligation to the world's poorest and also support our national interest'.[12] As with the place-based research agenda, the underlying objectives of the funding scheme were transparently economic, with a strong emphasis on development: 'to generate innovative solutions to intractable development issues and to identify practicable pathways to healthier and safer lives, sustainable development and prosperity for all, equal and effective education, social justice and human rights, and stable institutions'.[13] The six UKRI 'strategic GCRF portfolios' were global health, education, sustainable cities, food systems, conflict and resilience. The UN's seventeen Sustainable Development Goals (SDGs) provided the wider international context to these strategic priorities, as did a desire to build the capacity of, and partnerships with, researchers in ODA-eligible countries.

Although the future of this research agenda is somewhat uncertain in light of the sudden cut to GCRF funding from February 2022, and reductions to overall UK ODA budgets announced in 2025, the global challenge discourse nonetheless launched a cluster of research institutes, teaching initiatives and modes of policy engagement in UK higher education. As with the place-based agenda, there are both risks and affordances. The role played by the notion of the 'global challenge' in shaping research and policy is open to critique: Ludwig and others highlight the fact that 'global challenges are most commonly highlighted together with the solutions offered by dominant actors' – that is to say, global challenge thinking does not necessarily lead to better or even more innovative solutions, but tends to support the implementation of ideas already favoured by those with power.[14] Similarly, Isakova and others, in an illuminating examination of the social construction of the global challenge discourse, find that research in this area commonly reinforces, rather than challenges, the dominant global order.[15]

Moreover, given the profound entanglement between global challenge thinking – particularly the way such thinking conceives of the nature of the global – and discourses of 'sustainable development', this framing is open to the same critiques that have been made of the UN SDGs and the wider ODA context. Namely, as Seema Arora-Jonsson puts it: that they conceal 'a universalist agenda underpinned by Global North and neoliberal interests' which is imposed upon, rather than shaped in dialogue with, the Global South; and that this universalist agenda, as has been noted elsewhere, takes for granted the notion of economic development as a general good, as well as assuming it to be compatible with environmental sustainability.[16]

Humanities thinking has the potential to expand and redefine the terms of the global-challenge debate. There are alternative ways of understanding the notion of the global and the framing of crisis, catastrophe or 'challenge' that draw on critical traditions including post-structuralism, eco-theory and post-colonialism. One example is Gayatri Spivak's emphasis on the 'planetary' as the lived corollary of the abstract-economic 'global'; another is Achille Mbembe's analysis of planetary 'necropolitics' as an alternative conceptualisation of global power and violence.[17] Such approaches insist on an attention to the marginalised people and epistemologies that can be rendered invisible by the 'universalising' framing of the global challenge.

These two trends, towards place-based research on the one hand and global-challenge thinking on the other, both require input from humanities disciplines in order to make their core assumptions visible and connect them meaningfully with social and cultural realities. Although both clearly have the potential to serve as powerful framings that allow researchers to engage with policy contexts at various scales, the current orthodoxy in which 'place-based' means 'relating to a (more or less) deprived regional community in the UK' and 'global' means 'relating to the Global South without calling into question the power held by the Global North' is not intellectually satisfactory.

Place and planet

Questions also arise as to how the place-based and global-challenge research agendas relate to each other. Global challenges have numerous and complex local causes and effects (think, for example, of the 'think global, act local' slogan of climate activism), and all lived experience of place is affected by global phenomena, world politics and economics. These relationships between the place-based or local and the global or planetary are far from straightforward: they are always mediated by intangible social and political formations such as nations, regions, provinces, continents and cultures.[18] However, as yet, no research, policy or impact analysis has explored the 'gap' that springs up between these two trends in research funding and framing – which is all the more striking considering that many shared themes shape both agendas. Climate-change adaptation, mitigation and resilience; urban life, policy and planning; health and well-being; gender, racial and other forms of inequality are some of the common areas of focus. And yet little consideration is given, by policymakers and research-funding bodies at least, to how specific place-based interventions or understandings sit within a regional, national, continental or cultural context; and, in turn, how questions of cultures, epistemologies, power dynamics and identities at a global level inform and affect local contexts. Without a clear understanding of how the local and the planetary affect and modify one another via intermediate structures, the place-based research agenda risks parochialism, irrelevance and/or political naivety, and the global challenge agenda risks neocolonialism, instrumentalism and perpetuating inequality.

There are, of course, many rich bodies of theory on the local/global interface that might usefully inform an attempt to mediate between these competing scales – many of which come directly from humanities disciplines, within which the supra-local, sub-national framings, such as community, region, nation and culture, are central considerations. Two examples of thinkers in the post-colonial tradition have already been cited (Spivak and Mbembe) but other fields, including eco-theory and comparative literature, also have much to say about these dynamics. 'Think global, act local' has long been a central principle of environmental action. Ursula Heise explores how aesthetics have long been a key means by which the relationship of local to global is negotiated, arguing that literary and filming strategies, such as fragmentation, montage, collage and zooming, are some of the ways in which we imagine the connection between our felt, local places and the abstract, invisible reality of global systems.[19] Heise writes of 'eco-cosmopolitanism' as a way of describing the responsibility we each have to ecosystems beyond our immediate place in a planetary context; Anna Tsing and others prefer the concept of 'patchiness' to describe the combination of local realities and global frameworks, thinking of systems not as composed of pre-existing structures, but rather conceptualising the systems, including world systems, as 'thought experiments with which to make sense of structures' at a local level.[20] At this local level, 'patches' are components of what they term 'landscape structures' (borrowing from the language of ecology) and provide space for thinking about differentiated human experience in ways that reject the problematic Anthropocentrism of some attempts to theorise social injustice in the era of humans as geological agents, the so-called Anthropocene.

New theories of world and comparative literature, too, scrutinise the idea of world systems and their relation to local experience. Emily Apter's polemic against world literature contends that incommensurability and, ultimately, untranslatability, are overlooked realities undermining any vision of a universal *Weltliteratur*.[21] There are strong echoes here of Arora-Jonsson's critique of the 'global challenge' as a front for a post-Enlightenment universalist agenda grounded in 'Western values' – crucially, however, Apter's work also offers something like a solution in thinking of language in all its differentiated reality as a useful impediment to the complete proliferation of an undesirably homogenous global culture. Language, Apter's work implies, is valuable not because it allows us to communicate with one another across local boundaries, but because it highlights what Tsing might call the 'patchiness' of the world and its cultures.

Jennifer Wenzel tackles the problem of 'world literature' in the context of global environmental change, describing literature (alongside other cultural forms such as photography and film) as a form of what she terms 'world-imagining'; the literary, for Wenzel, is part of a 'mesh of relations in which the liberatory and immiserating implications of globalisations – old and new – are knit and can be laid bare'.[22] By offering close readings of texts which navigate a variety of routes through this mesh, navigating different spatial scales, her world demonstrates how literature and culture allow writers – and, more importantly, readers – to overcome the 'quarantines of imagination' that might restrict thinking to homogenous linguistic, cultural, geographical or social bubbles, while also allowing for an uneven (or 'patchy') conceptualisation of the global. As for Heise, literary form is central to Wenzel's thinking, since it is form that situates both writers and readers within this dynamic of uneven globalisation and that (via strategies of reflexivity in particular) makes this position visible to them during the process of world-imagining she describes.

Case study: Wetland Times

According to these recent theories of comparative and world literature, then, language, and especially the literary use of language, is a key means by which the imaginative projections that connect the local to the planetary are generated, mediated and problematised. Literary research thus has a central role to play in ensuring that place-based research addresses and informs global challenges, and that the sense of the global implied by the global challenge discourse remains attentive to social and cultural differences and power dynamics.

My own ongoing research project explores the role of the literary and linguistic imagination in navigating the spatialised temporality of a particular sort of landscape, the wetland. The project, funded by a British Academy International Interdisciplinary Knowledge Frontiers grant since 2023, is concerned with the 'temporal ecosystems' of three global wetland sites (Morecambe Bay, UK; the northern European Wadden Sea; and Dja Faunal Reserve in southern Cameroon). Its central aim is to investigate the different ways in which time is conceptualised, experienced and described in these vulnerable and complex landscapes, using an interdisciplinary approach combining methodologies from both arts and humanities and social science.

Wetland Times is a project about both place and time. These three very different places are brought into dialogue by examining a shared global issue, that of time and how it is conceptualised in the context of environmental change. Time is central to conversations about climate change and conservation practice, which is constantly reflecting on temporal phenomena: how to model future scenarios, how to ensure sustainable land use and management, and how to protect or preserve past and existing landscapes and habitats. One central question conservationists face, for example, hinges on the problem of 'baselines': given that unmanaged landscapes are constantly in flux, how do conservation practitioners charged with restoring or maintaining a place decide which is the 'correct' version of the landscape to preserve or reconstruct?[23] (This happens to be particularly challenging when it comes to wetlands, which are some of the most unstable of landscapes and highly variable: Annie Proulx likens global wetlands to 'wallpaper samples, each with its own design and character'.)[24]

The project is interested in both local and global times. In terms of global (and globalising) time, we focus partly on the idea of the Anthropocene, which unsettles human narratives of progress, development and freedom at a planetary level. But we are implicitly critical of this move towards a totalising planetary time, since the accompanying prescription for 'deep time' and planetary thinking to solve ecological problems often threatens to dominate and overwrite the messy, locally specific and culturally sensitive times that underpin the human relationship with nature which Wetland Times seeks to recuperate and foreground.

How does the project conceive of the relationship between the local and the global, between the 'place-based' studies of Morecambe Bay, the Wadden Sea and the Dja Faunal Reserve on the one hand, and the 'global challenge' of environmental change, wildlife conservation and habitat preservation on the other? The primary way in which we understand this connection is via language and, more specifically, via concepts or *Begriffe*, contested words and phrases that have accumulated and reflect complex webs of social and cultural meaning.[25] 'Anthropocene', 'conservation' or 'development' are three English-language examples that play an important role in academic and technical discourse about global challenges; we situate these in dialogue with concepts that occur in specific local contexts, including in languages other than English. We adopt a variety of strategies for exploring which concepts are locally meaningful to communities in Morecambe, the Wadden and the Dja. These include fieldwork interviews and participatory arts methodologies, but also – and most importantly for the purposes of this chapter – we look at literary texts, which are a rich source of data for understanding how time concepts are developed, understood and contested within particular local languages and contexts.

One useful example of this in the German-language context is the poet Ulrike Draesner's long poem *Doggerland* (2021).[26] This experimental, book-length text describes the development and collapse of a Mesolithic hunter–gatherer (and later settled agricultural) civilisation occupying the territory that today lies submerged between the east coast of Britain and the northern coast of the European landmass (spanning Germany, Denmark and the Netherlands). Doggerland is, therefore, bordered by the English fens on the one hand and the Wadden Sea coast on the other, and is often described as a kind of invisible, primordial wetland landscape, deep time in an imagined place. 'Before the Fens there was Doggerland', as Proulx puts it.[27]

Draesner's poem is a complex, multi-layered and multilingual text that comprises three columns: a column of modern English words to the left, a column of modern German words to the right and in the centre, the 'main' text that switches freely between these and other languages, including proto-Indo-European. The text, showing as it does the emerging glossaries of contemporary English and German, which encompasses words like *Vergangenheit* [past], *Erzählung* [narrative] or *Geschichte* [story or history], dramatises the coming into being and contestation of time concepts. At the same time, it also presents time and temporal concepts for the reader's consideration; not least the idea of history itself, including and in relation to pre-history. The poem asks at what point in human evolution a sense of historicity emerges and how, and seems to posit a connection between this and the development of agriculture, as the shift to settlement is also accompanied by a formal shift in the poem to more regular line lengths and rhythms. Other time concepts are also scrutinised and given specific meaning in relation to Doggerland and, by extension, the modern Wadden Sea coast: the concept of the archive, for example, as a storehouse of historical data that lays itself open to (re)interpretation. The Wadden, or the North Sea, seabed is revealed by Draesner's text to be a rich cultural and linguistic archive. 'Deep time', a phrase that occurs often in the text, is also given particular meaning here in ways that connect with and enrich the global discourse around geological temporality: Draesner's deep time is not only the time of inert rocks and geological processes, but also of early humans and the non-human creatures with which they lived in close proximity.

In all of these cases, a specific artistic engagement with place yields new insights that can usefully be put into dialogue with insights from other cultures, other places, to gain a deeper understanding of a global phenomenon, that of time in landscapes affected by environmental change. Moreover, the language arts have a specific role to play precisely because they, more than any other realm of human activity, are capable of staging the complexity of concepts and animating linguistic concepts with rich and subtle meanings. Language reflects, but also shapes, the 'patchiness' of which Tsing and others write: it is a phenomenon that connects, but that also allows for difference and separation to be acknowledged.

Conclusion

The study of literature, including literary research, has long been felt to achieve what Collini argues ought to be the central task of universities, the 'deepening [of] human understanding'. Until relatively recently, literary scholars were rarely called upon to explain precisely how it does so, let alone in terms that appeal to research funding bodies and prospective students alike. The place-based research agenda has the potential to underpin both moral and practical arguments for the value of a certain kind of literary study interested in places local to any given HEI, that can then be leveraged in the service of an argument about greater cultural understanding leading to improved economic productivity or social cohesion. But this place-based approach alone is not sufficient to explain the value of literary research that goes beyond certain regional literary traditions in the UK: which is global or comparative in scope, which is interested in languages, literatures and cultures other than English and, perhaps in the 'other' more broadly, that which lies outside the realm of our immediate local experience. Where once this openness to global cultures might have been understood as an end in itself, now those who wish to study them are frequently asked: why here? Why not leave the study of literature in any language to the nation or community of 'native' speakers? The agenda of the 'global challenge' – or, indeed, the market logic of internationalisation – is not seen as enough justification for an in-depth understanding of the languages, literatures and cultures of other places. On the contrary, as discussed above, this way of understanding social and environmental problems is frequently accompanied by a resurgent universalism, an assumption that the 'challenges' of one culture or community are the same as the challenges of another.

In response to this challenge, literary researchers must argue strongly that our research, especially that which looks across linguistic and cultural boundaries, can add much-needed nuance to our sense of both the local and the global. Drawing on my own current research, I have given one example of how it does this, by revealing and reshaping the concepts via which we communicate within and beyond our local contexts. There are many other literary methodologies that provide a similarly productive means of revealing how literature, language and culture supply a vital perspective on the relationship between the local and the global. And it is, arguably, in these many layers – not only literature but also history, culture, politics, society and community – between place on the one hand and planet on the other where the most is at stake.

Notes

1 Philip McCann, *UK Research and Innovation: A Place-Based Shift?*, July 2019, McCann_-_UK_Research_and_Innovation_-_A_Place-Based_Shift_vFinal.pdf [accessed 17 June 2026].

2 The British Academy, *Place-Based Approaches to Research Funding* (The British Academy, 22 March 2021), doi:10.5871/place/9780856726576.001.

3 'Place Matters: The Arts and Humanities and the Place Agenda', 2021, https://www.ukri.org/blog/place-matters-the-arts-and-humanities-and-the-place-agenda/ [accessed 25 September 2024].

4 Stefan Collini, *Speaking of Universities* (Verso, 2017), p. 127.

5 'Universities, Economic Development and "Levelling Up" – How Can Universities Make a Positive Impact on Their Local Areas?', *Impact of Social Sciences*, 2021, https://blogs.lse.ac.uk/impactofsocialsciences/2021/11/16/universities-economic-development-and-levelling-up-how-can-universities-make-a-positive-impact-on-their-local-areas/ [accessed 25 September 2024]. See also Louise Kempton and others, *Putting Universities in Their Place: An Evidence-Based Approach to Understanding the Contribution of Higher Education to Local and Regional Development* (Routledge, 2021), doi:10.4324/9781003198154.

6 'Universities, Economic Development and "Levelling Up" – How Can Universities Make a Positive Impact on Their Local Areas?'

7 Collini, *Speaking of Universities*, p. 126.

8 'University of Glasgow Place-Based Research Programme Hub: About the Programme', https://www.gla.ac.uk/schools/socialpolitical/research/urbanstudies/activities/projects/place-basedresearchprogramme/abouttheprogramme/ [accessed 28 September 2024].

9 'Place Matters'.

10 Nicky Marsh, Michael Howcroft, and Joseph Owen, *'Pride in Place' Beyond the Metrics: Insights from the Feeling Towns Project* (University of Glasgow, 14 March 2024), doi:10.36399/gla.pubs.321921.

11 'Funding boost and expertise to level up places around the UK', 2022, https://webarchive.nationalarchives.gov.uk/ukgwa/20250107101250/https://www.ukri.org/news/funding-boost-and-expertise-to-level-up-places-around-the-uk/ [accessed 3 June 2026].

12 Department for Business, Energy and Industrial Strategy, *UK Strategy for the Global Challenges Research Fund (GCRF)*, 2017.

13 Department for Business, Energy and Industrial Strategy. It is worth noting that projects actually funded by the GCRF interpreted these objectives in a range of ways, and some were implicitly or explicitly critical of the 'global challenge' discourse in ways that align with my argument.

14 David Ludwig and others, 'What's Wrong with Global Challenges?', *Journal of Responsible Innovation*, 9.1 (2022), pp. 6–27, doi:10.1080/23299460.2021.2000130.

15 *Constructing Global Challenges in World Politics*, ed. by Alina Isakova and others (Routledge, 2024), doi:10.4324/9781003452348.

16 Seema Arora-Jonsson, 'The Sustainable Development Goals: A Universalist Promise for the Future', *Futures*, 146 (2023), p. 103087, doi:10.1016/j.futures.2022.103087.

17 Gayatri Spivak, '"Planetarity" (Box 4, WELT)', *Paragraph*, 38.2 (2015), pp. 290–2; Achille Mbembe, *Necropolitics*, Theory in Forms series (Duke University Press, 2019).

18 For one example of a call for 'interconnectedness' in place-based research from beyond the arts and humanities, see Patricia Balvanera and others, 'Interconnected Place-Based Social–Ecological Research Can Inform Global Sustainability', *Current Opinion in Environmental Sustainability*, 29 (2017), pp. 1–7, doi:10.1016/j.cosust.2017.09.005.

19 Ursula K. Heise, *Sense of Place and Sense of Planet: The Environmental Imagination of the Global* (Oxford University Press, 2008).

20 Anna Lowenhaupt Tsing, Andrew S. Mathews, and Nils Bubandt, 'Patchy Anthropocene: Landscape Structure, Multispecies History, and the Retooling of Anthropology: An Introduction to Supplement 20', *Current Anthropology*, 60.S20 (2019), pp. S186–97, doi:10.1086/703391.

21 Emily S. Apter, *Against World Literature: On the Politics of Untranslatability* (Verso, 2013). For other, related, critiques of the resurgence of interest in 'world literature' since 2000, see Pheng Cheah, 'What is a World? On World Literature as World-Making Activity', *Daedalus*, 137.3 (2008), pp. 26–38, doi:10.1162/daed.2008.137.3.26; Sharae Deckard, *Combined and Uneven Development: Towards a New Theory of World-Literature*, Postcolonialism across the Disciplines, Volume 17 (Liverpool University Press, 2015).

22 Jennifer Wenzel, *The Disposition of Nature: Environmental Crisis and World Literature* (Fordham University Press, 2019), p. 8.

23 See Jamie Lorimer and others, 'Rewilding: Science, Practice, and Politics', *Annual Review of Environment and Resources*, 40.1 (2015), pp. 39–62, doi:10.1146/annurev-environ-102014-021406.

24 Annie Proulx, *Fen, Bog and Swamp: A Short History of Peatland Destruction and its Role in the Climate Crisis* (Simon and Schuster, 2023), p. 18.

25 Our theoretical framework here draws on the work of Reinhart Koselleck. See Reinhart Koselleck, 'Introduction and Prefaces to the *Geschichtliche Grundbegriffe*', *Contributions to the History of Concepts*, 6.1 (2011), pp. 1–37, doi:10.3167/choc.2011.060102.

26 Ulrike Draesner, *Doggerland: Gedicht* (Penguin, 2021).

27 Proulx, *Fen, Bog and Swamp*, p. 44.

References

Apter, Emily S., *Against World Literature: On the Politics of Untranslatability* (Verso, 2013)

Arora-Jonsson, Seema, 'The Sustainable Development Goals: A Universalist Promise for the Future', *Futures*, 146 (2023), p. 103087, doi:10.1016/j.futures.2022.103087

Balvanera, Patricia, and others, 'Interconnected Place-Based Social–Ecological Research Can Inform Global Sustainability', *Current Opinion in Environmental Sustainability*, 29 (2017), pp. 1–7, doi:10.1016/j.cosust.2017.09.005

The British Academy, *Place-Based Approaches to Research Funding* (The British Academy, 22 March 2021), doi:10.5871/place/9780856726576.001

Cheah, Pheng, 'What is a World? On World Literature as World-Making Activity', *Daedalus*, 137.3 (2008), pp. 26–38, doi:10.1162/daed.2008.137.3.26

Collini, Stefan, *Speaking of Universities* (Verso, 2017)

Deckard, Sharae, *Combined and Uneven Development: Towards a New Theory of World-Literature*, Postcolonialism across the Disciplines, Volume 17 (Liverpool University Press, 2015)

Department for Business, Energy and Industrial Strategy, *UK Strategy for the Global Challenges Research Fund (GCRF)* (2017), https://assets.publishing.service.gov.uk/media/5a822337e5274a2e87dc156d/global-challenges-research-fund-gcrf-strategy.pdf [accessed 5 May 2026]

Draesner, Ulrike, *Doggerland: Gedicht* (Penguin, 2021)
Heise, Ursula K., *Sense of Place and Sense of Planet: The Environmental Imagination of the Global* (Oxford University Press, 2008)
Isakova, Alina, and others (eds), *Constructing Global Challenges in World Politics* (Routledge, 2024), doi:10.4324/9781003452348
Kempton, Louise, and others, *Putting Universities in Their Place: An Evidence-Based Approach to Understanding the Contribution of Higher Education to Local and Regional Development* (Routledge, 2021), doi:10.4324/9781003198154
Koselleck, Reinhart, 'Introduction and Prefaces to the *Geschichtliche Grundbegriffe*', *Contributions to the History of Concepts*, 6.1 (2011), pp. 1–37, doi:10.3167/choc.2011.060102
Lorimer, Jamie, and others, 'Rewilding: Science, Practice, and Politics', *Annual Review of Environment and Resources*, 40.1 (2015), pp. 39–62, doi:10.1146/annurev-environ-102014-021406
Ludwig, David, and others, 'What's Wrong with Global Challenges?', *Journal of Responsible Innovation*, 9.1 (2022), pp. 6–27, doi:10.1080/23299460.2021.2000130
Marsh, Nicky, Michael Howcroft, and Joseph Owen, *'Pride in Place' Beyond the Metrics: Insights from the Feeling Towns Project* (University of Glasgow, 14 March 2024), doi:10.36399/gla.pubs.321921
Mbembe, Achille, *Necropolitics*, Theory in Forms series (Duke University Press, 2019)
McCann, Philip, *UK Research and Innovation: A Place-Based Shift?*, July 2019, https://www.ifm.eng.cam.ac.uk/uploads/Research/CSTI/UKRI_Place/McCann_-_UK_Research_and_Innovation_-_A_Place-Based_Shift_vFinal.pdf [accessed 5 May 2026]
'Place Matters: The Arts and Humanities and the Place Agenda', 2021, https://www.ukri.org/blog/place-matters-the-arts-and-humanities-and-the-place-agenda/ [accessed 25 September 2024]
Proulx, Annie, *Fen, Bog and Swamp: A Short History of Peatland Destruction and its Role in the Climate Crisis* (Simon and Schuster, 2023)
Spivak, Gayatri, '"Planetarity" (Box 4, WELT)', *Paragraph*, 38.2 (2015), pp. 290–2, *JSTOR*, http://www.jstor.org/stable/44016381 [accessed 5 May 2026]
Tewdwr-Jones, Mark, and Louise Kempton, 'Universities, Economic Development and "Levelling Up" – How Can Universities Make a

Positive Impact on Their Local Areas?', *Impact of Social Sciences*, 2021, https://blogs.lse.ac.uk/impactofsocialsciences/2021/11/16/universities-economic-development-and-levelling-up-how-can-universities-make-a-positive-impact-on-their-local-areas/ [accessed 25 September 2024]

Tsing, Anna Lowenhaupt, Andrew S. Mathews, and Nils Bubandt, 'Patchy Anthropocene: Landscape Structure, Multispecies History, and the Retooling of Anthropology: An Introduction to Supplement 20', *Current Anthropology*, 60.S20 (2019), pp. S186–97, doi:10.1086/703391

'University of Glasgow Place-Based Research Programme Hub: About the Programme' https://www.gla.ac.uk/schools/socialpolitical/research/urbanstudies/activities/projects/place-basedresearchprogramme/abouttheprogramme/ [accessed 28 September 2024]

Wenzel, Jennifer, *The Disposition of Nature: Environmental Crisis and World Literature* (Fordham University Press, 2019)

Chapter 5

Translating the past: literary research, public history and the heritage of Wales

Carol Tully

> *O wad some Pow'r the giftie gie us*
> *To see oursels as others see us!*
>
> ROBERT BURNS, 'To a Louse. On Seeing One on a Lady's Bonnet at Church' (1786)

Being relevant

We find ourselves in strange times. The geopolitical landscape is in turmoil, climate change is ever-more apparent and the ripple effect of the COVID-19 pandemic is yet to subside. As we seek to negotiate this seemingly endless series of obstacles, our individual mental health, societal wellbeing and core cultural values increasingly find themselves in the spotlight as a means to reset and become more resilient. We are encouraged to reflect, take time out and connect, with ourselves, with each other and, importantly, with what we have in common, not what divides us. Central to this are the ways in which we spend our leisure time, broaden our horizons and find our place in the world. The value of visiting heritage sites, art galleries and museums, exploring our family genealogy, joining book groups and finding our creative selves, is an ever-present topic in media lifestyle features. Increasingly, media content explores our shared past, through the houses we lived in, the clothes we wore and the work we did as the turn to social history reaches its logical destination: we, and our place in the world we have inherited, have become the subjects of our own personal research. Underpinning this is the broad span of the arts and humanities disciplines and the work that we as professional researchers produce as historians, musicologists, biographers and, of course, literary scholars. The study of literature – past and present – enables us to reflect on and engage with the issues that affect our daily lives. Modern languages literary research brings the added dimension of intercultural understanding, opening up new vistas and ways of understanding the interconnectedness of the world in which we live. Yet, as the arts and humanities find themselves under increasing pressure, these interdependent aspects of scholarly endeavour need championing more than ever. The question we face as experts is how to do this.

Sometimes it is that very expertise that gets in the way. We have all been there, planning a research project on a topic about which we are passionate and the value of which is patently obvious to us and our academic peers. As academics, we are trained to see the broader significance and perhaps we take that for granted. After all, arts and humanities research is all about us as humans and the world we have created for ourselves, so clearly it must be important. Then we try to explain it to someone else, over dinner perhaps or making conversation at a family event. The blank faces and conversation-stopper moments are frustrating but ultimately understandable. Most people are too polite to ask the burning question: why on earth are you working on that? Extrapolate this up to governmental level and the questions become more probing. To those beyond the arts and humanities academy, the idea of spending time, and being paid, to research in depth what appears to be an entirely random, esoteric topic, even in the best of economic times, seems outlandish to say the least. What is it all for? Why should public money be given over to such projects when there is so much else at stake? What is the point? It was partly to answer questions just like these that funding bodies and government came up with the notion of showing demonstrable impact, a move that threw the ball right back into the academic court. We, as literary researchers, faced a new challenge: to make the work we do speak to new audiences and change lives, giving it value beyond the still-crucial enhancement of human knowledge. Tricky. This dilemma is explored by Rick Rylance in his 2016 discussion *Literature and the Public Good*, where he describes the opposing camps:

> The use of measurement data and justificatory requirements of this kind are ubiquitous in public life and rile humanistic opinion. When decision-makers demand 'value assurance', humanists see a category mistake. The *intrinsic* value of art, or scholarly learning, or abstract ideas, or faith beliefs, or one's inwardness with foreign languages, for example, are said to be good in themselves. They demonstrate their worth by existing, and only incidentally through worldly activity stimulated by them.[1]

The humanistic view outlined here has its place. After all, not all research can be immediately assigned an economic value, but that does not mean that it might not in time contribute to the development of future economies, not least through the 'softer' elements such as wellbeing and cultural identity. So, as for Rylance, for me the dichotomy is a false one. Some things take time for their 'value' to emerge. It does not mean it is not there. What our commodity-driven age lacks, perhaps, is the patience to wait. Rylance is right to argue for the role of literature (and the arts and humanities more broadly) in ensuring we are able to rebalance our view of the world and of ourselves.

Nonetheless, the arrival of 'value assurance' has had its benefits, however uncomfortably it might sit. We, as researchers, now behave differently. It is, I think, fair to say that many modern languages researchers struggled initially with this shift. Some disciplines – take the natural sciences or medicine – have it relatively easy when it comes to demonstrating the societal impact of their work. It is a little harder to argue when your research focus is on, say, Middle-High German poetry or the Portuguese novel. How can the study of these add value to the life in the anglophone world? To some extent, it has to do with the inherent interdisciplinarity of the methodology. Although it sits at the heart of many modern languages degrees, the combination of language and literature is not always obvious to those on the outside. Reading literature is for leisure, surely? Language is about grammar, vocabulary and translation, is it not? Why combine the two, beyond the obvious fact that the deployment of one makes the other accessible to a larger audience? There is no obvious public benefit. The brave new world of impact forced us to challenge that assumption head on. Over time, this has brought not only a benefit to wider society but also a fresh impetus to modern languages literary research that has challenged us to see our own connections with and value to wider society with fresh eyes.

This finds us working in ways which earlier generations of researchers would have found hard to countenance. Our work has become increasingly visible and important, not just because we think it is but because, with our help, others are beginning to understand it better for what it can contribute. In a highly commodified world, like it or not, relevance comes from impact, not just from hard work and insight. To be recognised as important, modern languages literary research has had, more than ever, to prove its relevance. The trick is to achieve this without compromising the integrity of the fundamental research or selling our souls in an impact-driven Faustian pact.

One area which can benefit from modern languages research is that of public history, which *The Historical Association* defines as 'bring[ing] together heritage, archives, museums, local history societies, history professionals, and active amateurs' and 'the engagement with history for different groups and professionals but with a level of expertise outside of the fixed university environment'.[2] This group of practitioners is central to the curation and interpretation of the sites that underpin the heritage tourism economy. Within this cultural ecosystem, Faye Sayer sees the public historians as enablers:

> Critically, public history is not history becoming heritage, but is a merging of the two. As such, public history enables history to be valuable to a broad audience and to have significance in the present, beyond the creation of knowledge, providing broader social, political and economic value. Subsequently, a crucial part of a public historian's role is in decoding history's underlying significance to people outside the profession. To do this, many public historians and those working in sectors of public history, such as the media, listen to stories, and ensure, where possible, that the multiple voices are heard as part of the narrative of the past. This leads to new avenues for historical dialog through the understanding that 'there is not a single unitary voice on the history of a site'. Public historians are not arbiters of the 'past', rather they are providers of present past narratives.[3]

Notably, there is no mention here, or indeed in most studies of public history, of a transnational, multilingual perspective. Yet, some of those 'multiple voices' and 'present past narratives' are embedded in the literature (broadly defined) and cultural material that sit at the heart of what we as modern languages researchers do when we interrogate literary texts in other languages and from other cultural perspectives. The past is reflected in prose, theatre and poetry, as well as travel writing, journalism and written ephemera. Of course, film and media, too, have their place. Yet, these foreign language sources can remain hidden, closed or inaccessible without the right expertise to mediate and interpret them – 'decoding [their] underlying significance' as Sayer would have it. Public historians and the fields they help to support, such as the heritage tourism industry, are, then, key potential beneficiaries of modern languages literary research.

The past is a foreign country

Imagine rummaging in the attic of the family home and coming across a suitcase full of letters and diaries in a foreign language where the only discernible words are the names of places and long-deceased relatives. What secrets might be contained in these forgotten documents? What might you learn about your own past if you were able to read them? This hypothetical scenario reflects, at a hyper-local level, the reality of our understanding of countless archives, libraries, collections and other ephemera held by all manner of cultural institutions across the UK. Be it letters, books, foreign periodicals, diaries or visitor books, there remains a wealth of information that is yet to see the light of day or be understood, even when its presence is known. The assumption that awareness of a resource signals understanding of its content is a dangerous one to make. As a frequent visitor to the British Library, I have lost count of the times a book, more often than not a foreign language title published in the nineteenth century, has arrived from the stacks uncut, simultaneously catalogued and present while inaccessible and absent. This begs the question, how much more is there to understand about our past, from even the most well-researched and not-so-distant periods? This is one area where modern languages literary research can make a real difference in opening up and interpreting previously hidden resources. What we uncover is a potential gold mine for the fields of public history and heritage tourism. In terms of practical, commodifiable value, literary research into foreign language sources can contribute new data, visual material, stories and ideas. It also brings a sense of connectedness, highlighting the value of the local to the global. Unheard narratives emerge through storytelling, and new and fascinating artefacts surface. This new material can, as Barbara Kirshenblatt-Gimblett puts it, 'raise the threshold of wonder',[4] unlocking sources, as well as foregrounding once-hidden witnesses to the changes to our world. The resource is there in plain sight, but it needs modern languages researchers to unlock the content.

My own experience of the value of literary research to public history and heritage tourism centres on the field of travel writing and my work on the Arts and Humanities Research Council-funded project 'European Travellers to Wales: 1750–2010'. This was a collaborative project, led by Bangor University along with Swansea University and the University of Wales Centre for Advanced Welsh and Celtic Studies, based in Aberystwyth, that ran from 2013 to 2018.[5] We explored the representation of Wales and 'Welshness' in texts by European travellers from 1750 to the present day, homing in on key points in the period of Welsh modernisation from the Industrial Revolution to the post-devolution era. The idea was to challenge perceptions of Wales in European travel writing as 'unknown' and 'invisible' by uncovering, collating and interpreting accounts of travel to Wales in languages other than English. In so doing, we were able to challenge notions of hegemony and identity within the genre of travel writing, relating both to the places visited and the places of origin of the diverse travellers we encountered. Our research, including the co-authored book *Hidden Texts, Hidden Nation. (Re)Discoveries of Wales in French and German Travel Writing (1750–2018)*, presented an important case study of a culture often minoritised in the field by providing a telling illustration of the dynamics of European intercultural relations and representation.[6] The writers we identified ranged from more famous public figures, such as Madame de Genlis,[7] Felix Mendelssohn[8] and Hermann von Pückler-Muskau,[9] to travelling scholars, industrial spies, exiles and professional travel writers. The range of accounts painted a picture of Wales over two and a half centuries and held a mirror up to the changing value systems and shifting social structures across Europe. Some played to the stereotypes: Genlis was enchanted by the harp, Mendelssohn hated the weather, Pückler-Muskau cavorted with champagne on the summit of Eryri, his hyperbole rendering the scene as an imaginative Friedrichesque feast of the sublime:

> Aussichten entschädigten mich nicht, den von Wolken ganz umschleiert, konnte ich kaum 20 Schritt weit vor mir sehen, und in diesem geheimnißvollen clair obscur erreichte ich auch den ersehnten Gipfel, zu dem man über einen schmalen Felsenkamm

> gelangt. Ein Steinhaufen, in dessen Mitte eine hölzerne Säule steht, ist als Wahrzeichen aufgerichtet. Ich glaubte hier der Erscheinung meines Doppelgängers zu begegnen, als ein junger Mann aus dem Nebel hervortrat, der mir selbst völlig glich, NB. wie ich aussah, als ich vor 16 Jahren in den Schweizer-Alpen umherirrte.[10]
>
> [I was not compensated for my sufferings by the view, for, shrouded as I was in clouds, I could hardly see twenty paces before me. In this mysterious *clair obscur* I reached the wished-for summit, the way to which lies over an irregular wall of rocks. A pile of stones, in the centre of which is a wooden pillar, marks the highest point. I thought I met my *wraith*, as a young man emerged from the mist who precisely resembled me, that is to say when I wandered over the Swiss Alps sixteen years ago.][11]

Others resisted the temptation to romanticise quite so much and instead saw a side to Wales that would have been entirely new to their contemporary readers. For example, Christian August Gottlieb Goede, writing in 1804, took aim at the English mismanagement of the principality, noting that 'sich die Englische Regierung nicht gleichgültiger gegen die Cultivirung des Welschen Volkes hätte zeigen können, als es bis jetzt geschehen ist' [the English government could not have been more disinterested in the cultivation of the Welsh people than it has been up to now],[12] while French industrialists, father and son Georges and Achille Dufaud, visiting in the 1820s, marvelled at the advanced technology and sublime grandeur of the Dowlais iron works at Merthyr Tydfil, highlighting the skilled workforce found there: 'Le pays de Galles et Cyfarthfa surtout a et conserve les meilleurs puddleurs du monde, un puddleur ordinaire et non soigneux n'est pas admis' [Wales and Cyfarthfa in particular has and retains the best puddlers in the world, an ordinary, careless puddler is not admitted].[13]

As this brief overview suggests, the range of material uncovered was incredibly varied and of potential value to diverse stakeholders. The multilingual aspect of the project brought an added and hugely significant dimension by opening up new perspectives and uncovering previously unheard voices. Beyond the co-authored volume mentioned above, we undertook a number of academic activities during the three years of the main project, including journal articles, blogs, a conference and two doctoral theses. As these elements developed, they provided the raw material for the impact activities that were central to the main project and formed the basis of the follow-on activities. These ranged from an exhibition and educational materials to tourist information and public history resources and involved a number of formal and informal partners across Wales, including Visit Wales, the National Library of Wales, the Royal Commission on the Ancient and Historic Monuments of Wales, the Ceredigion Museum, Storiel (Bangor), the Swansea Museum, the People's Collection Wales and individuals such as creative writers, artists and local historians. Despite the breadth of impact and engagement activities, it must be stressed that the project was first and foremost a study of literature. The underpinning research focused on the discovery, analysis and contextualisation of travel writing as a literary genre. The ideas around impact generation emerged once the methodological direction had been set and were driven by the primary material as it emerged. It is on this basis that I want to make the case for literary research: our exploration of the travellers' voices has been at the root of this project that – ultimately – touched so many lives through impact and engagement activities; in other words, it was the ultimate enabler for this project.

From page to public

So how did we translate the 'multiple voices' and 'present past narratives' we uncovered into accessible public history and heritage tourism resources? This was an organic rather than a linear process. Faced at the outset with the set of questions outlined at the beginning of this chapter – What is it all for? Why should public money be given over to projects like this when there is so much else at stake? What is the point? – we had to think hard about the ways in which our collaborative research was going to matter beyond the academy. Some things were immediately clear. We had the huge advantage of working on a topic that would be of interest to the public locally and that fitted with the needs of various Welsh Government departments and cultural institutions, so an approach focused on public history feeding into heritage tourism made sense. An exhibition involving regional museums would work for local audiences given the large number of artists and other creatives among our group of travellers; the National Library of Wales would be an excellent partner given their educational remit; working with Visit Wales was obvious for a project largely focused on travellers and tourists; and the Royal Commission's interest in the built environment made them a clear candidate for collaboration given the detailed descriptions of the changing face of Wales found in our corpus. But we still had to persuade these institutions to come on board and explain what was in it for them. This is quite hard to do when you are at the beginning of a project and not entirely sure what might emerge. Pilot events and persistence were crucial to the process of persuading third-sector organisations such as Visit Wales and the Ceredigion Museum to come on board at an early stage, not least as supportive partners in the grant application process. Other relationships were more serendipitous such as our work with the Royal Commission whose offices happened to be in the same building as the Aberystwyth-based colleagues on the project.

Underpinning our activities, and perhaps of most importance for public history in particular, was the development of the searchable database of travel accounts hosted on the project website.[14] When we began work on our project, we expected, based on an initial scoping exercise, to find around 100 travel narratives dealing with Wales. To date, the number is just short of 500 with new texts still surfacing. In part this is due to the mislabelling of Wales as England in many book titles and catalogue entries, which rendered the nation hidden, as we note in our book, but perhaps the key development is the enhanced discoverability brought by more efficient search engines and the digitalisation of older material. We were able to build on this to showcase the stories and maximise their accessibility to a range of users. The database provides links to original texts where possible and also to translations where they exist. A mapped itinerary, information on the travel writer and a summary of each text are provided to enable users to gauge the value of a given text to their needs, thus providing a useful tool for local history groups, other researchers and students. Notably, the resource aided consultants in preparing the successful bid to recognise the Slate Landscape of Northwest Wales as a UNESCO World Heritage Site by helping them to draw out the international significance of the area through detailed information gleaned from texts by the likes of Johann Georg Kohl, visiting in 1844,[15] and L. Smyers, who described Penrhyn Quarry near Bangor as 'pas pareil dans le monde' [unparalled in the world].[16] The caveat for others aiming to replicate our approach is the issue of defining, or at least estimating, the extent of the corpus (which we failed to do!). By its very nature, the untapped potential of foreign language material in libraries and archives is predicated on the Rumsfeldian principle of unknown unknowns. You simply do not know how much there is until you look, and this can command a huge amount of research time.

Equally time-consuming is the curation of an exhibition. We worked with the Ceredigion Museum to curate 'EurÔlwg/EuroVisions', an exhibition of art and artefacts relating to the experiences of travellers to Wales with accompanying information drawing on the travel narratives we had uncovered. Exhibits ranged from paintings by well-known exiled twentieth-century artists such as Karel Lek, Josef Herman and Heinz Koppel to drawings by Felix Mendelssohn, foreign-language tourist brochures and posters, and even the outfit worn by the Breton onion sellers, once a familiar sight on the streets of South Wales. Following its run in Aberystwyth, the exhibition then travelled to Storiel in Bangor and the Swansea Museum and remains partly available through the project website.[17] In terms of the benefit to public history, the exhibition enabled all three museums to enhance their outreach programmes through related events such as talks and school visits, as well as increasing footfall from the local community. The idea for the exhibition title, which also worked bilingually, was inspired by a well-known multilingual song contest, emphasising the transnational nature of the content, while the local aspect was enhanced by the gathering of visitor feedback on luggage labels. Although successful, the event was not a straightforward undertaking, especially in relation to the artworks. Permissions from multiple lenders, some of whom charged a fee, took time to arrange, as did the careful logistical planning involved in moving valuable exhibits from one location to another. Working with experienced curators was essential in this regard but the planning was complex and time consuming. The assumption that your project is top of the list is a dangerous one to make as partner institutions negotiate their own competing demands.

Over the first two years of the project, we became increasingly aware of the potential value of our work for the interpretation of the history of Wales, in terms of both the understanding of Welsh heritage and the impact that it might have on heritage tourism. This led to our successful Follow-On Funding application for the more simply titled 'Travellers to Wales' project. For this, we worked with the Royal Commission and Visit Wales to produce the 'Journey to the Past' website.[18] The website, which is fully multilingual throughout (Welsh, English, French and German) combines fifty-four travel destinations, with over seventy heritage sites across Wales arranged into nine themed trails. As well as showcasing a range of materials from the Royal Commission's extensive archives, the page for each location includes translations of excerpts from French and German travel texts translated into both Welsh and English, making them accessible to new audiences for the first time. For example, the entry for Capel Curig in Gwynedd showcases narratives by Goede, Samuel Heinrich Spiker, Jules Gourdault and J. Menard, all of whom would be new to the majority of tourists today but whose commentary relates to their own experiences. For example, Spiker describes the view visible from above the Capel Curig Inn, built by Lord Penrhyn in 1801, in terms which underline the sublime grandeur of the landscape for which North Wales remains so famous:

> Die Aussicht auf die umliegende Gegend, und namentlich nach Westen zu, zu genießen, muß man vor das Haus gehen und eine gegenüberliegende Anhöhe ersteigen. Hier entfaltet sich ganz die wilde Schönheit der Gegend: überall nichts als Klippen und Schluchten: gegen Westen die beiden kleinen Seen, welche am Fuße des Snowdon, nicht weit von einander, liegen, und über ihnen der dunkele Snowdon selbst, mit seinen zwei dicht neben einander emporstarrenden Spitzen!
>
> [In order to enjoy the prospect of the surrounding country, and especially to the west, we must ascend an eminence in front of the house. Here the country spreads itself out before us in all its wild beauty; in every direction we see nothing but rocks and ravines. To the west we perceive two little lakes at the foot of Snowdon, not far from each other; and above them the dark Snowdon itself, with its two closely approximating points.][19]

As well as enabling us to surface to a broader public the materials we had discovered and interpreted, our partner organisations also benefitted from involvement in the project. Visit Wales embedded the website into their own, having committed to the project as partners based on the value of the research to their promotion of Wales, in particular in relation to their key German market.[20] The Royal Commission was able to further develop and disseminate its holdings to audiences beyond Wales, in particular through the creation of new digital artefacts such as the animated film about the Cyfarthfa Ironworks at Merthyr Tydfil that featured excerpts from the vivid narratives of Carl Gustav Carus, Carl Klocke, Louis Simenon and Alphonse Esquiros, who was much affected by the experience:

> J'étais couché depuis quelques heures déjà lorsque je me sentis réveillé en sursaut par un éclat d'incendie. Je courus à ma fenêtre,

> vis le ciel rouge comme s'il eût été enflammé par une aurore boréale. J'étais sur le point de crier: au feu! Mais comme personne ne bougeait dans l'hôtel et que tout était tranquille dans le voisinage, je me rassurai, et bientôt je me souvins que je vivais cette nuit-là dans le pays des foreges. La lueur sanglante qui empourprait les ténèbres était en effet une réverbération des ironworks.
>
> [I had already been in bed a few hours when a flash of fire woke me with a start. I ran to my window, saw the sky all red as though ablaze by an aurora borealis. I was about to cry out: fire! But as nobody was moving in the [Castle] hotel and that all seemed calm nearby, I reassured myself and remembered that I was living in the land of forges that night. The blood-coloured light that reddened the darkness was in fact a reflection of the ironworks.][21]

Again, success was down to securing the right partners. Working with a well-known and respected body such as the Royal Commission gave us access to a range of material and contacts which we would never have been able to garner ourselves, while Visit Wales enabled us to access audiences beyond Wales through its various channels. Dealing with such high-profile partners is, however, not always straightforward. While the Royal Commission, based in the same building as two of the project team, was always on hand and accessible, working with Visit Wales was made more complicated by frequent changes in personnel, as is often the case with government departments. The will to collaborate was always there but the case had to be made more than once before commitment was secured. Nonetheless, the impact generated by the project was notable. The economic benefit is hard to quantify but it is clear that there was a long-term contribution to the economy of North Wales in particular through the successful UNESCO bid and to the Welsh economy more broadly as a result of our work with Visit Wales, all the more so given the need to attract European tourists back to Wales following the pandemic.

A plea for us

The crucial role of modern languages literary research in uncovering lost stories lies at the heart of the success of this project. The material and our interpretation of it enabled a deeper understanding and provided extra layers of knowledge. This can be seen as part of a process of democratisation, adding additional, previously unheard or long-forgotten voices to the narrative of Wales. Reflecting the fragmentary nature of heritage, this newly (re)discovered material constitutes another element of the value matrix through which we understand the heritage of Wales and its place in the world. This metonymic process was not only able to surface commodifiable, practical new resources for the fields of public history and heritage tourism but, significantly, also fostered new areas of cultural connectivity that enhanced individual and societal wellbeing by reinforcing a sense of belonging and revalidation of already known cultural value from a new perspective. Yet, despite offering such value, research in the field of heritage tourism seems to focus on language as a means to communicate with visitors, not as a factor in the curation of sites. There is a notable absence as the implications of linguistic diversity and translation remain largely unconsidered. Underlining this, Kirshenblatt-Gimblett lists a plethora of 'instruments' available to heritage industry in interpreting sites:

> Dance teams, heritage performers, craft cooperatives, cultural centers, arts festivals, museums, exhibitions, recordings, archives, indigenous media, and cultural curricula are not only evidence of heritage, its continuity, and its vitality to the present, they are also instruments for adding value to the cultural forms they perform, teach, exhibit, circulate, and market. Much is made of the traditions themselves, as if the instruments for presenting them were invisible or inconsequential.[22]

Although the transnational, transcultural aspect of the heritage industry is implicit here, not least through the mention of 'indigenous media', the role of linguistic and cultural-specific knowledge in producing material and curation is largely, if not entirely, unacknowledged. Modern languages research and its value to heritage tourism is, it seems, entirely 'invisible or inconsequential'. There is a worry also that the potential perspectives such research might offer are neglected on purpose. Discussing the approach to presenting heritage sites as multi-sensory experiences, Kirshenblatt-Gimblett suggests that '[the] expressed desire to make sites real and vivid indicates that sites cannot do this for themselves. The inability of sites to tell their own story authorizes the interpretation project itself.'[23] This shifts the power dynamic markedly when considering the inclusion of or interest in foreign-language resources in the presentation of a site. There is an implicit ethical choice to be made in bringing in a new set of voices.

Things have moved on. Kirshenblatt-Gimblett was writing in the late 1990s but generally, heritage tourism research continues to discuss globality, identity, the past with no or little reference to linguistic diversity. The existence of translation and transcultural understanding is generally taken for granted. This has prompted a recent turn in the field of translation studies that seeks to question this approach.[24] Viewing places and artefacts through the prism of modern languages research can lead to a process of transvaluation, a change in the type of value assigned to an object, and recent research on public history suggests a shift that modern languages researchers will no doubt welcome. Discussing 'emerging trends in public history', Sayer notes that:

> [l]ocalized and socially engaged approaches are needed for projects to have positive and transformative impacts on the public. This enables localized micro approaches to public history theory and practice to be situated within a wider global framework of public history, supporting critical dialog and collaborative reflection as well as challenging English-speaking perceptions that dominate master public history narratives.[25]

This sounds promising. We, as researchers, have the means to help achieve these aims but to do so, those working in the fields of public history and heritage tourism need a better understanding of the ways in which modern languages research can enable but also be enabled to challenge and confront accepted views and suggest new systems, taxonomies and perspectives. By showing how the study of literature and other aspects of our research can have impact and are, therefore, highly relevant, we can forge important and productive partnerships. In these strange times, and perhaps particularly so, the work we do as modern language researchers has a crucial role to play in connecting cultures. There is no better argument for literature than that.

Notes

1 Rick Rylance, *Literature and the Public Good* (Oxford University Press, 2016), p. 14.

2 https://www.history.org.uk/historian/categories/public-history [accessed 27 April 2026].

3 Faye Sayer, *Public History: A Practical Guide* (Bloomsbury, 2015), p. 5.

4 Barbara Kirshenblatt-Gimblett, *Destination Culture: Tourism, Museums, and Heritage* (University of California Press, 1998), p. 72.

5 My colleagues on the project were co-investigators Kathryn N. Jones (Swansea) and Heather Williams (CAWCS), Research Assistant Rita Singer, and PhD students Christina Les (Bangor) and Anna-Lou Dijsktra (Swansea). We were fortunate to receive two tranches of Arts and Humanities Research Council (AHRC) funding over that period in the form of a Research Grant and then Follow-On Funding for Impact.

6 Kathryn N. Jones, Carol Tully and Heather Williams, *Hidden Texts, Hidden Nation: (Re)Discoveries of Wales in French and German Travel Writing (1750–2018)* (Liverpool University Press, 2020).

7 Stéphanie-Félicité du Crest de Saint-Aubin, Comtesse de Genlis, *Mémoires inédits de Madame la Comtesse de Genlis, sur le dix-huitième siècle et la révolution française, depuis 1756 jusqu'à nos jours*, 8 vols (Ladvocat, 1825).

8 Felix Mendelssohn Bartholdy, *Briefe*, ed. by Rudolf Elvers (Fischer, 1984).

9 Hermann von Pückler-Muskau, *Briefe eines Verstorbenen: Ein fragmentarisches Tagebuch aus England, Wales, Irland und Frankreich; geschrieben in den Jahren 1828 und 1829* (Hallberger, 1836).

10 Pückler-Muskau, *Briefe eines Verstorbenen*, p. 69.

11 Translation taken from Hermann von Pückler-Muskau, *A Tour in England, Ireland and France in the Years 1828 and 1829 with Remarks on the Manners and Customs of the Inhabitants, and Anecdotes of Distinguished Public Characters in a Series of Letters by a German Prince* (Carey and Lea, 1833), p. 295. Note the omission of Wales from the title in translation.

12 Christian August Gottlieb Goede, *England, Wales, Irland und Schottland: Erinnerungen an Natur und Kunst aus einer Reise in den Jahren 1802 und 1803*, 5 vols (Arnoldische Buch- und Kunsthandlung, 1804–5), V, pp. 360–1.

13 See Guy Thuillier, *Georges Dufaud et les débuts du grand capitalisme dans la métallurgie, en Nivernais, au XIXe siècle* (SEVPEN, 1959), p. 225.

14 See: http://etw.bangor.ac.uk/accounts [accessed 27 April 2026].

15 Johann Georg Kohl, *Reisen in England und Wales* (Arnold, 1844).

16 L. Smyers, *Essai sur l'état actuel de l'industrie ardoisière en France et en Angleterre, suivi de quelques observations pratiques sur la formation du schiste ardoisier* (Poulet-Malassis, 1858), p. 8.

17 http://eurovisions.bangor.ac.uk/index.php.en [accessed 27 April 2026].

18 https://footsteps.bangor.ac.uk/en/ [accessed 27 April 2026].

19 https://footsteps.bangor.ac.uk/en/location/capel-curig [accessed 27 April 2026].

20 https://www.visitwales.com/de/info/Streifz%C3%BCge-durch-vergangene-Zeiten [accessed 27 April 2026].

21 https://footsteps.bangor.ac.uk/en/location/merthyr-tydfil [accessed 27 April 2026].

22 Kirshenblatt-Gimblett, *Destination Culture*, p. 156.

23 Kirshenblatt-Gimblett, *Destination Culture*, p. 168.

24 See Sharon Deane-Cox and Pauline Côme, 'Heritage Interpretation(s): Remembering, Translating, and Utilizing the Past' in *The Routledge Handbook of Translation and Memory*, ed. by Sharon Deane-Cox and Anneleen Spiessens (Routledge, 2022), pp. 186–209.

25 Faye Sayer, 'Open Dialogues and Localized Approaches: Reflections on International Public History Perspectives and Practices', *International Public History*, 5 (2022), pp. 53–5 (p. 53).

References

Deane-Cox, Sharon, and Anneleen Spiessens (eds), *The Routledge Handbook of Translation and Memory* (Routledge, 2022)

European Travellers to Wales, 'Accounts of Travel', http://etw.bangor.ac.uk/accounts [accessed 27 April 2026]

European Travellers to Wales, 'Eurovisions', http://eurovisions.bangor.ac.uk/index.php.en [accessed 27 April 2026]

Genlis, Stéphanie-Félicité du Crest de Saint-Aubin, Comtesse de, *Mémoires inédits de Madame la Comtesse de Genlis, sur le dix-huitième siècle et la révolution française, depuis 1756 jusqu'à nos jours*, 8 vols (Ladvocat, 1825)

Goede, Christian August Gottlieb, *England, Wales, Irland und Schottland: Erinnerungen an Natur und Kunst aus einer Reise in den Jahren 1802 und 1803*, 5 vols (Arnoldische Buch- und Kunsthandlung, 1804–5)

Historical Association, https://www.history.org.uk/historian/categories/public-history [accessed 27 April 2026]

Jones, Katherine N., Carol Tully, and Heather Williams, *Hidden Texts, Hidden Nation. (Re)Discoveries of Wales in French and German Travel Writing (1750–2018)* (Liverpool University Press, 2020)

Journey to the Past, Wales in Historic Travel Writing from France and Germany, https://footsteps.bangor.ac.uk/en/ [accessed 27 April 2026]

Kirshenblatt-Gimblett, Barbara, *Destination Culture: Tourism, Museums, and Heritage* (University of California Press, 1998)
Kohl, Johann Georg, *Reisen in England und Wales* (Arnold, 1844)
Meethan, Kevin, *Tourism in Global Society: Place, Culture, Consumption* (Palgrave Macmillan, 2001)
Mendelssohn Bartholdy, Felix, *Briefe*, ed. by Rudolf Elvers (Fischer, 1984)
Pückler-Muskau, Hermann von, *Briefe eines Verstorbenen: Ein fragmentarisches Tagebuch aus England, Wales, Irland und Frankreich; geschrieben in den Jahren 1828 und 1829* (Hallberger, 1836)
Pückler-Muskau, Hermann von, *A Tour in England, Ireland and France in the Years 1828 and 1829 with Remarks on the Manners and Customs of the Inhabitants, and Anecdotes of Distinguished Public Characters in a Series of Letters by a German Prince* (Carey and Lea, 1833)
Rylance, Rick, *Literature and the Public Good* (Oxford University Press, 2016)
Sayer, Faye, *Public History: A Practical Guide* (Bloomsbury, 2015)
Sayer, Faye, 'Open Dialogues and Localized Approaches: Reflections on International Public History Perspectives and Practices', *International Public History*, 5 (2022), pp. 53–5
Smyers, L., *Essai sur l'état actuel de l'industrie ardoisière en France et en Angleterre, suivi de quelques observations pratiques sur la formation du schiste ardoisier* (Poulet-Malassis, 1858)
Thuillier, Guy, *Georges Dufaud et les débuts du grand capitalisme dans la métallurgie, en Nivernais, au XIXe siècle* (SEVPEN, 1959)
Timothy, Dallen J., and Stephen W. Boyd, *Heritage Tourism* (Pearson Education, 2003)
Visit Wales, 'Journeys Through Bygone Eras', https://www.visitwales.com/de/info/Streifz%C3%BCge-durch-vergangene-Zeiten [accessed 27 April 2026]

Chapter 6

Towards sustainable practices in the 'post-museum': object lessons from contemporary literature

Emma Bond

In August 2023, the British Museum became embroiled in scandal when it emerged that over one and a half thousand items from its collections, including gold, jewellery and semi-precious stones dating back to the fifteenth century B.C., had been stolen by an employee and re-sold on eBay. What is perhaps more scandalous than a curator siphoning off ancient objects for personal gain is that the theft also exposed systemic weaknesses in the British Museum's catalogues and record-keeping practices. The website that the museum launched the following month with the aim of finding the missing objects listed items 'similar to' those missing, rather than the exact objects themselves.[1] This is because the majority of the missing artifacts had never been registered. At the time of writing, around half of the British Museum's collections, in fact, remained uncatalogued – approximately four million objects. This is less surprising than it might seem, since inadequate resourcing, combined with a sheer excess of things, means that cataloguing has become a near-impossible task for many of today's world museums to keep up with. If we add to this the fact that most museums in the Global North only have capacity to display a maximum of around five per cent of their collections,[2] leaving the rest in storage – which is expensive, environmentally unsustainable and exclusive in terms of access – we can see precisely why the contemporary museum sector is facing what has been termed a 'crisis of accumulation'.[3]

This chapter draws on material first published in my recent monograph *Curating Worlds: Museum Practices in Contemporary Literature*, which proposes that a number of museum techniques (such as collecting, curating, display, storage, preservation and deaccession) can be seen as narrative strategies that offer up new ways of reading, interpreting and understanding literary texts.[4] The final chapter of the book, on object deaccession, takes its cue from the 'crisis' of accumulation described above to explore how museums might envisage post-object futures, and how contemporary novels might offer a framework for reading modes of degrowth through their own moves towards post-representation.[5] It is this link between literature and museums that I want to explore further in the present chapter, in order to foreground the value of literary research for other fields and disciplines. In *Curating Worlds*, I identify parallels between museum debates on deaccession and a waning of the solidity of material referents in an emerging genre of novels that Timothy Bewes has recently termed 'post-fictional'. These are novels that stretch and exceed genre boundaries, 'formally ambiguous modes of writing with ontological implications that extend beyond the practice of literature',[6] which therefore, I argue, offer themselves as potential models for imagining new modes of (narrative) representation within museum futures.

In what follows here, I will focus my analysis on the rupture between form and content that museum paradigms of loss, disposal and deaccession imply, in order to identify what sorts of analogous modes of reading *beyond the object* we might be able to use when approaching contemporary novels. In terms of literature, these new, liminal forms of representation are emerging to occupy a 'fringe' position in terms of genre and, in particular, are muddling modes of fiction and non-fiction. These are literary forms 'that cross the borders between styles, genres and media, between real-life events and imagined ones'.[7] Using a term coined by the Italian author collective Wu Ming, Kate Willman refers to such texts as 'unidentified narrative objects' (UNOs). My chapter will identify instances in post-fictional UNOs where the ties between an object and its representation become loosened in such a way as to activate our understanding of the narrative potential of spaces such as museums and other heritage sites that exist, in Bewes's words cited above, 'beyond the practice of literature'.[8]

This is an especially timely intervention since deaccession is a growing contemporary concern for museums, and one that holds high emotional, even existential, stakes. In recent years, top US institutions, such as the

Baltimore Museum of Art and the Brooklyn Museum, have come under fire for selling high-value artworks in order to raise funds for the care of collections and for diversity initiatives. As Christopher Bedford, director of the Baltimore Museum of Art, explained at the time, 'my greatest act of creativity is now an economic one'.[9] Deaccession thus threatens the foundations of our current understanding of the museum as an institution and as a concept but, in selected cases, it could potentially open up new avenues and new directions for museum futures. Indeed, in the current crisis of heritage sites holding on to 'too much stuff', Eilean Hooper-Greenhill's declaration that the 'great collecting phase of museums is over' has ushered in the idea of the 'post-museum', which forecasts a focus on object re-*use* and adaptation rather than on the further accumulation of things.[10] This post-museum is envisaged less as a sited building and more as a scripted process that can be experienced 'within a variety of architectural forms'.[11] In the analysis that follows, I will suggest that one of these forms that the post-museum might take could be the post-fictional novel, inspired by Wolfgang Ernst, casting the design of the earliest object collections as a 'space of contemplation' or 'a cognitive field of ideas': not so much a place, then, as a text or a semiotic-led space.[12] This chapter will make the case for the value of literary research by exploring whether contemporary works of post-fiction can hint at what might happen if the absolute primacy of the object collection in the museum begins to wane.

This sense of a growing flux and uncertainty in visions of museum object futures has been a long time in the making. Dayna L. Caldwell offers a bleak picture of museums in the grip of an obsessive-compulsive crisis, with their backrooms and basements now resembling 'the slowly expanding burden within a hoarder's domain'.[13] But how did they arrive here? The crisis of object accumulation is perhaps best explained by the heritage explosion of the twentieth century, which saw the global number of museums increase exponentially, coupled with an 'ethics of memory' which arose in response to the traumas of a century characterised by loss. This combination of factors gave rise to something of a 'Noah complex', where museums felt compelled to first collect and then retain unsustainable numbers of objects in order to preserve memories of the past.[14] Only over the past twenty years have the first steps towards implementing a solid framework for getting rid of objects occurred, spurred by the publication of the National Museum Director's Conference reports entitled 'Too Much Stuff' in 2003, and the issue of a revised Museums Association 'Disposal Toolkit' in 2014.

Yet curators must still confront anxieties around which objects to collect in order to preserve a representative sample of the present for the future, since we never know for sure what is going to be valuable, and to whom, beyond our own lifespans. Do we thus need to whittle down some existing collections of past material to make more space for the present in the future? On the one hand, museums poised towards disposal risk damaging public trust in their stewardship, thereby putting the notion of museums as institutions bound to survive time into doubt. For if its foundational collections can be dismantled, the museum is no longer a fixed entity for perpetuity. On the other hand, museums have a responsibility to future generations not to become unmanageable. But what happens to the spaces left behind by objects that are delisted, deaccessioned and ultimately disposed of: victims of processes of decluttering in public museums and private homes alike? And what sort of narratives emerge in the gaps, the blank spaces and the empty display cases they leave behind?

As far back as 1968, the Smithsonian-based historian Wilcomb Washburn posed the provocative question that if the primary purpose of the museum is to store and transfer knowledge and information, 'need one save objects at all?'.[15] In an era of three-dimensional digitisation and reproduction such as the present one, representations of what and how museum objects can *mean* has necessarily been diversified. The focus on the (digitised) preservation of information rather than objects themselves has brought about the risk of things being transformed into images and the museum itself becoming a data bank, 'taking apart', as Ernst warns, 'the hermeneutic distinction between memory and waste'.[16] Concerns about object overflow have affected the contemporary novel in much the same way as they have today's museums. Many novels of the twentieth century have been categorised as having functioned like a 'storage medium' for the flotsam and jetsam of history.[17] So if the task of the postmodern museum was, in the eyes of some theorists, 'to teach the user how to cope with information',[18] can more contemporary, twenty-first century, post-fictional novels show them how to do so, precisely by moving beyond object reliance? As we shift away from relying on museums and novels to provide figural representations of reality, new locations for meaning-making are emerging within the residual or blank spaces freed up after objects become frail or fail in other ways to deliver what is desired of them. In the analysis that follows, I will probe these ideas in readings of contemporary novels that interrogate objects in fruitless quests to answer unresolved questions, and in so doing privilege instances of failure, forgetting and loss over memory, conservation and further accumulation.

The ability to forget is becoming increasingly rare, both on a personal and institutional level, in today's digitised world where everything can be archived for future reference. This is because fetishising what remains of history has led to memory becoming akin to a 'new religion of the past', as Maria Stepanova remarks in her astounding, genre-bending book *In Memory of Memory*: '(i)n comparison with a future we don't want to inhabit, what has already happened feels domesticated – practically bearable'.[19] Personal pasts become a safe harbour, a foreign country that can be colonised, modified and then mobilised for present and future needs. Published by Fitzcarraldo in 2021 in a translation by Sasha Dugdale, Stepanova's volume has the white cover reserved for non-fiction works, rather than the distinctive blue shade of the imprint's fiction range, yet inside, it is characterised – somewhat confusingly – as 'Essay/Fiction'. It also bears the tantalising subtitle of *A Romance*. *In Memory of Memory* thus destabilising our readerly expectations from the off: the slash separating but also conjoining genres; the 'romance' label providing a bewildering angle. This hybrid labelling anticipates the author's interventionist approach to personal essay-writing that sees her constantly cast doubt on the material she lays before us until we, as readers, are ultimately left grasping at nothing more than her words. Stepanova's broad mission in *In Memory of Memory* is to oppose any comfortable retreat into the past by consistently showing how her attempts to revive and narrativise her own family history lead to nothing meaningful at all. Much of this work of letting go takes place within the relationship the narrator tries to form with objects. By gathering up her recently deceased Aunt Galya's belongings into detailed descriptions but simultaneously pointing to their lack of transferable meaning, Stepanova uses *In Memory of Memory* to show how post-fictional texts can serve as a particular kind of archive, both for things and for their disappearance, thus calling the reader's attention to the generative capacities of loss. Letting go of material remnants thus becomes a creative response to a contemporary necessity, allowing us to shed comforting, but maybe unrealistic, fantasies, whether these are of 'permanence, of national coherence, of a universal subject, (or) of a particular future'.[20]

Museums might well heed Sarah Wasserman's words quoted here. In the same way as the realist novel or the archive, the modern museum once represented an 'organizational principle for the content of cultural identity and scientific knowledge',[21] one built on practices of collecting, ordering, categorising, displaying and preserving past things. It has thus assumed the function of externalising memory: we can relegate our memorial function to museums because the physical content of memory is (supposedly) stored there in perpetuity. Traditional museums, memorials and even novels are all, in Pierre Nora's felicitous term, *lieux de mémoire*, or sites of memory, that in effect replace active processes of memorialisation.[22] However, faced with the 'profusion struggle' of overflowing reserves and storerooms, heritage institutions are now recognising the need to consciously define the life cycle of objects as bookended by moments of birth and death, foreclosing the possibility of endlessly preserving memory for future generations.[23] Calls for degrowth in heritage collections thus align museum priorities with economic and social agendas that attend more closely to utility and to the potential future benefits of actions and acquisitions rather than seeing a priori value in the act of accumulation itself. With the advent of the post-fictional novel and the post-museum, the old regime of using traditional museal and literary forms as storage emporia for representative memorialisations of the past is now changing. This 'implosion of the mnemonic museum frame has consequences for the form of representation of the past',[24] and making difficult decisions about deaccession and disposal can allow us to open up space for more sustainable modes of remembering through forgetting and letting go of material props and anchors in heritage and narrative settings alike.

Even given this, the reader, and indeed the museum visitor, still has a crucial (albeit malleable) role in the interpretation of objects and texts, respectively. Stepanova would say this is because pasts are 'submissive': 'they reject no interpretation, endure any amount of humiliation'.[25] We can (re-)fashion them however we like. On finding a mystery man's name written on a piece of paper inside a lace purse belonging to her grandmother, the narrator pesters her mother for ideas of who it might be. 'I wanted to know what to make of it. "Make of it what you will," said my mother, and ended the conversation.'[26] What are the implications of this refusal of the potential to find meaning in our relationships with objects? Can achieving liberation from such a search allow us to be more creative, and more generative, in our interpretation of things? If in the Western tradition to date, material objects were assumed to act as analogues of human memory, then, as Adrian Forty shows, they also used to 'stand in for memories and thus preserve them'.[27] Yet now this is no longer the case, since in standing in for memories, objects have succeeded in substituting them, thereby weakening our ties with the past. The more time Stepanova's narrator spends in her family's archive of objects and photographs, the less she finds she knows or remembers. 'The history of a family which I had at the outset learnt at the speed of a straight line was now fragmenting in my head into tesserae, into notes indicating textual omissions, into hypotheses there was no one left to prove.'[28] Fact has turned into fiction, and all that remains to her are 'unverifiable stories, fables, fairy tale elements, embryos of a novel'.[29]

If our reliance on material objects to help us remember the past starts to wane, so the emphasis on recognising the value of letting go of some of its associated objects might well increase. As Wasserman says: '(d)oing away with fantasies of durability means rejecting damaging nostalgia and accepting constant change; it also means recognizing that even temporary formations can carry within them the possibility of real action'.[30] Discarding materials and information allows for greater latitude in opening up gaps where creativity might spark new ideas, new connections and new content. Yet in *In Memory of Memory*, the silence of family memories stored in cupboards, albums and cemeteries mimics the futility of the narrative drive to complete histories, and speaks instead of the impossibility of saving anything at all. The forgotten art of decomposition means that too much past lingers in the here and now, and the stories we tell about that past are themselves beyond repair. When confronted with her failure to make the mute objects in her family archives communicate, Stepanova's narrator concludes that in the end, nothing revealed itself to her, and 'the less I can say about them, the closer they come'.[31] We have seen how in *In Memory of Memory*, a 'register of narrative certainty gives way to one of crisis and disorientation in which authenticity not only of the account but also of the experience falls into doubt'.[32] We now inhabit a world where preservation at all costs is a concern of the past, and where objects have lost their primacy in our efforts to connect with and memorialise collective and personal pasts. Even narrative efforts at connection are, indeed, also in decline, and evidence the fact that 'deflections, refusals, even failures and incapacities are as important to the story of the novel as insights, revelations, intuitions, and enigmas – or more so'.[33]

In this new era of Hooper-Greenhill's post-museum, we can thus see how the erosion of object primacy may, in some select instances, be reconfigured as a positive outcome, since objects can tie memory down, fixing it into an unnatural stasis that limits its natural capacity for movement. As Michel de Certeau says, 'memory is a sort of anti-museum: it is not localizable'.[34] Perhaps it is in the post-fictional spaces between objects, spaces in which we can move, walk and think beyond the fixity of representation, that we can relocate new museological priorities and practices to come: practices that privilege various modes of reuse, and potentially also of global redistribution. For in an era where the idea of 'forever pollution' currently haunts our futures, the crisis of accumulation that affects both the public and the private spheres in the Global North is exacerbated by ever-more-sophisticated modes of technological hoarding. Perhaps acknowledging a broader range of creative methods for representing and imagining the past, as are envisaged in the post-museum and in post-fictional narratives, might also offer something of a response to urgent issues of sustainability in our planet's fight for climate survival.

Post-apocalyptic imaginings seem less distant and more imaginable in the aftermath of the COVID-19 pandemic, and narratives such as Emily St. John Mandel's 2014 novel *Station Eleven* provide a glimpse of what our relationships to things might look like in the wake of a disaster to come. When a group of stranded air travellers sets up camp in the fictional Severn City Airport after a flu pandemic eliminates 99% of the Earth's human population, a lawyer named Clark takes over the Skymiles Lounge with an object collection that becomes known as the Museum of Civilization. News of the airport museum spreads far and wide, with visitors coming to the airport to view, and sometimes add to, the collection on display. But although the objects have a consolatory power for Clark, their curator, the 'civilization' they represent is shown to be extinct, replaced by new scales of humanity and inhumanity as those left in the world jostle for survival. Its futility is made clear in the following exchange, where the characters of August and Kirsten are asked to explain what the Museum of Civilization is to a passer-by.

> 'I heard it's supposed to be a place where artifacts from the old world are preserved,' August said. The man laughed [. . .]. 'Here's the thing, kids, the entire world is a place where artifacts from the old world are preserved. When was the last time you saw a new car?'[35]

It is, rightly, the conservation of the planet itself that must concern us now, not the shoring up of individual components of its material contents.

Given this, can museums design and envisage new future-oriented practice that will see us all transition beyond object dependence? And can literature help to show how they can do so? Contemporary works of literature gesture towards the possible contours of a post-museal future where the potential of objects is imagined as lying beyond their figural properties. The landscape of ontological doubt sketched by texts such as *In Memory of Memory* and *Station Eleven* further calls into question both the value of the physical space of the museum and the representational powers held within the material contours of the museum object. Recent calls for deaccessioned museum objects and objects marked for disposal to be transformed into art or even into working objects make us further query what the value of static, 'forever' collections is now. This value, I would argue, is contingent on factors of external necessity which are constantly changing. Outside the Severn City airport in *Station Eleven*, and, thus, far from the Museum of Civilization's collection of obsolete objects, lies the graveyard where those who have died there since the outbreak of the flu pandemic are laid to rest. Between two obsolete runways, a series of aeroplane tray tables have been repurposed as grave markers, 'driven into the ground, details of the deceased carved into the tray's hard plastic'.[36] In both literary and museum settings, we should be looking for such examples of future-oriented practice in the adaptive reuse of objects that works to find meaning in loss.

The residues of material and memorial loss exist in multiple forms: in texts, in objects, in modes of intangible heritage and, most of all, in stories. Kevin Walsh is right when he makes the point that a new museology must involve people 'in the production of their own pasts'.[37] This is an active process, distinct from any traditional passive experience of didactic learning in the museum. Reading post-fictional literature offers us the tools to produce our own pasts in this way because, as Judith Schalansky writes in *An Inventory of Losses*, another work of contemporary post-fiction, when all else is lost, or threatened with destruction, '(w)riting survives. By writing, as by reading, one can pick one's own ancestors and establish a second, intellectual hereditary line to rival conventional biological heritage'.[38] Museums can use literary imaginings to find solutions to the challenges to come as we contemplate post-object futures and move beyond current preservation paradigms. Likewise, care can be reimagined within processes of letting go, of forgetting and of leaving spaces uncurated in order to spark creative twists and trails of fantasy and look toward new post-object futures in twenty-first-century museums and literature alike.

But we can also locate examples of how to figure museal and material degrowth into readings of contemporary novels that allow us to identify more radical shifts in narrative trends. In order to do so, we need to turn back to Bewes's idea that the post-fictional signals some sort of dissolution of the novel's claim to representativeness. Bewes claims that a shift has taken place in the register of contemporary narrative: from certainty to crisis and disorientation, so that ultimately, 'the authenticity not only of the account, but also of the experience falls into doubt'.[39] Alongside this, the formal principles and qualities of the work have become fragile, allowing writing itself to become a 'prominent and intrusive element in the consciousness of fictional protagonists' in a cycle of awareness that 'renders indeterminate the distinction between reality and fiction'.[40] Finally, Bewes notes that the post-fictional novel 'unthinks or deauthorizes the very claims made by the work',[41] making 'deflections, refusals, failures and incapacities as important to the story of the novel's thought as insights, revelations, intuitions and enigmas – or more so'.[42] These reflections chime with the recent trend toward radical autofiction in contemporary narrative, and reveal how autofictional methods might help us configure practices aimed at post-representativeness in other settings as well, such as museums and heritage sites. In contemporary Italian author Walter Siti's pamphlet *Il realismo è impossibile* [Realism is Impossible], the autofictional voice is described as one that 'esige partecipazione e consenso. Esibizionismo ricattatorio che funziona come "intimazione di realtà"; l'autore di autofiction, mentre dice al lettore "credimi", gli comunica con altrettanta sfacciataggine "sto mentendo' [requires participation and consensus. An exhibitionist blackmail that functions like a 'summons to reality'; the writer of autofiction, at the same time as saying to the reader 'believe me', breezily admits to him, 'I'm lying'].[43]

Siti is perhaps the most famous of a growing number of contemporary Italian novelists who instrumentalise the instability of the autofiction genre in order to dismantle the distinction in the reader's mind between reality and fiction.[44] As Raffaele Donnarumma has said: 'In Italy, Siti represents, in the most eloquent and considered way, how the hypermodern subject constructs and reflects on itself. He believes that a story cannot exist outside the despotism of the subject.'[45] What is more, Siti's autofiction is emptied of the usual kinds of material indicators that one would expect to find in a novel that was making serious attempts to reproduce a world. By this, I don't just mean a literal sense of object decluttering, degrowth or deaccession, although these features are also present in Siti's work, especially in his 2014 novel *Exit Strategy*. The title evokes a clear drive towards narrative modes of deferral, evasion and refusal, while the cover art features Pere Borrell del Caso's 1874 painting *Huyendo de la critica* [Escaping Criticism], which depicts a figure literally climbing out of a frame of representation. The novel begins as the protagonist, also named Walter, is emptying out his old flat in Rome, helped by some friends of his ex-partner Marcello: 'Vedo il mio appartamento sparire pian piano inghiottito dalla finestra e ricomparire in cortile sotto forma di scatoloni [. . .]. Nessun rimpianto è più possibile, né tornare indietro' [I watch my apartment disappear slowly, swallowed up by the window, and then reappear in the courtyard below in the form of boxes. No regrets are possible anymore, nor is turning back in time].[46] What is more, the death of Walter's sexual desire for Marcello, a desire that underpinned Siti's preceding trilogy *Il dio impossibile*,[47] is signified in the disposal of one particular object: Marcello's boxer shorts, that Walter notices 'avevano l'elastico allentato e lui li maneggiava dubbioso: "Quasi quasi li butto . . ."' [had lost their elastic and he fingered them uncertainly: 'Maybe I should throw them away'].[48] Later, 'buttando le bucce di pera nel secchio della spazzatura vedo i boxer bianchi e verdi, lì appallottolati come una bestia morta' [while throwing some pear skins in the rubbish bin I see the white and green boxer shorts there, rolled up into a ball like a dead animal].[49]

Discarding his investment in this relationship along with their own material referent opens up a space of ontological doubt that throws Siti's novel itself into a genre spin. The narrator states, a few pages after this episode, that the work will not be autofictional and warns the reader, 'non date retta alla dicitura "romanzo" sulla copertina' [pay no attention to the word 'novel' on the cover].[50] He says, instead, that this will be 'un diario banale, pane al pane e vino al vino' [an ordinary diary, where a spade is called a spade].[51] And yet, once again, the narrator is unreliable. He cannot seem to fix an endpoint to the diary, adding first a 'post scriptum', then an 'addendum in extremis' and a final 'nota', in which he again addresses the reader, saying in a voice that removes agency from the narrator and reassigns it to the text itself: 'domando scusa, sembra che questo libro non voglia finire' [apologies, it seems this book doesn't want to finish].[52] Finally, in the last note, he negates all the previous statements he has made on the genre of the work:

> Nonostante la forma diaristica, questo non è un diario: non il mio, almeno. Io non voglio più parlare di me, ma il personaggio a cui ho prestato il mio nome ha esigenze di coerenza e di radicalità a cui fortunatamente nella vita non devo sottostare; quando esisto in carne e ossa, mi riservo di mutare in modo nebuloso e reversibile. Il mio io da esportazione [. . .] sosteneva di essersi convertito e così gli ho affidato il compito di scrivere un diario di cui porta intera la responsabilità. Romanzo in forma di diario, dunque, [. . .] che mostra il protagonista definitivamente invecchiato; arricchito ma anche stremato da esperienze fatte in altri libri.[53]
>
> [Despite the diary form, this isn't a diary: or at least, it's not my diary. I don't want to talk about myself anymore, but the character to whom I've lent my name needs a coherence and radicality that luckily I don't have to obey in real life; when I exist in flesh and blood, I reserve the right to change in murky and reversible ways. My externalised self claimed to have been converted and so I entrusted him with the task of writing a diary which he took total responsibility for. A novel in the form of a diary, therefore, [. . .] that shows the protagonist irrevocably aged; enriched but also worn out by his experiences in previous books.]

I'm interested in the way that Siti's statements cited here chime with Bewes's notion of post-fiction, and particularly in how the self-positioning of the writer within a text weakens its own programme; thereby definitively blurring the distinction between reality and fiction. This is mirrored in Siti's wider personal and political writing project, that seeks to indicate (and indict) a weakening of society's own relationship with reality through our increased dependence on the artificiality we experience through engaging with reality television, mass tourism and social media. Crucially, this break with reality also plays out in terms of (narrative) form. As Walter walks through the city's historic cemetery at the end of *Exit Strategy*, he notices that the old kiosk outside it has been burned down in a fire, creating a landscape in a state of permanent destruction and re-elaboration: 'la plastica annerita ingombra il marciapiede; le lamiere della metro in costruzione sono ostaggio di writers di opposte bande, i disegni sovrapponendosi si annullano. Nessuna forma è più possibile' [blackened plastic blocks the pavement, the metal sheets of the metro under construction are hostage to battles between rival graffiti bands, drawings accumulate to cancel each other out. No form is possible anymore].[54] The reader, and indeed the writer, are both lost in a landscape of overabundant signs that have lost any solidity of meaning.

What are the implications of us losing faith in the certainty of finding meaning in our relationships with external objects; objects which we have, to date, used to stand in for reality itself? And can halting or rediverting our search for meaning in objects offer up a liberation from now-obsolete attempts to reproduce images of a fixed material reality? As I hope to have shown in this chapter, reducing our reliance on over-accumulated materials and information to represent the past can allow for greater formal latitude, perhaps even leading us towards new ways of re-imagining the future of the novel as a genre, and of the museum as a concept and as an institution. The spaces of doubt that lie in the post-fictional grooves between material objects, which include doubts about form, programme and mission, are where I believe some of the most intriguing links between museums and contemporary narrative now lie, since the 'insistent quality' of post-fictional works of literature is 'not only refusing to connect the work and the world, but thinking, inhabiting, even forging the space of their disorientation'.[55] As I hope to have shown, the value of literature, and thus also of literary research, lies precisely in its ability to help us navigate new ways of reading the world in all of its rich disjointedness and abundance.

Notes

1 British Museum, 'Recovery of Missing Items', https://www.britishmuseum.org/our-work/departments/recovery-missing-items [accessed 14 August 2024].

2 Steven Lubar, *Inside the Lost Museum: Curating, Past and Present* (Harvard University Press, 2017), p. 97.

3 Rodney Harrison, 'Forgetting to Remember, Remembering to Forget: Late Modern Heritage Practices, Sustainability, and the "Crisis" of Accumulation of the Past', *International Journal of Heritage Studies*, 19.6 (2013), pp. 579–95.

4 Emma Bond, *Curating Worlds: Museum Practices in Contemporary Literature* (Northwestern University Press, 2024). I am very grateful to Northwestern University Press for granting me permission to reproduce material from the book here.

5 This chapter was drafted long before the politically motivated attacks on heritage institutions in the US in Spring 2025, most notably the Smithsonian, which I fully denounce. These attacks, alongside images of the devastating looting of Sudan's National Museum by the Rapid Support Forces (RSF) that emerged around the same time, make clear the fundamental curatorial role of museums, and the crucial part collections have in providing an evidence base for history.

My theoretical ideas here pivot on the potential ecological and narratological value of selected acts of conscious, self-determined deaccession, and are in no way meant to undermine the significance and enduring value of museum object collections overall.

6 Timothy Bewes, *Free Indirect: The Novel in a Post-fictional Age* (Columbia University Press, 2022), p. 9.

7 Kate Elizabeth Willman, *Unidentified Narrative Objects and the New Italian Epic* (MHRA Legenda, 2022), p. 1.

8 Bewes, *Free Indirect*, p. 9.

9 Andrew Russeth, 'As Museums Push to Sell Art, Competing Ideas About Deaccessioning are Playing Out in Public', *ARTnews*, 8 February 2021, https://www.artnews.com/art-news/market/museum-deaccessioning-coronavirus-pandemic-1234583143/ [accessed 21 April 2026].

10 Eilean Hooper-Greenhill, *Museums and the Interpretation of Visual Culture* (Routledge, 2000), p. 152.

11 Hooper-Greenhill, *Museums*, p. 152.

12 Wolfgang Ernst, 'Archi(ve)textures of Museology', in *Museums and Memory*, ed. by Susan A. Crane (Stanford University Press, 2000), pp. 17–34 (p. 18).

13 Dayna L. Caldwell, 'Disposing Material: Information Lost or New Perspectives Gained?', in *Museums and the Disposal Debate*, ed. by Peter Davies (Museums Etc., 2011), pp. 44–55 (p. 45).

14 Cornelius Holtorf, 'Averting Loss Aversion in Cultural Heritage', *International Journal of Heritage Studies*, 21.4 (2015), pp. 405–21 (p. 407).

15 Cited in Bjørnar J. Olsen, 'Manker's List: Museum Collections in the Era of Deaccessioning and Disposal', *Nordic Museology*, 1 (2018), pp. 62–73 (p. 67).

16 Ernst, 'Archi(ve)textures', p. 26.

17 Sarah Wasserman, *The Death of Things: Ephemera and the American Novel* (University of Minnesota Press, 2020), p. 4.

18 Ernst, 'Archi(ve)textures', p. 18.

19 Maria Stepanova, *In Memory of Memory*, trans. by Sasha Dugdale (Fitzcarraldo Editions, 2021), p. 105.

20 Wasserman, *The Death of Things*, p. 28.

21 Susan A. Crane, 'Introduction: Of Museums and Memory', in *Museums and Memory*, ed. by Crane, pp. 1–13 (p. 2).

22 Pierre Nora, 'Between Memory and History: Les Lieux de Mémoire', *Representations*, 26 (1989), pp. 7–24 (p. 7).

23 Jennie Morgan and Sharon Macdonald, 'Degrowing Museum Collections for New Heritage Futures', *International Journal of Heritage Studies*, 26.1 (2020), pp. 56–70 (p. 61).

24 Ernst, ‘Archi(ve)textures’, p. 32.

25 Stepanova, *In Memory of Memory*, p. 133.

26 Stepanova, *In Memory of Memory*, p. 369.

27 Adrian Forty, ‘Introduction’, in *The Art of Forgetting*, ed. by Adrian Forty and Susanne Küchler (Berg, 1999), pp. 1–18 (p. 2).

28 Stepanova, *In Memory of Memory*, p. 47.

29 Stepanova, *In Memory of Memory*, p. 47.

30 Wasserman, *The Death of Things*, p. 37.

31 Stepanova, *In Memory of Memory*, p. 500.

32 Bewes, *Free Indirect*, p. 2.

33 Bewes, *Free Indirect*, p. 4.

34 Michel de Certeau, *The Practice of Everyday Life*, trans. by Steven Rendall (University of California Press, 1984), p. 108.

35 Emily St. John Mandel, *Station Eleven* (Picador, 2014), p. 146.

36 Mandel, *Station Eleven*, p. 276.

37 Kevin Walsh, *The Representation of the Past: Museums and Heritage in the Post-modern World* (Routledge, 1992), p. 161.

38 Judith Schalansky, *An Inventory of Losses*, trans. by Jackie Smith (MacLehose Press, 2020), p. 24.

39 Bewes, *Free Indirect*, p. 2.

40 Bewes, *Free Indirect*, p. 2.

41 Bewes, *Free Indirect*, p. 10.

42 Bewes, *Free Indirect*, p. 4.

43 Walter Siti, *Il realismo è impossibile* (nottetempo, 2013), p. 75. No English language translations of Siti’s works have yet been published; those included here are my own.

44 I include in this group Claudia Durastanti’s 2019 novel *La straniera*, Veronica Raimo’s *Niente di vero* (2023), Maria Grazia Calandrone’s 2023 *Dove non mi hai portata: mia madre, un caso di cronaca* and even Elena Ferrante’s self-reflective non-fiction works such as *Frantumaglia* (2003; 2016), *L’invenzione occasionale* (2019) and *I margini e il dettato* (2021), which detail close relations between biographical details and her fictional novels.

45 Raffaele Donnarumma, ‘Constructing the Hypermodern Subject: *Troppi paradisi* by Walter Siti’, *The Italianist*, 35.3 (2015), pp. 440–52 (p. 450).

46 Walter Siti, *Exit Strategy* (Rizzoli, 2014), p. 10.

47 *Il dio impossibile* (Rizzoli, 2014) is made up of three of Siti’s preceding novels: *Scuola di nudo*, first published in 1994, *Un dolore normale* (1999) and *Troppi paradisi* (2006).

48 Siti, *Exit Strategy*, p. 29.

49 Siti, *Exit Strategy*, p. 30.

50 Siti, *Exit Strategy*, p. 34.

51 Siti, *Exit Strategy*, p. 34.

52 Siti, *Exit Strategy*, p. 213.

53 Siti, *Exit Strategy*, p. 221.

54 Siti, *Exit Strategy*, p. 218.

55 Bewes, *Free Indirect*, p. 6.

References

Bewes, Timothy, *Free Indirect: The Novel in a Post-fictional Age* (Columbia University Press, 2022)

Bond, Emma, *Curating Worlds: Museum Practices in Contemporary Literature* (Northwestern University Press, 2024)

British Museum, 'Recovery of Missing Items', https://www.britishmuseum.org/our-work/departments/recovery-missing-items [accessed 14 August 2024]

Caldwell, Dayna L., 'Disposing Material: Information Lost or New Perspectives Gained?', in *Museums and the Disposal Debate*, ed. by Peter Davies (Museums Etc., 2011), pp. 44–55

Crane, Susan A., 'Introduction: Of Museums and Memory', in *Museums and Memory*, ed. by Susan A. Crane (Stanford University Press, 2000), pp. 1–13

de Certeau, Michel, *The Practice of Everyday Life*, trans. by Steven Rendall (University of California Press, 1984)

Donnarumma, Raffaele, 'Constructing the Hypermodern Subject: *Troppi paradisi* by Walter Siti', *The Italianist*, 35.3 (2015), pp. 440–52

Ernst, Wolfgang, 'Archi(ve)textures of Museology', in *Museums and Memory*, ed. by Crane, pp. 17–34

Forty, Adrian, 'Introduction', in *The Art of Forgetting*, ed. by Adrian Forty and Susanne Küchler (Berg, 1999), pp. 1–18

Harrison, Rodney, 'Forgetting to Remember, Remembering to Forget: Late Modern Heritage Practices, Sustainability, and the "Crisis" of Accumulation of the Past', *International Journal of Heritage Studies*, 19.6 (2013), pp. 579–95

Holtorf, Cornelius, 'Averting Loss Aversion in Cultural Heritage', *International Journal of Heritage Studies*, 21.4 (2015), pp. 405–21
Hooper-Greenhill, Eilean, *Museums and the Interpretation of Visual Culture* (Routledge, 2000)
Lubar, Steven, *Inside the Lost Museum: Curating, Past and Present* (Harvard University Press, 2017)
Mandel, Emily St. John, *Station Eleven* (Picador, 2014)
Morgan, Jennie, and Sharon Macdonald, 'Degrowing Museum Collections for New Heritage Futures', *International Journal of Heritage Studies*, 26.1 (2020), pp. 56–70
Nora, Pierre, 'Between Memory and History: Les Lieux de Mémoire', *Representations*, 26 (1989), pp. 7–24
Olsen, Bjørnar J., 'Manker's List: Museum Collections in the Era of Deaccessioning and Disposal', *Nordic Museology*, 1 (2018), pp. 62–73
Russeth, Andrew, 'As Museums Push to Sell Art, Competing Ideas About Deaccessioning are Playing Out in Public', ARTnews, 8 February 2021, https://www.artnews.com/art-news/market/museum-deaccessioning-coronavirus-pandemic-1234583143/ [accessed 21 April 2026]
Schalansky, Judith, *An Inventory of Losses*, trans. by Jackie Smith (MacLehose Press, 2020)
Siti, Walter, *Exit Strategy* (Rizzoli, 2014)
Siti, Walter, *Il realismo è impossibile* (nottetempo, 2013)
Stepanova, Maria, *In Memory of Memory*, trans. by Sasha Dugdale (Fitzcarraldo Editions, 2021)
Walsh, Kevin, *The Representation of the Past: Museums and Heritage in the Post-modern World* (Routledge, 1992)
Wasserman, Sarah, *The Death of Things: Ephemera and the American Novel* (University of Minnesota Press, 2020)
Willman, Kate Elizabeth, *Unidentified Narrative Objects and the New Italian Epic* (MHRA Legenda, 2022)

Chapter 7

What literature can do for health: a spotlight on eating disorders in men and boys

Heike Bartel

'I didn't have the vocab to explain anorexia'.[1] This is how the I-narrator in Dave Chawner's autobiographical illness narrative *Weight Expectations. One Man's Recovery from Anorexia* (2018) describes the central problem of understanding and seeking help for a complex health problem: having an eating disorder as a man and how his lack of words to grasp, articulate and communicate this disorder has affected his life for years. The author describes how the lack of words that came from his lack of understanding of a slowly unfolding mental health crisis was further exacerbated by a lack of awareness in society in general and, specifically, even in healthcare. That a man could have an eating disorder was not on his own or anybody else's radar – and largely, it still is not.

This chapter aims to contribute to making the case for literary research by outlining what can be gained from an interdisciplinary approach linking literature, medicine and health. The spotlight is on a very particular issue: eating disorders and their effect on a cohort that clinical researchers recognise as neglected, under-represented and under-diagnosed yet vulnerable – men and boys. As a scholar working at the meeting point between literary studies, medical research and patient-centred healthcare design,[2] I hope that findings from engaging with this specific topic may instigate further interdisciplinary dialogue. Literature, like many other art forms, can present new perspectives on the world and human experiences, and interrupt stereotypical and limiting understandings of what is perceived as being 'healthy' or 'normal'. And literary research can facilitate a greater understanding of how, why and when literature makes the invisible seen, lends attention to what seems to be mute and gives word to experiences that cannot be articulated otherwise. In turn, this understanding can add to healthcare practice and training, and also create greater public awareness.

This chapter draws on examples from thirty-nine published books on eating disorders, authored by men, from English-speaking and other countries. Recent examples include the text by British-born Chawner, cited above, *Heavy: An American Memoir* (2018) by African-American author Kiese Laymon and Aron Boks's German book *Luft nach unten: Wie ich mit meiner Magersucht zusammenkam und mit ihr lebte* [Room For Less: How I Got Together With My Anorexia and Lived With Her] (2019).

Reasons behind the emergence of this cluster of texts, mostly independent from each other, can be seen in an increased awareness of men's health along with new orientations around masculinity and a rising interest in the topic of eating disorders that emerged in the 1970s, mainly with focus on females and anorexia.[3]

Narratives of lived experience

The connection between literature, health, illness and medicine has a long and rich history. In the introduction to a scholarly survey on *Dionysus in Literature: Essays on Literary Madness* (1994), the editor, Branimir M. Rieger, emphasises the role of literature by asking: 'from what better source could one learn about madness, violence, murder, deceit, betrayal, lust, greed, loneliness and depression?'.[4] Ranging from canonical classics to contemporary bestsellers, the choice of authors presented in this collection reminds us of the potential of literature to represent and communicate ways of understanding elementary male human experiences. Rieger's approach of thirty years ago concentrates mainly on the well-known male authors of the Global North (with Virginia Woolf being the only female author given a chapter of her own).

The following contribution, by contrast, will focus on a type of literature that is not (yet) part of the canon, yet is of growing importance at the interface between literary scholarship and medical research and practice and 'worthy of its own branch of study':[5] contemporary writing about the direct experience of illness. 'Illness narrative', 'autopathography' or 'narrative of lived experience' are terms used to systematise writings that typically combine 'an auto/biographical narrative about living with an illness with reflections on the wider implications of a particular disease, treatment, recovery and interactions with medical professionals'.[6] Since the 1960s, and spurred by an increased interest in personal narratives of illness and health as part of a broader, political, social and scientific interest in medicine and its organisation in healthcare systems, there has been a growth of scholarship advancing research into such writings. Feminist scholarship has played an important role here in amplifying marginalised (health) experiences. The genre is becoming richer, more prominent and increasingly important both as a field opening up new areas of literary research, for example in autobiographical and life-writing[7] or in narratology.[8] It is also a growing source of information, education and self-help for health issues. Evolving scholarship on this genre offers interdisciplinary approaches that connect, among others, the fields of literature and health.[9]

A girls' illness?

There is a small, yet growing, number of illness narratives on eating disorders written by men, available in English and German, that have emerged since the 1990s.[10] The texts differ in style and content but at the centre of all of them is a man or a boy with an eating disorder.

But what are eating disorders and why is this topic of interest with regards to men, illness narratives and a dialogue between literature, medicine and health? Eating disorders – anorexia nervosa, bulimia nervosa and binge-eating disorder to list the most commonly known – are complex psychiatric disorders believed to be caused by a combination of biological, psychological, genetic and socio-cultural factors. What causes eating disorders, who develops them, how and why is not fully understood. Yet, when compared with other psychiatric illnesses, research on eating disorders is underfunded and only slowly evolving.

Eating disorders can range from mild to severe, with anorexia nervosa having the highest mortality of all mental health conditions. They can affect anybody regardless of gender, age, background or body shape. Yet eating disorders are still widely perceived by the public and by many healthcare professionals as only affecting females, the group that has, according to available statistics, the highest prevalence. While the focus on females in research, treatment and general awareness is much needed, it has also caused a 'glaring gender disparity'.[11] Medical researchers and cultural scholars, such as Susan Bordo, recognise that a growing number of boys and men are affected by 'the eating and body image disorders that we once thought only girls had'[12] and that this comes at considerable personal and healthcare cost.[13] In the UK, between ten and twenty-five per cent of the approximately 1.25 million people diagnosed with an eating disorder are male.[14] Experts warn that these available figures are only the tip of the iceberg and that many more men and boys are affected. John F. Morgan warns of the 'invisibility' of these men and boys due to a widespread labelling of the disorder as a 'women's and girl's Illness',[15] and several of the illness narratives by men illustrate the personal effects of this invisibility. For example, when I-narrator Jim in Jim Kohl's autobiographical text picks up the courage to talk to his doctor about his problems, he is met with the rebuff: '"Well, first of all, you don't have anorexia because men don't get anorexia"'.[16] That the term 'girls' illness' – or the German *Mädchenkrankheit* – is used as a problematic label for eating disorders in several narratives raises related issues. The term marks linguistically the exclusion of men and boys from the very concept of eating disorder and increases stigma and shame. Researcher Russell Delderfield emphasises that constructing eating disorders as a 'girls' illness' perpetuates the view of 'feminine-as-flawed' that leads men and boys to regard being affected by such illnesses as shameful and even 'a threat' to a particular concept of male identity. It appears to suggest that eating disorders 'challenge the very essence of identity, of a man's masculinity (including sexuality) itself'.[17]

Illness narratives of eating disorders by men

Illness narratives authored by men with lived experience of an eating disorder can play an important role in raising awareness and knowledge of this 'underdiagnosed, undertreated, and misunderstood' health topic.[18] The texts by men in the spotlight in this chapter share central themes beyond mere clinical diagnoses that literary scholarship in English and other languages can help to understand and convey. Themes include food, eating and health, the challenges of being 'seen' and helped by healthcare professionals, as well as struggles with recovery. Other themes emerging across this corpus paint an even richer and more complex tableau that includes representations of: food and family, culture, religion and communities; difficult family relations especially struggles with the father – some including violence; being bullied for weight; body image problems; wanting to be more 'manly' or muscular; pressure to be better at sports; problems around romantic relationships; alcohol and drug misuse; experiences of coming out as gay; crisis caused by a loved one's death; the stress caused by major life changes; and a range of mental health issues such as depression, neurodivergent conditions and substance dependency. Autobiographical writings on the topic – such as the titles by Chawner, Laymon and Boks mentioned above, as well as Bernhard Wappis's *Darüber spricht man(n) nicht . . . !* [Men Don't Talk About This . . . !] (2005) or Frank Bruni's *Born Round: The Secret History of a Full-time Eater* (2009) cited below – can function as a seismograph. This means that, given the lack of empirical data on the pressing issue of eating disorders in men and boys, these literary texts can chronicle existing and imminent problems that are not (yet) on the bigger radar of societies.[19]

A comparative approach across national and linguistic boundaries highlights the international significance of the topic and uncovers further nuances. One particular point of comparison is the function food, eating and feeding have for men from different backgrounds and how this is played out in eating disorders and concepts of masculinity. For example, a rural Austrian village in the 1980s is the specific cultural, historical and political setting of the unfolding anorexia of Wappis's I-narrator. This context is reflected in a particular 'order' of food and eating that the protagonist disrupts through his eating disorder. He rejects the traditional 'Essen für die Kärntner Männer' [food for the men from the Austrian region of Carinthia], heavily meat-based, regional dishes of *Knödel und Gulasch* [dumplings and goulash], *Schweinsbraten* [roast pork] and *Wiener Schnitzel*.[20] This food is served up in large quantities and at strictly regular mealtimes by the housewife-mother. Mealtimes are portrayed as tense family scenarios dominated by the working-class father whose national pride and childhood experiences of food scarcity after the Second World War shape his attitude towards eating. By rejecting food, the I-narrator is confronting particular gender roles and concepts of masculinity and national identity. Writing about food and eating means – here and in many other narratives – also engaging in critical socio-cultural and historical commentary and with concepts of hegemonic masculinity.

Another example is the I-narrator in Bruni's *Born Round* for whom the regional dishes cooked by his father and grandmother are closely connected to the struggle to assimilate into US society as Italian immigrants.[21] The large family's extensive feasts and cooking rituals are part of the desire to (re)create a lost cultural legacy and a sense of belonging. In the family's new environment, food functions as what Maud Ellmann calls 'currency': the acts of feeding and eating read as the 'prototype of all transactions with the other'.[22] The overemphasis on food as part of the developing binge-eating disorder by Bruni's I-narrator is set in the context of family and cultural legacy, migration and identity-formation. Bruni's story mirrors the stories of several other men (and women) where eating disorders are connected with personal stories of migration and displacement.[23] A third example, Laymon's *Heavy: An American Memoir* (2018), is one of the few texts that speaks to the experience of a Black male with an eating disorder.[24] Laymon interweaves his personal experiences of excessively bingeing and severely restricting food with American history and problems of social inequality, sexual violence, institutional racism and 'the racial and gendered terror that controlled and contorted the bodies of our family'.[25] These three examples offer an impression of how narratives – and their mediation through literary analysis – can help 'to understand the meaning of people's experiences without reducing these to statistical values about aetiology, epidemiology, psychopathology or treatment'.[26] However, these texts also show that literature and literary analysis can bring much more into the discussion than merely adding to an inventory of illness profiles. Literary studies open other fields of enquiry such as history, cultural politics, gender studies, masculinity studies, migration and trauma studies, or critical race studies – to name but a few.

The disciplines of literary studies are crucial contributors here to enable international research and to engage fully with the transculturality of the topic across linguistic, cultural and national boundaries. International research on autofiction, memory studies and life-writing is enhancing our understanding of how autobiographical narratives are always embedded in wider cultural and social texts and debates. The growing interest in life-writing within the humanities and beyond over the last two decades is one example of how academic disciplines not only respond to cultural debates and social phenomena but also help to establish new cultural spaces within which autobiographical texts can be produced and received. Literary accounts of illness, their analyses in literary scholarship and recognition as distinct genres have opened new trajectories to understand what it means to live with an illness or a chronic condition – not only for philologists but also for health professionals and the lay reader.

Furthermore, these narratives have the potential to expand and advance literary scholarship itself. In an article in the journal *Literature and Medicine*, the renowned literary theorist and narratologist Shlomith Rimmon-Kenan highlights the potential of illness narratives to expand notions of the narrative. She reads illness narratives as texts that can teach us to consider 'the complex interaction between the collapse of the body and that of the narrative, the problem of narrating the unnarratable'. She encourages us to look at the contributions such texts can make to our literatures and our thinking 'in terms of contingency, randomness, and chaos rather than order and regularity'.[27] It is against such contexts that so-far-unheard voices – both from the past and the present – become (re) publishable and gain new attention. And it should not be forgotten that such new perspectives are standing on the pioneering shoulders of critical feminist interventions in the literary canon.

Better health through literature?

When it comes to health, literature that links health issues and medical encounters with personal stories can provide access to topics otherwise inaccessible for many readers.[28] Done sensitively, this can contribute significantly to raising awareness and increasing knowledge. To maximise the power of literature for better health seems to be an important way forwards given strained public health systems nationally and internationally and the fact that waiting lists for treatment are becoming longer. Programmes such as the UK National Health Service's (NHS) 'Books on Prescription' that build on the role of literature and reading for better health aim to bridge this gap to 'help people who may be experiencing stress, anxiety, depression or other psychological problems' including eating disorders.[29] Another project, 'Reading Well', reports its success in delivering starting points for further engagement with 'things that are difficult to discuss', especially within the ten minutes maximum that UK patients have with a doctor.[30] While there is a clear need to take a decisive stance where 'traditional' healthcare services need to step up to deliver care, there is a strong case to be made for the use of literature for better health. Literature-based projects provide anecdotal evidence for the success of such an approach for eating disorders in men (Hungry for Words, n.d.).[31] Research on self-help and guided self-help (with the help of a therapist) speaks to the benefits of using select literature that allows individuals to work privately and at their own pace – reading online and offline.[32]

However, there can also be problems with this 'prescribing' of literature. The topic raises questions regarding who reads, when, why and how, and who doesn't in the light of education, language, diversity, age and gender, and particularly how to engage boys as (perceived) 'reluctant readers'.[33] The closure of libraries is one practical concern. Moreover, research has identified the need to investigate how this kind of approach affects different reader cohorts.[34] Regarding eating disorders, Emily Troscianko makes a strong case for critical and empirical evaluation of how reading texts about eating disorders – self-help books, autobiographical illness narratives and fictional accounts – may affect readers with past or current experiences of the disorder. Based on an empirical study, she stresses the need to acknowledge that literature 'is not a transparent vehicle for CBT [cognitive behavioural therapy]' or other therapies but rather 'a richly selective and associative medium capable of generating a variety of specific (wanted and unwanted) responses in readers'.[35] With regards to the reading behaviours of men and boys and other types of eating disorders than anorexia there is a need for more research, particularly regarding social media, but these findings raise important questions for our topic.[36]

We are reminded that literary texts that explore the human experience can be a powerful tool in reading for better health that has a strong capacity to speak to its readers, to engage and create responses. Clinical studies in recovery narratives raise 'connectedness, understanding, reduction in stigma, and validation' as benefits of reading and writing sensibly used and carefully screened personal narratives.[37] There is clear scope for collaborative work between clinicians, scientists, people with lived experience and literary scholars to develop a more nuanced understanding of reading for better health, particularly when it comes to eating disorders. Clinical researchers looking for the 'active ingredients'[38] in self-help using literary texts can benefit from the insights into such texts offered by literary scholars regarding stylistic dimensions, use of language and metaphor, linguistic characteristics, questions around fiction and authenticity, narrative strategies or the creation of ambiguities. Rather than restricting reading lists or censoring texts, such collaborations can lead to designing tools that 'unpack' texts and provide both reading in private and reading in groups in schools or healthcare settings with insights, information, questions and further material.

In the field of eating disorders in men, the text *Schlagmann* [Strokeman] by Evi Simeoni (2012), based on the life story of Olympic rower Bahne Rabe, and the accompanying teachers' handbook[39] are examples of such fruitful work across the disciplines. For instance, the handbook introduces Gottfried Benn's 1953 poem *Nur zwei Dinge* [Just Two Things] to engage students in further discussion of the topic of addiction and identity raised in the text. Furthermore, it encourages an exploration of the genre of letters, its particular style and cultural significance regarding letters by *gescheiterte Helden* [failed male heroes] and across linguistic boundaries, adding to the letters from the text other German and English examples, including the suicide note of Nirvana lead singer Kurt Cobain (1967–94).[40]

Better healthcare through literature?

Literature can not only give voice to but can also amplify the personal experiences of those affected by poor health and contribute to shaping healthcare, training of practitioners and planning clinical research. Driven since the 1970s by the emergence of patients' rights activism, the disability movement and the emphasis of recent UK healthcare policies on PPE (Public & Patient Engagement), contributions by people with lived experience are starting to be acknowledged in healthcare and medical research. As stated, current medical classifications that underpin diagnoses of eating disorders are presently mostly geared towards females, and gender diversity is 'not accommodated in current classification schemes'.[41] This may directly affect the risk of under- or misdiagnoses. Illness narratives by men based on their personal experiences can contribute to change here.

While quantitative evidence-based research is the main driver of specialised scientific enquiry, qualitative research is becoming increasingly important to develop effective treatment for health problems. Some approaches in qualitative research consider accounts of individual experiences, including those delivered in literary form,[42] and rely on interpretative tools and thematic analysis[43] to describe patterns of illness profiles. Here, the potential of interdisciplinary work lies not in assimilating literary scholarship into medicine but in recognising its distinct value and bringing the two disciplines into dialogue.

Individual projects and whole programmes have emerged that aim to drive such dialogue in various ways.[44] The American journal *Literature and Medicine*, founded in 1982, has played an important role in developing an interdisciplinary research agenda and is still driving strategies, methodologies and engagement. The teaching programme of 'Narrative medicine', pioneered at Columbia University by physician and literary scholar Rita Charon, emphasises the importance of literature for medical practitioners towards developing 'narrative competence' as a skill to improve their understanding of patients and increase their empathy and self-understanding. She describes it as the capacity 'to recognize, absorb, interpret, and be moved by the stories of illness'[45] – those stories that physicians hear from their patients but also those that they read. Her programme aims to fortify the work of health professionals using narratives for clinical practice training. Reading together or alone for them to become 'more attentive to patients, more attuned to patients' experiences, more reflective in their own practice, and more accurate in interpreting the stories patients tell of illness'.[46] Charon cites from Virginia Woolf's essay 'How Should One Read a Book?' as a guiding principle: 'Open your mind as widely as possible, then signs and hints of almost imperceptible fineness . . . will bring you into the presence of a human being unlike any other'.[47] Other programmes have developed similar concepts further for the use of literature in the education of current and future healthcare staff, and examples include *Teaching Literature and Medicine* (Hawkins, 1999), *The Chief Concern of Medicine* (Schleifer and Vannatta, 2013) or *Poems for Health Professionals* (Bartel, n.d.). While urging the connection between the disciplines, Charon and others also warn against the danger of using literature merely to award medical professionals 'a civilizing veneer'.[48] Just as literature is not a straightforward tool for better health, neither is it a magic tool that turns practitioners into more empathetic and humane healthcare professionals. However, engaging deeply and in the fullest sense with the struggles expressed in texts such as *Weight Expectations* (Chawner, 2018) or *Luft nach unten* [Room for Less] (Boks, 2019) can give those involved in healthcare insights into experiences of illness and recovery that reach beyond medical case studies. To open up narrative medicine towards more contemporary texts and to international contexts, to include more non-English titles (in translation if necessary) and texts at the margins of traditional literary genres, including those produced and self-published by former patients such as Wappis (2005), have been identified as ways to improve this programme.[49] Yet such connecting of literature, health and medicine is only possible if institutions are willing to invest time and resources and find in their curricula and training some opportunities for interdisciplinary engagement within the main specialist pathways.

On a disciplinary level, the subjects of medical humanities and the subsequently established health humanities explore systematically the connections between arts and humanities and medicine and healthcare. The shift from 'medical' to 'health' marks the recognition of *all* fields and the sheer variety of people that are involved in healthcare – not purely medics. It also acknowledges that 'medicine is only a minor determinant of health in populations alongside other factors such as class, education, occupation, environment, race, and stigma',[50] let alone gender and sexuality. The disciplines have emerged through research that is available in English and German and are still driven by research in the US and the UK. Yet international academia is now employing this interdisciplinary framework to drive innovative research agendas around the globe. Stephanie Hilger, the editor of the first edited volume on health humanities in *German* studies (emphasis: HB) with contributions from scholars working in many different countries, invites readers to reflect on the 'ensuing productive transformations that the Health Humanities undergoes when it [. . .] takes on different terminologies and incarnations across geographical and linguistic boundaries'.[51] Reflecting on such new international directions also shows the need to open up the discipline and our investigations into the connections between literature, health and medicine beyond North American, German and British contexts and beyond research that we can find in English translation.

Better health through writing?

In his research into illness narratology, medical anthropologist Arthur W. Frank has coined the term 'quest narrative'. The reference is to one of the oldest models of storytelling about an individual's often arduous journey in pursuit of a particular goal, usually with a focus on learning, self-reflection, questioning and overcoming obstacles. Quest narratives ultimately 'accept illness and seek to use it'; illness becomes 'quest' and 'journey',[52] and such stories 'imply that the teller has been given something by the experience, usually some insight that must be passed on to others'.[53] Unsurprisingly, given their focus on recovery, 'quest' narratives are the ones predominantly used for teaching, self-help purposes and 'prescribed books' in the field of eating disorders and in other health fields. However, while such thinking highlights the pragmatic benefits of literature for better health, literature, of course, cannot be reduced to this. An interdisciplinary dialogue should not limit itself to one-sided 'medically productive borrowings from the humanities'.[54] Instead, literary texts that disrupt and question reader expectations towards progress, healing or some kind of closure, and that therefore resist typecasting as quest narratives, also provide important contributions. These often challenge the boundaries of narrative typology through aesthetic complexity and ambiguity, through their 'contingency, randomness, and chaos'.[55] For example, the 1996 autobiographical account of anorexia by American Michael Krasnow, *My Life as a Male Anorexic*, is marked by permanent resistance to and distrust of healthcare professionals and their institutions. The text challenges its readers by generating two conflicting discourses that ask to be navigated. For example, in one passage, the severely ill and undernourished I-narrator resists violently to being restrained and force-fed with feeding tubes. He aims to regain his autonomy and voices his anger about what he perceives as an abusive breach of trust. He is '"talking back" to the authority of medical doctors' and speaks out against what reads here as an account of 'dehumanizing treatment accorded by institutions to vulnerable people'.[56] However, the medical documents inserted into Krasnow's text that chronicle his illness from the perspective of various clinicians present a different perspective. They speak to the immediate threat to the patient's life and to tube-feeding as a life-saving intervention. Rather than presenting a quest for better health, the narrative encourages critical engagement with a conflicted medical scenario and stimulates reflection as to which account to privilege. Furthermore, the ambiguity of diverging interpretations may also open the possibility of not arriving at one 'truth' – with all its ethical consequences.

Ambivalence and uncertainty are also integral to texts where loss of mental or language facility, having unusual sensory experiences, memory loss or other experiences present considerable challenges to narration. Boks's *Luft nach unten* [Room for Less] (2019), Jim Kohl's *Skeletal Marriage* (2009) and Gary Grahl's *Skinny Boy* (2007) all engage with the experience of hearing and talking to an eating-disorder voice.[57] Krasnow's 1996 text navigates memory loss as a result of electric shock treatment, and Benjamin von Stuckrad-Barre's *Panikherz* [Panic Heart] (2016) deals with blackouts due to drugs and alcohol.[58]

It is the strength of literary studies to train readers to do justice to the uncertainties and ambivalences resulting from such conditions as presented in narrative texts; they learn how to be open to a text's loud silences and its use of language; to recognise and accept a text's polyphony and heterogeneity, its conflicting voices, its dialogism and, what Mikhail Bakhtin called, heteroglossia: that is, to acknowledge that any word, any speech is already multi-vocal. Having such analytical devices in the healthcare toolkit may help in expanding and deepening interdisciplinary learning for a better understanding of illness

Conclusion

This chapter argues that literature, creative writing and literary research provide a path in the quest to find better health outcomes in treating eating disorders in men and boys. It advocates the therapeutic uses of reading and writing towards improving healthcare training and research, changing perceptions and even clinical classifications, and raising awareness of health issues in an international context. The exploration of literature in dialogue between literary scholars, healthcare practitioners and individuals with lived experience can contribute to real health outcomes through improving the visibility of, language for and treatment approaches to eating disorders in males. To achieve and maintain good health is one goal here. However, another goal is thinking about creative openness and resistance to narrative typecasting that both open up questions about the 'other sides' of literature. That a dialogue between literature, healthcare and medicine can bring very real, positive changes in medical practice is also highly relevant to educational policy at a time when the arts and humanities must constantly defend their value for and impact on society. As noted earlier, literature opens up other fields of enquiry such as history, cultural politics, gender studies, masculinity studies, migration and trauma studies, or critical race studies and, importantly, access to other languages. Accordingly, the practical suggestions offered here in support of literary studies and their impact in the medical realm lead on to a multitude of other aspects of what literature can be and do towards gaining knowledge and stimulating analytical competence, critical intelligence and creative imagination.

Notes

1 Dave Chawner, *Weight Expectations: One Man's Recovery from Anorexia* (Jessica Kingsley, 2018), p. 97.

2 The author is Professor of German Studies and Health Humanities. She works on the interdisciplinary projects Hungry for Words (University of Nottingham, n.d.) and EDIFY (EDIFY, n.d.). The author's research in this field is supported by UK Research and Innovation as part of the interdisciplinary EDIFY programme (grant number: MR/W002418/1).

3 See Bianca Sukrow, *Der Fall des Falles: literarische Phänomene in psychiatrischen und autobiografischen Fallgeschichten* (Olms, 2015), p. 15. There is considerable scholarship on the topic of eating disorders in women and girls. Three seminal examples from the extensive list of titles are: Susie Orbach's *Fat is a Feminist Issue: The Anti-Diet Guide to Permanent Weight Loss* (1978), Susan Bordo's *Unbearable Weight: Feminism, Western Culture, and the Body* (2003) and Isabelle Meuret's *Writing Size Zero: Figuring Anorexia in Contemporary World Literatures* (2007).

4 Branimir M. Rieger, *Dionysus in Literature: Essays on Literary Madness* (Popular Press, 1994), p. 3.

5 Paul Crawford, and others, *Health Humanities* (Palgrave Macmillan, 2015), p. 59.

6 Stella Bolaki, *Illness as Many Narratives: Arts, Medicine and Culture* (Edinburgh University Press, 2016), p. 4.

7 See Alfred Hornung, 'North America', in *Handbook of Autobiography/Autofiction*, ed. by Martina Wagner-Egelhaaf, vol. II (de Gruyter, 2019), pp. 1205–61 (pp. 1250–3).

8 See Shlomith Rimmon-Kenan, 'What Can Narrative Theory Learn from Illness Narratives?', *Literature and Medicine*, 25.2 (Fall 2006), pp. 241–54.

9 Seminal studies that have advanced the field include, but are not limited to, Arthur Kleinman's *The Illness Narratives* (1988); Arthur Frank's *The Wounded Storyteller: Body, Illness and Ethics* (1995); Ann Hunsaker Hawkins's *Reconstructing Illness: Studies in Pathography* (1993); Rita Charon's *Narrative Medicine: Honoring the Stories of Illness* (2006); Stella Bolaki's *Illness as Many Narratives: Arts, Medicine and Culture* (2016); G. Thomas Couser's *Signifying Bodies: Disability in Contemporary Life Writing* (2009); and Ann Jurecic's *Illness as Narrative* (2012).

10 The author has explored this body of work in detail in a book-length study on autobiographical writing and in a co-authored volume. See Heike Bartel, *Men Writing Eating Disorders: Autobiographical Writing and Illness Experience in English and German Narratives* (Emerald, 2021); Heike Bartel, James Downs, and Georgios Paslakis, *Masculinities and Mental Health: Eating Disorders in Men's Lived Experience and Contemporary Discourse* (Routledge, 2026).

11 Russell Delderfield, *Male Eating Disorders: Experiences of Food, Body and Self* (Palgrave Macmillan, 2018), p. 2.

12 Susan Bordo, *Unbearable Weight: Feminism, Western Culture, and the Body* (University of California Press, 2003), p. xxii.

13 Leigh Colin and Raymond Lemberg, *Current Findings on Males with Eating Disorders* (Routledge, 2014), p. 195.

14 https://www.beateatingdisorders.org.uk/media-centre/eating-disorder-statistics/ [accessed 19 August 2024].

15 John F. Morgan, *The Invisible Man: A Self-help Guide for Men with Eating Disorders, Compulsive Exercise and Bigorexia* (Routledge, 2008), pp. 6–7 and p. x.

16 Jim Kohl, *Skeletal Marriage* (Lightning Source, 2009), p. 128.

17 Delderfield, *Male Eating Disorders*, p. 13 and p. 6.

18 Eric Strother, and others, 'Undertreated, Underdiagnosed and Misunderstood', *Eating Disorders*, 20.5 (2012), pp. 346–55 (p. 346).

19 The metaphor of literature as a seismographic instrument to indicate, measure and warn against socio-cultural and political shifts and 'earthquakes' was first introduced by cultural sociologist Siegfried Kracauer (1889–1966) and has been introduced in the context of health problems in societies by von Jagow and Steger; see Bettina von Jagow and Florian Steger, *Was treibt die Literatur zur Medizin? Ein kulturwissenschaftlicher Dialog* (Vandenhoek & Ruprecht, 2009), p. 35.

20 Bernhard Wappis, *Darüber spricht man(n) nicht . . . ! Magersucht und Bulimie bei Männern. Ein autobiographischer Erfahrungsbericht und Ratgeber* (Books on Demand, 2005), p. 19.

21 See Frank Bruni, *Born Round: The Secret History of a Full-time Eater* (Thorndike Press, 2009).

22 Maud Ellmann, *The Hunger Artists: Starving, Writing and Imprisonment* (Virago, 1993), p. 53.

23 See, for example, Dennis Henning with P. Woods, *Hiding Under the Table* (Americana Publishing, 2004); and Heike Bartel, 'Rewriting Illness from the Turkish-German Margins', in *The Health Humanities in German Studies*, ed. by Stephanie M. Hilger (Bloomsbury, 2024), pp. 173–88.

24 Medical researchers stress that more insight into experiences of eating disorders by Black men – and other 'minority ethnic patients' – are needed (Chukwuemeka Nwuba and Bailey Spinn, eds, *Eating Disorders Don't Discriminate: Stories of Illness, Hope and Recovery from Diverse Voices* (Jessica Kingsley, 2024), p. 81). In 2019–20, hospital admissions in England saw a sharp rise 'for people from a black African background . . . , increased by a staggering 216%'. This is particularly relevant given research findings indicating that clinicians may be less likely to recognize eating disorders in Black patients compared to white patients (see Kathryn H. Gordon, Marisol Perez and Thomas E. Joiner Jr, 'The Impact of Racial Stereotypes on Eating Disorder Recognition', *International Journal of Eating Disorders*, 32.2 (September 2002), pp. 219–24).

25 Kiese Laymon, *Heavy: An American Memoir* (Simon and Schuster, 2018), p. 198.

26 Delderfield, *Male Eating Disorders*, p. 2.

27 Rimmon-Kenan, 'What Can Narrative Theory Learn', pp. 241 and 243.

28 Von Jagow and Steger, *Was treibt die Literatur*, p. 11.

29 NHS, 'Books on Prescription', https://www.nhsborders.scot.nhs.uk/patients-and-visitors/our-services/general-services/wellbeing-service/books-on-prescription/ [accessed 20 August 2024].

30 National Academy for Social Prescribing, 'Books Can Help Get Us Through Tough Times', https://socialprescribingacademy.org.uk/resources/books-on-prescription/ [accessed 20 August 2024].

31 See University of Nottingham, 'Hungry for Words: Creative Approaches to Shape Healthcare and Address Health Inequalities', https://www.nottingham.ac.uk/research/groups/hungry-for-words/ [accessed 19 August 2024].

32 See Chris Williams, 'New Technologies in Self-help: Another Effective Way to Get Better?', *European Eating Disorders Review*, 11.3 (May/June 2003), pp. 170–82; and Sarah J. Perkins, and others, 'Self-help and Guided Self-help for Eating Disorders', *Cochrane Database of Systematic Reviews*, 3 (2006), pp. 1–60 (p. 10).

33 International Literacy Association, 'Effective Approaches to Motivate and Engage Reluctant Boys in Literacy', https://ila.onlinelibrary.wiley.com/doi/abs/10.1002/TRTR.01107 [accessed 19 August 2024].

34 See Kerryn Husk, and others, 'What Approaches to Social Prescribing Work, for Whom, and in What Circumstances? A Realist Review', *Health & Social Care in the Community*, 28.2 (2020), pp. 309–24.

35 Emily T. Troscianko, 'Literary Reading and Eating Disorders: Survey Evidence of Therapeutic Help and Harm', *Journal of Eating Disorders*, 6.8 (April 2018), pp. 1–17 (p. 2).

36 See also Heike Bartel and James Downs, 'Opening a New Space for Health Communication: Twitter and the Discourse of Eating Disorders in Men', in *Masculinities and Discourses of Men's Health*, ed. by Gavin Brookes and Małgorzata Chałupnik (Palgrave Macmillan, 2023), pp. 77–100.

37 Stefan Rennick-Egglestone, and others, 'Mental Health Recovery Narratives and Their Impact on Recipients: Systematic Review and Narrative Synthesis', *The Canadian Journal of Psychiatry*, 64.10 (2019), pp. 669–79 (p. 671).

38 Perkins, and others, 'Self-help and Guided Self-help', p. 10.

39 See Christoph Kunz, *Evi Simeoni, Schlagmann. Lehrerhandbuch* (Klett, 2013).

40 Kunz, *Evi Simeoni*, p. 22 and pp. 31–3.

41 Stuart B. Murray, Scott Griffiths, and Jonathan M. Mond, 'Evolving Eating Disorder Psychopathology: Conceptualising Muscularity-oriented Disordered Eating', *The British Journal of Psychiatry*, 208.5 (2016), pp. 414–15.

42 See, for example, Priyanka Thapliyal, Deborah Mitchison, and Phillipa Hay, 'Insights into the Experiences of Treatment for an Eating Disorder in Men: A Qualitative Study of Autobiographies', in *Advances in the Prevention and Management of Obesity and Eating Disorders. Special Issues Edition of Behavioural Sciences*, ed. by Amanda Sainsbury and Felipe Q. da Luz (MDPI, 2018), pp. 107–23.

43 See, for example, Virginia Braun and Victoria Clarke, 'Using Thematic Analysis in Psychology', *Qualitative Research in Psychology*, 3.2 (2016), pp. 77–101.

44 For an overview see Hilger, 'Introduction', pp. 1–22.

45 Rita Charon, *Narrative Medicine: Honoring the Stories of Illness* (Oxford University Press, 2006), p. vii.

46 Charon, *Narrative Medicine*, p. 107.

47 Charon, *Narrative Medicine*, p. 109.

48 Charon, *Narrative Medicine*, p. 226.

49 See von Jagow and Steger, *Was treibt die Literatur*, pp. 11–12; also, Heike Bartel, *Men Writing Eating Disorders: Autobiographical Writing and Illness Experience in English and German Narratives* (Emerald, 2021), pp. 125–6.

50 Therese Jones, and others, 'The Almost Right Word: The Move from Medical to Health Humanities', *Academic Medicine*, 92.7 (July 2017), pp. 932–5.

51 Hilger, 'Introduction', p. 10.

52 Frank, *The Wounded Storyteller*, p. 115.

53 Frank, *The Wounded Storyteller*, p. 118. Frank's approach has been taken up, extended and also critiqued by many subsequent scholars in ways that raise important questions for the connection of literary narratives and medicine (see, for example, Angela Woods, 'The Limits of Narrative: Provocations for the Medical Humanities', *BMJ Medical Humanities*, 37.2 (2011), pp. 73–8.

54 Stefani Engelstein, 'Foreword: Boundaries and Interdisciplines: Where Health Humanities Meets Literature & Science in German Studies', in *The Health Humanities in German Studies*, ed. by Stephanie M. Hilger (Bloomsbury, 2024), pp. x–xv (p. xxiii).

55 Rimmon-Kenan, 'What Can Narrative Theory Learn', p. 243.

56 Sidonie Smith and Julia Watson, *Reading Autobiography: A Guide for Interpreting Life Narratives* (University of Minnesota Press, 2010), pp. 146–7.

57 Aaron Boks, *Luft nach unten. Wie ich mit meiner Magersucht zusammenkam und mit ihr lebte* (Schwarzkopf & Schwarzkopf, 2019); Jim Kohl, *Skeletal Marriage* (2009); Gary Grahl, *Skinny Boy: A Young Man's Battle and Triumph Over Anorexia* (American Legacy Media, 2007).

58 Michael Krasnow, *My Life as a Male Anorexic* (Harrington Park Press, 1996); Benjamin von Stuckrad-Barre, *Panikherz* (Kiepenheuer & Witsch, 2016).

References

Primary sources

Boks, Aaron, *Luft nach unten. Wie ich mit meiner Magersucht zusammenkam und mit ihr lebte* (Schwarzkopf & Schwarzkopf, 2019)

Bruni, Frank, *Born Round: The Secret History of a Full-time Eater* (Thorndike Press, 2009)

Chawner, Dave, *Weight Expectations: One Man's Recovery from Anorexia* (Jessica Kingsley, 2018)

Grahl, Gary A., *Skinny Boy: A Young Man's Battle and Triumph over Anorexia* (American Legacy Media, 2007)

Henning, Dennis, with P. Woods, *Hiding Under the Table* (Americana Publishing, 2004)

Kohl, Jim, *Skeletal Marriage* (Lightning Source, 2009)

Krasnow, Michael, *My Life as a Male Anorexic* (Harrington Park Press, 1996)

Laymon, Kiese, *Heavy: An American Memoir* (Simon and Schuster, 2018)

Simeoni, Evi, *Schlagmann. Roman* (Klett, 2012)

Von Stuckrad-Barre, Benjamin, *Panikherz* (Kiepenheuer & Witsch, 2016)

Wappis, Bernhard, *Darüber spricht man(n) nicht . . . ! Magersucht und Bulimie bei Männern. Ein autobiographischer Erfahrungsbericht und Ratgeber* (Books on Demand, 2005)

Secondary sources

Bartel, Heike, *Men Writing Eating Disorders: Autobiographical Writing and Illness Experience in English and German Narratives* (Emerald, 2021)

Bartel, Heike, 'Rewriting Illness from the Turkish-German Margins', in *The Health Humanities in German Studies*, ed. by Stephanie M. Hilger (Bloomsbury, 2024), pp. 173–88

Bartel, Heike, and James Downs, 'Opening a New Space for Health Communication: Twitter and the Discourse of Eating Disorders in Men', in *Masculinities and Discourses of Men's Health*, ed. by Gavin Brookes and Małgorzata Chałupnik (Palgrave Macmillan, 2023), pp. 77–100

Bartel, Heike, James Downs and Georgios Paslakis, *Masculinities and Mental Health: Eating Disorders in Men's Lived Experience and Contemporary Discourse* (Routledge, 2026)

Beat, 'Eating Disorder Statistics', https://www.beateatingdisorders.org.uk/media-centre/eating-disorder-statistics/ [accessed 19 August 2024]

Beat, 'Male 40 Years Old, and Anorexic', https://www.beateatingdisorders.org.uk/your-stories/anorexia/male-40-years-old-and-anorexic/ [accessed 19 August 2024]

Bolaki, Stella, *Illness as Many Narratives: Arts, Medicine and Culture* (Edinburgh University Press, 2016)

Bordo, Susan, *Unbearable Weight: Feminism, Western Culture, and the Body* (University of California Press, 2003)

Braun, Virginia, and Victoria Clarke, 'Using Thematic Analysis in Psychology', *Qualitative Research in Psychology*, 3.2 (2016), pp. 77–101

Charon, Rita, *Narrative Medicine: Honoring the Stories of Illness* (Oxford University Press, 2006)

Colin, Leigh, and Raymond Lemberg, *Current Findings on Males with Eating Disorders* (Routledge, 2014)

Couser, G. Thomas, *Signifying Bodies: Disability in Contemporary Life Writing* (The University of Michigan Press, 2009)

Crawford, Paul, and others, *Health Humanities* (Palgrave Macmillan, 2015)

Delderfield, Russell, *Male Eating Disorders: Experiences of Food, Body and Self* (Palgrave Macmillan, 2018)

EDIFY, 'Shaping a Fresh Approach to Eating Disorders: Bringing Together Arts, Humanities and Sciences to Develop Personalised Care', https://edifyresearch.co.uk/ [accessed 19 August 2024]

Ellmann, Maud, *The Hunger Artists: Starving, Writing and Imprisonment* (Virago, 1993)

Engelstein, Stefani, 'Foreword: Boundaries and Interdisciplines: Where Health Humanities Meets Literature & Science in German Studies', in *The Health Humanities in German Studies*, ed. by Stephanie M. Hilger (Bloomsbury, 2024), pp. x–xv

Frank, Arthur, *The Wounded Storyteller: Body, Illness and Ethics* (University of Chicago Press, 1995 [2nd edition 2013])

Gordon, Kathyrn H., Marisol Perez, and Thomas E. Joiner Jr, 'The Impact of Racial Stereotypes on Eating Disorder Recognition', *International Journal of Eating Disorders*, 32.2 (September 2002), pp. 219–24

Hawkins, Anne Hunsaker, *Reconstructing Illness: Studies in Pathography* (Purdue University Press, 1999)

Hilger, Stephanie, 'Introduction: Intersections: Health Humanities and German Studies', in *The Health Humanities in German Studies*, ed. by Stephanie M. Hilger (Bloomsbury, 2024), pp. 1–22

Hornung, Alfred, 'North America', in *Handbook of Autobiography/Autofiction*, ed. by Martina Wagner-Egelhaaf, vol. II (de Gruyter, 2019), pp. 1205–61

Husk, Kerryn, and others, 'What Approaches to Social Prescribing Work, For Whom, and in What Circumstances? A Realist Review', *Health & Social Care in the Community*, 28.2 (2020), pp. 309–24

International Literacy Association, 'Effective Approaches to Motivate and Engage Reluctant Boys in Literacy', https://ila.onlinelibrary.wiley.com/doi/abs/10.1002/TRTR.01107 [accessed 19 August 2024]

Jones, Therese, and others, 'The Almost Right Word: The Move from Medical to Health Humanities', *Academic Medicine*, 92.7 (July 2017), pp. 932–5

Jurecic, Ann, *Illness as Narrative* (University of Pittsburgh Press, 2012)

Kleinman, Arthur, *The Illness Narratives: Suffering, Healing and the Human Condition* (Basic Books, 1998)

Kunz, Christoph, *Evi Simeoni, Schlagmann. Lehrerhandbuch* (Klett, 2013)

Morgan, John F., *The Invisible Man: A Self-help Guide for Men with Eating Disorders, Compulsive Exercise and Bigorexia* (Routledge, 2008)

Murray, Stuart B., Scott Griffiths, and Jonathan M. Mond, 'Evolving Eating Disorder Psychopathology: Conceptualising Muscularity-oriented Disordered Eating', *The British Journal of Psychiatry*, 208.5 (2016), pp. 414–15

National Academy for Social Prescribing, 'Books Can Help Get Us Through Tough Times', https://socialprescribingacademy.org.uk/resources/books-on-prescription/ [accessed 20 August 2024]

NHS, 'Books on Prescription', https://www.nhsborders.scot.nhs.uk/patients-and-visitors/our-services/general-services/wellbeing-service/books-on-prescription/ [accessed 20 August 2024]

Nwuba, Chukwuemeka, and Bailey Spinn, (eds), *Eating Disorders Don't Discriminate: Stories of Illness, Hope and Recovery from Diverse Voices* (Jessica Kingsley, 2024)

Orbach, Susie, *Fat is a Feminist Issue: The Anti-Diet Guide to Permanent Weight Loss* (Paddington, 1978)

Perkins, Sarah, and others, 'Self-help and Guided Self-help for Eating Disorders', *Cochrane Database of Systematic Reviews*, 3 (2006), pp. 1–60

Rakoš, Mafalda, ąnd Ruben de Theije, *A Story to Tell, or: Regarding Male Eating Disorders* (Fotohof edition, 2020)

Rennick-Egglestone, Stefan, and others, 'Mental Health Recovery Narratives and Their Impact on Recipients: Systematic Review and Narrative Synthesis', *The Canadian Journal of Psychiatry*, 64.10 (2019), pp. 669–79

Rieger, Branimir M., *Dionysus in Literature. Essays on Literary Madness* (Popular Press, 1994)

Rimmon-Kenan, Shlomith, 'What Can Narrative Theory Learn from Illness Narratives?', *Literature and Medicine*, 25.2 (Fall 2006), pp. 241–54

Schleifer, Ronald, and Jerry Vannatta, *The Chief Concern of Medicine: The Integration of the Medical Humanities and Narrative Knowledge into Medical Practice* (University of Michigan Press, 2013)

Smith, Sidonie, and Julia Watson, *Reading Autobiography: A Guide for Interpreting Life Narratives* (University of Minnesota Press, 2010)

Strother, Eric, and others, 'Undertreated, Underdiagnosed and Misunderstood', *Eating Disorders*, 20.5 (2012), pp. 346–55

Sukrow, Bianca, *Der Fall des Falles: literarische Phänomene in psychiatrischen und autobiografischen Fallgeschichten* (Olms, 2015)

Thapliyal, Priyanka, Deborah Mitchison, and Phillipa Hay, 'Insights into the Experiences of Treatment for an Eating Disorder in Men: A Qualitative Study of Autobiographies', in *Advances in the Prevention and Management of Obesity and Eating Disorders: Special Issues Edition of Behavioural Sciences*, ed. by Amanda Sainsbury and Felipe Q. da Luz (MDPI, 2018), pp. 107–23

Troscianko, Emily T., 'Literary Reading and Eating Disorders: Survey Evidence of Therapeutic Help and Harm', *Journal of Eating Disorders*, 6.8 (April 2018), pp. 1–17

University of Nottingham, 'Hungry for Words: Creative Approaches to Shape Healthcare and Address Health Inequalities', https://www.nottingham.ac.uk/research/groups/hungry-for-words/ [accessed 19 August 2024]

Von Jagow, Bettina, and Florian Steger, *Was treibt die Literatur zur Medizin? Ein kulturwissenschaftlicher Dialog* (Vandenhoek & Ruprecht, 2009)

Williams, Chris, 'New Technologies in Self-help: Another Effective Way to Get Better?', *European Eating Disorders Review*, 11.3 (May/June 2003), pp. 170–82

Woods, Angela, 'The Limits of Narrative: Provocations for the Medical Humanities', *BMJ Medical Humanities*, 37.2 (2011), pp. 73–8

Chapter 8

Reality, representation, resistance: a case study of an Arab cancer ethnodrama

Abir Hamdar

Introduction[1]

1. In her autobiography, *A Daughter of Isis* (1999),[2] the late Egyptian feminist and novelist Nawal el-Saadawi gives a brief but heart-rending account of her grandmother's experience with cancer. Writing of the old woman's unspoken diagnosis and treatment, el-Saadawi notes:

> They told her she had influenza and inflamed tonsils. She lay in bed for a whole year. Suffering mixed with sorrow accumulated in her body. The 'specialist in malignant tumours' sunk needles in her neck. Her neck was pierced with needles and wound up in gauze, so she could not move her head, but her ash-grey eyes kept moving around her, filled with helpless pain, and her finger pale and ghostlike kept pointing to the needles in her neck. A blurry finger pointing to the blurry mass of white gauze asking the question she could not ask: 'What is it then that I have in my neck?'.[3]

2. In 2004, a novel by Syrian Haifa Bitar entitled *Imraa' min Hadtha al-'Asr* [A Woman of This Modern Age] offered a detailed fictional account of a woman's experience with breast cancer.[4] Its publication marked one of the few (if not the first)

instances in which a woman writer addresses the experience of breast cancer in ways that are deeply unconventional in the modern Arabic literary tradition. But the well-known male Syrian writer and critic Yassin Refa'iyah was clearly uncomfortable with the ways in which Bitar's protagonist, Maryam, articulates her bodily configurations in times of illness. The critic violently argued in one review: 'This is not how a woman with breast cancer feels!'.[5]

3. In 2017, during a Q&A session that followed the staging of an ethnodrama based on Arab women's cancer testimonies entitled *Wasafuli al-Sabr* [I Am Waiting for You], a young man told the audience present of the anguish that still haunts him at being separated from his mother when the latter was experiencing cancer. The seventeen-year-old man recounted that when he was six years of age, his mother was diagnosed with cancer and his aunts kept the little boy away from her: 'They hid from me that she was unwell, they did not allow me to go into her room during her treatment and when she was dying I was not permitted to see her even when I cried and called for her. Then she died. I found out years later that my mother had lived with and died of cancer. But no one had said a word at the time' (23 July 2017).

Why begin this chapter with such random, disparate or fragmentary examples of women's cancer experiences drawn from creative fiction, real-life testimony and critical reception histories over a period of almost twenty years?

To read these different accounts together, we may begin to see them as episodes in a single story, namely the story of how the Arab world perceives and interprets women's cancer on the one hand and how it is counted, accounted and discounted. It also becomes clear how literary and socio-cultural representations of cancer are so deeply entangled with one another that it becomes impossible to tell where fiction ends and real life begins. As disability scholar Rosemarie Garland-Thomson puts it: 'Representation informs the identity—and often the fate—of real people with extraordinary bodies'.[6] In what follows, I want to argue that the account of the cancer experience of el-Saadawi's grandmother, the breast cancer representation of the protagonist of *A Woman of this Modern Age* and the young audience member's recollection of his mother's cancer experience do not 'tell the story of Arab women's cancer' so much as of its representational silence or absence.

This chapter gives a critical account of work undertaken on my ethnodrama *Wasafuli al-Sabr* [I Am Waiting for You] (2017), which seeks to explore the modern cultural history of women's cancer in the Arab world through a creative–critical engagement with fiction, criticism and real-life testimonies. It is my aim to exemplify the complex and multidimensional nature of literary research on the one hand and to underscore the latter's emancipatory capacity, especially for individuals and communities experiencing marginalisation. To quickly map my argument, the chapter will briefly reflect on the 'archaeology of silence' that marks Arab women's cancer experiences both in Arab society and in the modern Arabic literary tradition. I then highlight how the creative–critical approach this drama employed offered multiple perspectives on the question of speaking about, representing and embodying cancer, while also drawing attention to the social, cultural and political contexts that underpin these literary representations. In summary, the chapter highlights the ways in which the ethnodrama – and the employment of this genre – sought to critique and resist the marginalisation of women's cancer experience that extends from everyday phenomenological experience to literary and aesthetic representation.

The cancer taboo and silence

In many ways, and as I have shown elsewhere, cancer is perceived as a taboo in the Arab world, especially for women diagnosed with the disease.[7] If this taboo status has been unsettled in some Arab contexts, thanks to activist efforts and initiatives, the disease remains largely attached to a range of titles that ultimately steer away from mentioning it. To list but a few of the idiomatic placeholders that are still used to name it without naming it, cancer is often referred to as *haydek al-marad* [that disease]; *al-marad al-wehish* [the bad or nasty disease]; *al-marad al-'atel* [the dreadful or lousy disease]; *al-marad illi mabyitsama* [the disease not to be named]; and *haydek al-shi* [that thing]. If cancer is ever explicitly named, it is often in a foreign language: individuals who choose to identify the condition often resort to its French or English names *cancre* or 'cancer'.[8] Yet, as Jackie Stacey posits – in the context of their reflections on what they call the 'C' word during their own cancer treatment – the un-naming of cancer is a constant reminder that one has 'entered stigmatized territory'.[9] This linguistic evasion confronts us with what the critic calls 'a deep sense of the horrific': '[. . .] the terror directed towards people with cancer' is a clear indication of 'its taboo status'. For Stacey, 'what disturbs so deeply [. . .] is something which goes beyond rational or conscious responses, something which threatens most profoundly. We are haunted by the constancy of its tormenting presence and horrified by its particular manifestations'.[10] In Stacey's account, the 'power of cancer's horror is partly due to its association with death'[11] but also carries the 'physical disgust that marks [cancer's] impact'.[12]

It is important to stress that the linguistic erasure, negation or circumvention of women's cancer in Arab society extends into, and is mirrored by, Arabic literary representations of cancer. To examine the body of Arabic literary works on women's cancer – novels, short stories, plays and memoirs – that has been produced since the 1930s is to examine what I have previously called the history of an absence.[13] This absence stands in sharp contrast to the proliferation of cancer narratives in Western contexts.[14] If there have been a number of attempts to write fictional or autobiographical cancer narratives in more recent years – mainly on breast cancer – relatively limited critical and literary attention has been paid to these works in terms of their contribution to Arab and Arabic cancer narratives more widely or in terms of the insights they could give us to patient subjectivity and affect.[15] In this sense, the history of the absence or silence called 'cancer' persists today.

As I have argued elsewhere, this absence at the heart of the representation of women's cancer experiences is felt in various ways: the sheer lack of cancer narratives and memoirs, the dearth of representations of people with cancer, the failure to explore the subjectivity of those who have cancer and the refusal to even put a name to 'that disease' in those narratives where a character has cancer.[16] In many ways, this state of denial is perhaps best captured in el-Saadawi's words in *A Daughter of Isis*: 'No-one dared, no-one could bear to pronounce the word cancer. Death was a word that was easier spoken. When people spoke about cancer they said, "You know, that disease"'.[17]

For el-Saadawi herself,[18] as well as for a number of other Arab women writers and poets like the Moroccan writer Leila Hulw, the Egyptians Radwa Ashour[19] and Nemat al-Behairy,[20] the Iraqi Salima Saleh[21] and the Lebanese Nazik Saba Yared,[22] Arab women's cancer experiences have begun to emerge from the margins in recent years in different forms: fiction, autobiography and drama. To take just one of the most provocative contributions to this emerging field, the Syrian writer Haifa Bitar's *Imraa' min Hadtha al-'Asr* [A Woman of This Modern Age] (2004) offers a detailed account of a woman's experience with breast cancer, mastectomy and chemotherapy, told against the backdrop of the protagonist's past relationships with men. It is – to my knowledge – one of the earliest modern Arabic cancer accounts by a woman writer in the Arab world that breaks with the taboo surrounding the theme by addressing the experience of breast cancer in its acute corporeality. As a consequence, the novel was, despite positive reviews, attacked by a number of literary critics and on social media: the literary critic Refa'iyah (as noted above) argued that the narrative was in no way reflective of women's experiences of cancer. In order to prove his point, Refa'iyah compares the portrayal of the protagonist's experience of breast cancer with his own daughter's experience of the same disease: the critic revealed that his daughter was diagnosed with breast cancer while she was in her thirties and insisted that when 'she was ill she did not think of her past, her present or her future'.[23]

While I am obviously not in a position to comment on Refa'iyah's daughter's case, his review nonetheless serves – perhaps inadvertently – to highlight a number of key ethical and aesthetic issues surrounding the representation of women's cancer. To privilege his daughter's experience of breast cancer over Bitar's representation of this experience, the critic institutes an opposition and hierarchy between real-life experiences and literary representations, which he evidently perceives as being out of sync with, and inferior to, reality. However, there is at least an argument to be made here that the father's (Refa'iyah's) response to Bitar's novel says as much about the prevailing patriarchal normative discourses surrounding Arab women's cancer experiences, as it does about real-life empirical reality. For me, what is at issue here is not proving Refa'iyah right or wrong but rather exposing or questioning his underpinning normative assumption that there *is* a right or wrong – good or bad – way of living through the female cancer experience. In seeking to police the boundary between real life and literature, Refa'iyah's condemnation of the representation of a woman's breast-cancer experience in *A Woman of this Modern Age* ironically trespasses across that boundary: his depiction of a 'true' (and, by implication, also a 'false') cancer experience is every bit as fictional as the novel he derides.

In short, then, it is difficult, if not impossible, to challenge the culture of silence where Arab women's cancer experiences and representation are concerned. It is clear that a whole set of violent normative forces – social, gendered, political and religious – come into play in this story that is often of silent suffering. As we are beginning to see, this culture of silence has become so deeply ingrained that Arab women – especially those living outside the metropolis – still find it difficult to speak about their cancer diagnosis and treatment. To reinforce the problem, what we have seen to be the dearth of Arabic cancer accounts – whether literal, historical or autobiographical – makes the task of undertaking a comprehensive cultural archive of cancer representations even more challenging. What, then, might it mean to write a cultural history or genealogy of Arab women's cancer? How can it confront or overcome the discursive hole or lack at its core? To what extent might creative criticism be one way to fill or supplement that absence?

I Am Waiting for You and creative-critical fusion

In order to at least begin to answer these questions, I now want to turn to my ethnodrama *I Am Waiting for You* (2017). This play was written as part of a research project on a cultural history of cancer in the Arab world (funded by the Arts and Humanities Research Council as part of their Open World Research Initiative) and was first staged in Beirut, Lebanon, in the summer of 2017 in a production by the renowned Lebanese feminist theatre director Lina Abyad. In subsequent years, it has been performed to the wider public in Lebanon and to medical staff at various hospitals in Lebanon, including the Naef K. Basile Cancer Institute of the American University of Beirut Medical Center and Rizk Hospital, thus marking the first instance in the Arab world in which a play is performed in a hospital space to the medical community.

To offer some brief context, *I Am Waiting for You* builds on work published in my first monograph *The Female Suffering Body: Illness and Disability in Modern Arabic Literature* (2014) by seeking to fill, creatively, what that book called the 'absent presence' of women's illness in the Arabic novel. In order to understand and articulate how women in the region experienced cancer phenomenologically, I conducted ethnographic research in the form of a series of interviews with women who have or had cancer – as well as their family members – from Lebanon, Syria, Jordan, Iraq, Egypt and Palestine.

It will not be surprising to learn by now that most of the women I interviewed had not disclosed their cancer diagnosis to anyone except very close family members. As a matter of fact, certain women even hid their diagnosis from their family and loved ones, thus choosing to live their cancer experience in isolation because of the taboo surrounding the disease. Yet, as one Lebanese woman described the burden of this choice, at the start of the interview: 'I am tired. Tired of the silence' (Personal interview, April 2016). If this sentiment was repeated again and again by different interviewees, it should nonetheless be stressed that not everyone I contacted was willing to speak of their experience: requests for interviews were declined, postponed or cancelled at the last minute and, even during the interviews that proceeded, some interviewees found it impossible to speak of their experience or even name their disease. In this sense, every conversation took place against the background of a larger silence – which manifested itself as gaps, pauses and linguistic evasions that uncannily echoed the representations encountered in literary works – and it was this historical, social and literary silence that was the theme of *I Am Waiting for You*.

If my research sought to investigate Arab women's real and lived cancer experiences, it soon became clear that any empirical interrogation could not be independent of, and divorced from, the archive of literary and critical representations that, as we have seen, do so much to predetermine what forms that experience will take. To map what Jerome Klinkowitz calls the 'void' that lies between and within the archive of literary representations on the one hand and women's testimonies on the other, I sought to construct an exchange or interaction between (1) Arab women's testimonies of their cancer experience, (2) literary representations of women's cancer in modern Arabic literature and (3) the critical reception of those representations. This tripartite model not only enabled me to narrate the entanglement between the lived experience of cancer and the discourses that surround it in Arab societies at large, but also allowed the playscript to supplement and substitute the gaps in these different texts and contexts. In this creative–critical fusion, I found an artistic, methodological and critical medium that made it possible to 'speak' the silences in the different fictional and non-fictional accounts of women's cancer experiences.

What did this process look or sound like on stage? To briefly summarise how the play attempted to capture the testimonies of the women interviewed in dramatic form, *I Am Waiting for You* stages an encounter between a group of women (and one man) who sit and wait. Some have been waiting for weeks, others for years, still others seem to have been waiting forever. They wait patiently and impatiently, nervously and calmly, hopefully and resignedly. This mise-en-scène sought to capture what I found to be a recurring theme in the stories of the women who agreed to be interviewed. For these interviewees, their cancer experience was principally a form of prolonged waiting: waiting for test results, waiting to start treatment, waiting to finish treatment, waiting for partial or complete remission to be confirmed, waiting for one's hair to fall out or grow back, waiting for one's period to stop or return and for one's body to recuperate; waiting for the cancer to return, waiting to live and (at times) waiting to die.[24] In this sense, the 'you' in the title *I Am Waiting for You* remains open: it variously signifies health, illness, life and, indeed, death.

As this complex waiting experience is foregrounded, we also begin to witness how the different characters fill the silence by talking to each other, to themselves and to the space at large.[25] Their voices and stories become entangled with, and echoed by, the voices and stories of fictional characters, worlds and representations. To be clear, the playscript juxtaposes the voices of the real women who have or had cancer that I had interviewed with the voices of two literary protagonists who experience cancer in Arabic novels: Bitar's *A Woman of this Modern Age* and Betool Khedairi's *Ghayeb* [Absent] (2004). It thus created a kind of speculative 'dialogue' between Maryam (the cancer patient in Bitar's *A Woman of this Modern Age*) and Mona, a real-life Lebanese cancer patient. According to the same logic, Ilham (the Iraqi cancer 'victim' who disappears early in Khedairi's *Absent*) re-appears in a Beirut waiting room in 2017 and joins forces with the Iraqi actress Namaa al-Ward, who is herself a breast cancer survivor. In addition to these dialogic literary and real encounters, the characters also speak back to the negative literary review of Bitar's novel.

In bringing real and fictional narratives into dialogue in this way, *I Am Waiting for You* sought neither to dramatise real-life experience nor to realise drama but to expose the ways in which, once again, cancer experience has always been both fictional and real at the same time. It responds to, and engages with, the anthropologist Stuart McLean's theory of the imagination as 'an active component of experience and perception engaged in a constant set of interchange with the material textures of the existing world'.[26] Along a similar vein, Dara Culhane also notes in the introduction to the collection *A Different Kind of Ethnography* that 'the potentialities of the imagination' can 'force an alternative rendering of social lives, one that accounts for the forgotten, disappeared, hidden and lost'.[27] To write a work of fiction, as Ronald Sukenick reminds us in their *In Form: Digressions on the Act of Fiction*, thus does not mean abandoning the world of fact but rather realising how deeply the stuff of fiction is entrenched in our everyday lives:

> The great advantage of fiction over history, journalism, or any other supposedly 'factual' kind of writing is that it is an expressive medium. It transmits feeling, energy, excitement. [. . .] No other medium [. . .] can so well deal with our strongest and often most intimate responses to the larger and small facts of our daily lives. No other medium, in other words, can so well keep track of the reality of our experience.[28]

If cancer itself is defined medically or biologically as 'an abnormal and uncontrollable division of cells', as Brian Lobel argues, it is also what we might call an abnormal and uncontrollable division of meaning, of signification, of language: 'The word cancer quickly spins from being just a thing that happens to cells to being a language that one speaks, either fluently (like most cancer veterans), professionally (like most nurses, doctors and other healthcare staff), or like a new student in a language immersion class (like most of the newly diagnosed)'.[29] In *I Am Waiting for You*, I sought to show how one of the languages that cancer patients, nurses and doctors learn to speak or immerse themselves in is always, and also, the language of *fiction*.

Resisting silence

In order to resist the silence surrounding Arab women's cancer, I turned specifically to the genre of drama and I want to explain that choice, too. It is important to begin here with Kathleen Gallagher's claim that the use of traditional ethnographic methodologies 'often anchors researchers to only use those things that can be or were spoken in the given context rather than using stories – methodologically – as spaces for exploration and rival musings'. According to this scholar, ethnography's 'reductive and appropriating form of reporting' strips and divests 'experience of its ambiguities and contradictions'. To restore this symbolic dimension of lived experience, Gallagher turns to theatre: 'Storytelling through theatre that draws on symbol and metaphor, realism and abstraction can act as a "a methodological release point" to invite the unsaid, the masked, the contested, the contradictory.'[30] By 'methodological release point' Gallagher is here referring to Sara McClelland and Michele Fine's notion of the term to speak of 'the sometimes halting or uneven bursts of understanding that can result from innovative qualitative methodologies'.[31] If the identities of the women whose stories were told on stage remained anonymised in the play, I believe the dramatic genre enabled them to speak, not simply as a set of qualitative data points, but as embodied beings in all their messy complexity. In representing the ethnographic data through the medium of ethnodrama, *I Am Waiting for You* was paradoxically better able to do justice to the women's testimony than any straightforward traditional ethnography.

It is also important to stress that the ethnodrama was underpinned by an (inchoate, at times, but always indisputably present) *activist* spirit. After all, one of the key tropes that emerged from the individual interviews I conducted was the isolation of many of the women diagnosed with cancer: the taboo that often accompanied the diagnosis, the inability to talk openly about their treatment and the scarcity of support groups available (especially for those living in rural or conflict zones) imposed a corporeal, cultural and linguistic invisibility upon them. To bring these women's individual stories into conversation with one another in ethnodramatic form, I thus sought to create a virtual network or community of support for the women in question – and for other women with cancer who may see or read the play. By the same token, I think the collective testimonies we staged constituted a kind of virtual activist group or movement that sought to challenge prevailing taboos around women's cancer experience. In *I Am Waiting for You*, I tried to conceive of what Gallagher would describe as 'a place from which to begin inquiry' rather than 'a place at which to arrive':[32] the real and fictional stories we put on stage were a forum to invite critical and social questioning of the ways in which we speak, represent and cast women's cancer experiences.

If *I Am Waiting for You* was a place to begin inquiry, this inquiry took on a meaning beyond what we had all imagined and hoped for (researcher, theatre director, cast and production team). Its premiere in Beirut in 2017 was fraught with anxieties. As Lobel reminds us, performances about illness (especially cancer) are not a popular subject-matter for the stage and we worried that audiences would simply refuse to attend or respond negatively.

For the production team, Lobel's poignant critique of utopian theories of the theatre as a free democratic space resonated in the days leading up to the premiere: 'If the world that we live in finds it nearly impossible to embrace difference, fragility or vulnerability, how or why should we expect the theatre to be any better?'.[33] In staging the first play about cancer on an Arab stage, we had no idea what to expect and so were astonished and gratified that the run was a virtual sell-out.

What, then, was the audience response to *I Am Waiting for You*? To gauge audience reaction, we staged nightly post-performance Q&A sessions and invited spectators to give feedback via a number of identifiable and anonymous means (conversations, emails, sticky notes posted on a board in the foyer). It quickly became clear from both the quality and quantity of the feedback that the play struck an emotional chord with audience members – many of whom were themselves personally affected by cancer and who felt empowered to speak about it publicly for the first time. As the audience gathered around the stage after each performance, stories flowed and attempts to put into words what it has meant and means to be diagnosed with cancer for individuals, family members and carers unfolded. For one middle-aged woman, the play reignited a longstanding sense of guilt she felt over not disclosing her mother's cancer to friends and family even though the latter's self-imposed isolation had led to ugly rumours about her character:

> I should have defended her and told everyone she was hiding at home for fear of the taboo. And tonight I want to tell everyone who knew and did not know my mother that she had cancer and suffered from cancer and hid because of her cancer but people did not see this and assumed the worst of her. [. . .] They attacked her reputation and moral character! Why? Because she's a woman! (26 July 2017)

In another post-performance audience gathering, an older man with terminal cancer described how 'moved' he felt 'at being amongst the audience and listening to the accounts of women's cancer experiences': 'I don't have long to live,' the man announced, 'and I won't be around to see how our society will completely shatter this silence and taboo but I can only say that every story and every testimony has penetrated my very being' (29 July 2017).

In many ways, the audience reaction to the play testifies to the dramatic transformation of cancer from an isolated or atomised experience to a collective experience: 'The disease that sets the body apart from others,' as Arthur Frank observes, 'becomes, in the story, the common bond of suffering that joins bodies in their shared vulnerability'.[34] It also testifies to the power of modern theatre itself to break down the fourth wall that separates the performers from the audience. As Helena Grehan notes: 'Performance engages its spectators emotionally, viscerally and intellectually. It has the potential to generate a set of conditions within which linguistic or representational surfaces can be disturbed or interrupted in ways that allow spectators to reflect on and ask questions about the nature of any response to work.'[35] In the words of Dr Jacques Mokhbat, of LAUMC-Rizk Hospital, the play 'led us to question ourselves and to reevaluate our approach to patient care and self-education' (Email, 17 August 2017).

To draw this chapter to a close, though, I want to contend that the audience response – from both the general public and the medical community – testified to what the feminist writer and activist Audre Lorde calls 'the transformation of silence into language and action'. For Lorde, writing following their own breast cancer diagnosis and treatment, the speech act is also an act of community building:

> For every real word spoken, for every attempt I had ever made to speak those truths for which I am seeking, I had made contact with other women while we examined the words to fit a world in which we all believed bridging our difference . . . [I]n the transformation of silence into language and action, it is vitally necessary for each one of us to establish or examine her function in that transformation and to recognize her role as vital within that transformation.[36]

If every speech act is spoken to someone who, in turn, responds with their own speech act, then the response to *I Am Waiting for You* powerfully embodied this process: the cancer experiences embodied on stage generated a whole set of other stories about cancer experiences from members of the audience. In bearing witness to the creation of a – previously unspoken and inaccessible – archive of collective cancer stories, *I Am Waiting for You* testified to what Lorde calls – to repeat – 'the transformation of silence into language and action'.

Conclusion

To close, I recall the testimony of one of the women I interviewed whose first reaction upon learning of her cancer diagnosis was a strong desire to *read* about women's cancer – not in medical textbooks or on internet sites but in literary works, fiction and drama such as the texts discussed in this chapter. By reading about other women's experiences of cancer in this way, this particular young woman not only found a community of fellow cancer patients who simply did not exist in her own experience, but also a common language, imaginary and structure of feeling that paradoxically spoke more eloquently to her than her own raw or immediate experience of shock or trauma. In this way, the woman felt that her individual hermeneutic response to her cancer diagnosis was, from the beginning, mediated or refracted through this larger literary and cultural archive of other women (Personal interview, May 2016).

To answer the question of why literary research 'matters' – which this collection invites us to do – this chapter has argued that my ethnodrama *I Am Waiting for You* both describes and (quite literally) performs the power of the 'literary' – whether creative, critical or otherwise – to recover an archive of silent and silenced voices, to resist histories of silence and to find the words through which to tell the story of this past and present silence. It endeavours to participate in and expand a virtual community of support and empathy where all of us 'recognize our responsibility to seek those words out, to read them and share them and examine them in their pertinence to our lives'.[37] In challenging both a general and a specialised (medical) public to confront existing taboos around women's cancer, I also hope that my ethnodrama played some small role in enabling Arab women to speak 'that disease' with its proper name.

In this chapter, I have also sought to show that what we call 'Arab women's cancer' is *itself* a creative and critical work or labour that occupies a kind of middle ground between phenomenology and hermeneutics, experience and discourse, life and fiction. To ask the question of why literary research matters – at least as far as Arab women's cancer is concerned – is thus to approach the 'matter' from the wrong way around: what we call the real, lived or material experience of cancer is always already informed by, and entangled with, the literary in all its diverse forms. If I may return to the example of the woman with the cancer diagnosis I described above, I find it striking that her own cancer experience – her way of narrating her trauma to herself – effectively took the form of a kind of 'literary research'. In seeking to find the, so-called, real-world uses or value of literature in a world that is allegedly post-literary, we discover that there is, perhaps, already more literature in real life than we ever knew.

Notes

1 This chapter uses he/she to refer to individuals whose self-identified pronouns are known. I also use male/female adjectives where relevant and appropriate. When I refer to individuals whose identified pronouns are not known or when the gender of a person is irrelevant within the context, I use the singular 'they'.

2 This is one of the translations of el-Saadawi's three-volume autobiography which first appeared in Arabic as *Awraq Hayati*.

3 Nawal El-Saadawi, *A Daughter of Isis: The Early Life of Nawal El Saadawi* (Zed Books, 2009), trans. by Sherif Hetata, p. 208.

4 I use a general system of translation and only use the *ayn* (ʻ) and *hamza* (ʼ). I also present all Arabic names and titles of people, places and texts in the form most familiar to an English-speaking audience and/or the form used by the writers and the works under discussion.

5 Yassin Refaʻiyah, *'al-Ghiwaya fi Hudn al-Mawt'*, *al-Mustaqbal*, 14 January 2004, p. 20.

6 Rosemarie Garland-Thomson, *Extraordinary Bodies: Figuring Physical Disability in American Culture and Literature* (Columbia University Press, 1997), p. 15.

7 Abir Hamdar, 'Staging Silence: Arab Women's Cancer Experience', *Studies in Theatre and Performance*, 41.2 (2021), pp. 197–211, doi:10.1080/14682761.2019.1683348.

8 Hamdar, 'Staging Silence', p. 197.

9 Jackie Stacey, *Teratologies: A Cultural Study of Cancer* (Routledge, 2013), p. 70.

10 Stacey, *Teratologies*, p. 72.

11 Stacey, *Teratologies*, pp. 72–3.

12 Stacey, *Teratologies*, p. 74.

13 Abir Hamdar, *The Female Suffering Body: Illness and Disability in Modern Arabic Literature* (Syracuse University Press, 2014).

14 Mary K. DeShazer, *Fractured Borders: Reading Women's Cancer Literature* (University of Michigan Press, 2010).

15 One early exception is Fedwa Malti-Douglas's essay on Moroccan Leila Hulw's *Fa La Tansa Allah* [Do Not Forget God] (1984).

16 See, for example, Egyptian Mahmoud Taymur's 1969 novella *Wa Usdila al-Sitar* [And the Curtain is Lowered] and Yusuf al-Siba'i's 1969 two-volume novel *Nahnu La Nazra' al-Shawk* [We Do Not Sow Thorns], both of which depict women protagonists who suffer from a disease – the suggestion being cancer – but this disease is never identified or named.

17 El-Saadawi, *A Daughter of Isis*, p. 208.

18 See *Daughter of Isis* and her short story '*La Shaya' Yafna*' [Nothing Perishes] (1986).

19 See *Athqal min Radwa: Maqati' min Sira Thatiyya* [Heavier than Radwa: Excerpts from an Autobiography] (2013).

20 See *Yawmiyat Imraa' Mushi'a* [Chronicles of a Radiating Woman] (2006).

21 See *Aam al-Saratan* [The Year of the Cancer] 2017.

22 See *Taqasim 'ala Watarin da'i'* [Improvisations on a Missing String] (1997).

23 Refa'iyah, '*al-Ghiwaya fi Hudn al-Mawt*', p. 20.

24 Hamdar, 'Staging Silence', pp. 201–2.

25 Hamdar, 'Staging Silence', p. 201.

26 Stuart McLean, 'Introduction: Why Imagination?', *Irish Journal of Anthropology*, 10.2 (2007), pp. 5–9 (p. 6).

27 Dara Culhane, 'Imagining: An Introduction', in *A Different Kind of Ethnography* ed. by Denielle Elliott and Dara Culhane (University of Toronto Press, 2017), pp. 1–21 (p. 13).

28 Ronald Sukenick, *In Form: Digressions on the Act of Fiction* (Southern Illinois University Press, 1985), p. 242.

29 Brian Lobel, *Theatre & Cancer* (Red Globe Press, 2019), p. 10.

30 Kathleen Gallagher, *Why Theatre Matters: Urban Youth, Engagement, and a Pedagogy of the Real* (University of Toronto Press, 2014), p. 16.

31 Gallagher, *Why Theatre Matters*, p. 16.

32 Gallagher, *Why Theatre Matters*, p. 16.

33 Lobel, *Theatre & Cancer*, pp. 10–11.

34 Arthur W. Frank, *The Wounded Storyteller: Body, Illness and Ethics* (University of Chicago Press, 2013), 2nd edn, p. xix.

35 Helena Grehan, *Performance, Ethics and Spectatorship in a Global Age* (Palgrave Macmillan, 2009), p. 2.

36 Audre Lorde, 'The Transformation of Silence into Language and Action', in *Sister Outsider: Essays and Speeches* (Crossing Press, 1984), pp. 40–4 (p. 41 and p. 43).

37 Lorde, 'The Transformation of Silence', p. 43.

References

Al-Behairy, Nemat, *Yawmiyat Imraa' Mushi'a* [Chronicles of a Radiating Woman] (al-Haya al-Misriya al-'Ama li al-Kitab, 2006)
Al-Siba'i, Yusuf, *Nahnu la Nazra' al-Shawq* [We Do Not Sow Thorns] 2 vols (Dar Misr li-al-Tiba'a, 1969)
Ashour, Radwa, *Athqal min Radwa: Maqati' min Sira Thatiyya* [Heavier than Radwa: Excerpts from an Autobiography] (Dar al-Shorouk, 2013)
Bitar, Haifa, 'Excerpt from *A Woman of this Modern Age*', trans. by Issa J. Boullata (International Writing Program, University of Iowa, 21 May 2013 (Web))
Bitar, Haifa, *Imraa' Min Hadha al-'Asr* [A Woman of this Modern Age] (Dar al-Saqi, 2004)
Culhane, Dara, 'Imagining: An Introduction', in *A Different Kind of Ethnography*, ed. by Denielle Elliott and Dara Culhane (University of Toronto Press, 2017), pp. 1–21
DeShazer, Mary K., *Fractured Borders: Reading Women's Cancer Literature* (University of Michigan Press, 2010)
El-Saadawi, Nawal, *A Daughter of Isis: The Early Life of Nawal El-Saadawi*, trans. by Sherif Hetata (Zed Books, 2009)
El-Saadawi, Nawal, '*La Shaya' Yafna*' [Nothing Perishes], in *Lahzat Siddq* [Moment of Honesty] (Dar al-Adab, 1986), pp. 77–82
Frank, Arthur W., *The Wounded Storyteller: Body, Illness and Ethics.* 2nd edn (University of Chicago Press, 2013)
Gallagher, Kathleen, *Why Theatre Matters: Urban Youth, Engagement, and a Pedagogy of the Real* (University of Toronto Press, 2014)
Garland-Thomson, Rosemarie, *Extraordinary Bodies: Figuring Physical Disability in American Culture and Literature* (Columbia University Press, 1997)
Grehan, Helena, *Performance, Ethics and Spectatorship in a Global Age* (Palgrave Macmillan, 2009)
Hamdar, Abir, *The Female Suffering Body: Illness and Disability in Modern Arabic Literature* (Syracuse University Press, 2014)
Hamdar, Abir, *I Am Waiting for You*, directed by Lina Abyad, Madina Theatre, Beirut, 2017
Hamdar, Abir, 'Staging Silence: Arab Women's Cancer Experience', *Studies in Theatre and Performance*, 41.2 (2021), pp. 197–211, doi:10.1080/14682761.2019.1683348

Khedairi, Betool, *Absent*, trans. by Muhayman Jamil (The American University in Cairo Press, 2005)
Khedairi, Betool, *Ghayeb* [Absent] (al-Muassassa al-ʻArabiyya li-al-Dirasat wa-al-Nashr, 2004)
Klinkowitz, Jerome, *Structuring the Void: The Struggle for Subject in Contemporary American Fiction* (Duke University Press, 1992)
Lobel, Brian, *Theatre & Cancer* (Red Globe Press, 2019)
Lorde, Audre, 'The Transformation of Silence into Language and Action', in *Sister Outsider: Essays and Speeches* (Crossing Press, 1984), pp. 40–4
McLean, Stuart, 'Introduction: Why Imagination?', *Irish Journal of Anthropology*, 10.2 (2007), pp. 5–9
Refaʻiyah, Yassin, '*al-Ghiwaya fi Hudn al-Mawt*', *al-Mustaqbal*, 14 January 2004, p. 20
Saleh, Salima, *Aam al-Saratan* [The Year of the Cancer] (Dar al-Jamal, 2017)
Stacey, Jackie, *Teratologies: A Cultural Study of Cancer* (Routledge, 2013)
Sukenick, Ronald, *In Form: Digressions on the Act of Fiction* (Southern Illinois University Press, 1985)
Taymur, Mahmoud, '*Wa Usdila al-Sitar*' [And the Curtain was Lowered], in *Ana al-Qatil wa Qisas Ukhra* [I Am the Killer and Other Stories] (Dar Nahdat Misr. Yared, 1969), pp. 105–8
Yared, Nazik Saba, *Improvisations on a Missing String*, trans. by Stuart A. Hancox (University of Arkansas Press, 1997)

Chapter 9

Kalila wa Dimna and the arts of storytelling: conversations with medieval Arabic literature in contemporary London

Rachel Scott

In May 2006, the Barbican Theatre premiered *Mirror for Princes – Kalila wa Dimna*, a SABAB Theatre production by the Kuwaiti–British playwright Sulayman Al-Bassam.[1] The play was a dramatic reworking of an ancient collection of exemplary fables aimed at rulers and their courtiers – a kind of textbook of statecraft – known in Arabic as *Kalila wa Dimna*. An Arabic translation of a Persian translation of a Sanskrit book called the *Panchatantra*, the fables have existed in written form since the fourth century C.E. and almost certainly for far longer in oral form. Al-Bassam's retelling focuses on the context of their translation from Persian at the dawn of the Abbasid revolution in Iraq *c.*750 C.E. – one of the most turbulent moments in Islamic history, a period of Imperial expansion and the threat of civil war, as well as a golden age of Arab culture. The play follows the tragedy that unfolds around Ibn al-Muqaffa, a court scribe and scholar who translated the fables into Arabic for the Abbasid Caliph al-Mansur amid revolution and religious propaganda.

In publicity material, SABAB Theatre described the play as 'an exploration of the mechanics of Empire and the narratives of power, an argument for cultural and religious tolerance in the modern Arab and Western worlds'.[2] In interviews at the time, Al-Bassam also drew attention to the parallels with contemporary political events in the Middle East:

> I was looking for a way into some of today's ruined and chaotic and overcharged landscape of power and politics in my region [. . .] I found that through them I could find a very satisfying indirect way of addressing some of the issues that I want to explore today. [. . .] [The play is] not docu-drama, it's an approach to politics, religion and questions of social justices in the Middle East through history on one hand and fable on the other. Both of which are mechanisms to objectify and then perhaps distort and that you feel you're watching something that could very well be about now, that could very well be about this moment, that is in-fact about this moment.[3]

For Al-Bassam, the fables of *Kalila wa Dimna* provided a means of critiquing contemporary issues and events. The historical nature of the tales offers a 'long view' on the history of the Middle East and their fictional accounts of ethical and moral problems provide a means of gaining perspective on – 'objectifying' in Al-Bassam's words, that is, 'express[ing] (something abstract) in a concrete form; to render [it] objective'[4] – commonly held truths, established norms, practices and beliefs. Al-Bassam's use of the term 'distort' suggests that this process twists out of shape what is read (or viewed), until there arrives a sense of recognition; the issues being explored become magnified not as those of a distant past, but the here and now.

SABAB Theatre's *A Mirror for Princes* is not the only example of contemporary, creative responses that have sought to bring these ancient fables to new audiences and through them, to explore contemporary political and cultural themes. Others include Moneim Adwan's opera for the 2016 Festival d'Aix-en-Provence and the exhibition *Fables Across Time*, a collaboration between the Bahrain National Museum and the Children's Museum of Indianapolis which premiered in 2015 and 2016 respectively, and for which Tunisian artist Sabiha Al Khemir created original animated illustrations of several stories.[5] These cultural outputs are an example of what Clare Lees and Gillian R. Overing, in *The Contemporary Medieval in Practice*, call the 'ongoing critical conversation' between past and present, medieval and contemporary that has found expression in much recent practice-based and creative–critical research.[6] Lees and Overing consider the meanings of 'conversation' in its medieval English context (their particular specialism):

> The *Oxford English Dictionary* notes that in the fourteenth century 'conversation', derived from Latin via French, referred to 'the action

> of living, or having one's being in a place or among persons', or 'figuratively', to 'one's spiritual being', and also to dealing with others, living together, and to conduct, social as well as spiritual bearing, or behaviour in the world. A conversation in the Middle Ages required at least one other person (no talking to yourself, then), and also an awareness of community and place, whether social or spiritual.[7]

The concept of conversation as it is defined here, encompassing a sense of community and ethical behaviour, is useful when thinking about what we do as literary researchers, who we work with and speak to, and why it matters. Scholarly research does not take place in isolation but is rather part of 'a public conversation with a communal audience'.[8] While this statement is made in *The Contemporary Medieval in Practice* with specific reference to Old English poetry, it is also reflective (intentionally or not) of perceptions of the role and value of academic scholarship as something that is – or should be – in dialogue with wider society and that responds to and seeks to solve societal issues.[9]

The notion of the 'value' of the humanities and of literature and literary scholarship has been addressed in both academic and public discourse in recent decades. Essays in *The Public Value of the Humanities*, edited by Jonathan Bate, offer justifications of the public importance of the humanities to society using case studies that draw on a wide range of disciplines, including those that lie on the boundaries of the humanities and social sciences, such as law and geography.[10] In *Literature and the Public Good*, Rick Rylance likewise argues for the 'deeply embedded and consequential' nature of literature, whose benefits are not simply a matter of 'academic' debate but are discussed 'by practitioners, policymakers, and politicians daily as well as ordinary people'.[11] Rylance's reflections are notable for the emphasis he places on the monetary value of the literary economy, which he reasons has been significantly under-appreciated, although, ultimately, he defines its significant worth in broader terms than the economic rationale to which public debates frequently turn. Academic arguments such as these have been repeatedly borne out by research-led projects that engage directly with societal issues, as exemplified by Impact Case Studies submitted for the UK's 2014 and 2021 Research Excellence Frameworks (REF), which encompass improvements to health and wellbeing;[12] public understanding of critical social issues;[13] and the promotion of the value of diverse literatures and cultures and of cross-cultural communication and collaboration.[14] The activities that comprise literary scholarship – among which I include reading, transcribing, translating, writing, editing and teaching, though others may be added – play a critical role in the creation and dissemination of knowledge both within and beyond academia, in policy, schools and the cultural sector. These activities play a particularly vital role in increasing awareness of the literatures of earlier historical periods and of other languages and cultures; in doing so, they enable conversations between peoples and cultures across time, place and language.

In this chapter, I discuss another recent 'critical conversation' with *Kalila wa Dimna* that provides new and unique insights into the power of literature when approached through interdisciplinary and collaborative methods. *Ancient Tales for Troubled Times* was an ambitious collaboration between academic researchers, UK-based and international artists, curators, community arts organisations and charities, and primary school pupils. The project engaged creatively with *Kalila wa Dimna* to examine important societal realities and issues. At the heart of the project lay issues of identity, community, migration, and intercultural and interpersonal relations – themes that are highly relevant on a global level as well as more locally to a city like London. Storytelling was another central focus: sites of shared heritage, stories provide a space in which to imagine who we are, who we want to be and how we relate to others; myths, plays, pictures, novels and histories are all 'among humankind's chief instruments for understanding ourselves and our world'.[15] The project sought to foreground the importance of historical literatures and to disseminate knowledge of a globally significant text that influenced European forms of storytelling and yet remains relatively unknown in the UK.

Development of *Ancient Tales for Troubled Times* began in 2019 as part of the Arts and Humanities Research Council project *Language Acts and Worldmaking* and culminated in a series of public events and an exhibition at the P21 Gallery in London, a charitable trust promoting contemporary Arab art and culture, between 12 May and 11 June 2022.[16] The exhibition was curated by Ghazaleh Zogheib and Rania Mneimneh and included artworks by artists DemaOne, Ali J. Dalloul, Rayan Elnayal, Alice Kettle in collaboration with 'Anna', a refugee from Syria, Jean Morris, Dima Nachawi and Vaishali Prazmari; members of East London Textile Arts (ELTA), a participatory project involving local communities in Newham led by artists Sonia Tuttiett and Celia Ward; a group of young people working with artist Dima Karout and musicians at Play for Progress, a Croydon-based charity that delivers therapeutic and educational music and arts programmes, advocacy and wellbeing support for unaccompanied young people seeking asylum in the UK; and a group of Year 6 pupils from Sir John Heron Primary School in Newham. The programme of online and in-person public events included creative workshops and demonstrations and conversations with artists, curators and researchers that focused on different thematic strands underpinning the exhibition: 'Reimagining spaces and restoring lost histories', 'Threading stories of friendship in textile art', 'Art practice in challenging environments' and 'Cross-cultural encounters in the medieval world'.[17]

Conversation, in both the modern and the medieval sense, lies at the heart of *Kalila wa Dimna*. The fables it relates are framed by a dialogue between a ruler and his counsellor, wherein the ruler asks questions or poses a problem to which the counsellor replies with an exemplary tale that provides guidance or resolution. The tales told by the counsellor frequently contain further nested stories, told in dialogue between characters to elucidate the ruler's conundrum, which often boils down to the very issues suggested by the medieval notion of 'conversation' given in the *OED*: 'dealing with others, living together, and to conduct, social as well as spiritual bearing, or behaviour in the world'. Many of the tales are narrated by animals, an ancient technique for thinking about and representing society and the nature of truth. Social relations are a core thematic concern: alliances and coexistence between different groups are shown to be possible, albeit sometimes only temporarily, under certain conditions – namely, the recognition and understanding of the interests and natures of others. *Kalila wa Dimna* uses storytelling to understand the world and other people, revealing the messy complexity of life, the multiplicity of perspectives and voices that comprise it, and the fact that there exists not one single truth but many. This is mirrored in the book's structure: the tales echo and refract, and at times contradict each other, in a conversation that takes place across multiple narrative levels. The book's transmission might also be characterised as a type of dialogue: it has been translated into more than forty languages and stands, according to one critic, as 'a remarkable document of the history of contacts between civilisations' – a history that is narrativised in the prologues to many of its translations, which offer metafictional accounts of its origins and global dissemination.[18]

The type of 'critical conversations' that Lees and Overing discuss in *The Contemporary Medieval in Practice* are not only between past and present, but between text (literature) and image (visual arts). For large portions of its history, *Kalila wa Dimna* was not only a work of literature but a work of art: the fables were transmitted alongside rich illustrative traditions in Persian, Arabic and Turkish manuscripts and, while perhaps not as striking or richly decorated, there exist illustrated Latin, Spanish and German manuscripts, and printed editions in German, Spanish, Latin, Italian and English that include woodcuts.[19] In his introduction, Ibn al-Muqaffa, the eighth-century Arabic translator, explains that one of the book's aims is 'to demonstrate the images of the animals by various kinds of colors and tints so that they may be appealing to the hearts of kings, who should have a strong desire to enjoy such pictures',[20] underscoring how *Kalila wa Dimna* was intended to capture readers' interest visually as much as textually. Illustrations, illuminations, woodcuts, annotations and other marginalia work together and, at times, against each other to interpret the fables and impart meaning. It is precisely because earlier literary works such as *Kalila wa Dimna* so often blend the textual and the visual that I would argue they lend themselves to creative explorations and why, perhaps, they continue to hold appeal in the hyper-visual societies of the twenty-first century.

Kalila wa Dimna's own mixed-media reception history offers a persuasive example of the benefits of 'critical conversations' that bring together literature and the visual arts. Such interdisciplinary conversations are not only productive but potentially transformative; they can unearth new ways of thinking about the arts and literature and highlight different perspectives on a range of issues. Katja Hilevaara and Emily Orley suggest that putting the visual and material arts into dialogue with the theoretical or the textual (a process they describe as 'conversational sparring'), 'enables a form of thinking and articulation beyond what is often conceivable on one's own'.[21] Elizabeth Benjamin and Sophie Corser argue similarly that

> the reinterpretation of a text by an artist, or an art object by an author, provokes not only an assessment of the new and original work, but also a reappraisal of art, literature, and the process of adaptation. The relationship prompts evaluations, and therefore a self-consciousness of both or either medium.[22]

The type of interdisciplinary approach discussed in this chapter 'encourages a questioning of how the activities of artists/authors and viewers/readers are linked in a progression of interpretation, reinterpretation, rewriting, and reimaging'.[23] These encounters take on even deeper significance when they place the past into dialogue with the present, as Lees and Overing discuss: 'The profound human dilemmas we now experience', they write, 'whether these be political, racial or environmental, are brought into sharp relief and are given a new affective and potentially activist dimension'.[24] It is with this activist spirit that *Ancient Tales for Troubled Times* evolved.

In *Ancient Tales for Troubled Times*, participating creative practitioners and organisations became *hakawatis* or 'tellers of tales', continuing *Kalila wa Dimna*'s tradition of using storytelling to understand the world. The project focused on one chapter from the book: the 'Tale of the Four Friends', a story about looking beyond perceived differences and working together to overcome adversity and build successful relationships with others. Like all chapters in *Kalila wa Dimna*, the 'Tale of the Four Friends' begins with a brief dialogue between the ruler and his counsellor. The ruler states that he wishes to hear an example of true friendship. His counsellor responds with a tale about a crow, a mouse, a tortoise and a deer. On the surface at least, the four principal characters appear too different to get along, yet over time they recognise each other's worth and come to a mutual understanding. The four animals are faced with a series of threats, represented in the story by the figure of a hunter, which they overcome by working together, exemplifying the moral of the fable that true friendships are strengthened by adversity. The events of the chapter take place in a landscape of persecution and fear in which the animals travel repeatedly from place to place to find safety. Encounters with others are, at first at least, frequently the cause of anxiety and mistrust – emotions that are overcome through conversation. Along the way, the animals debate the different types of friendship, loyalty and the value of reciprocity in companionship, as well as philosophical questions of material wealth and poverty, misfortune, ambition, destiny and the acquisition of wisdom. In the 'Tale of the Four Friends', storytelling lies at the heart of the animals' ability to see beyond their differences. As they recount their own personal histories and the journeys that have brought them together, they find common ground and create a community in which they are finally able to find peace. The journeys undertaken by the four friends are not only physical – from one place to another – but symbolic: from pessimism to acceptance of help; from ignorance to wisdom; from fear and persecution to safety and tranquillity; and from exile to companionship.

The creative process that resulted in *Ancient Tales for Troubled Times* was similarly rooted in conversation: mirroring *Kalila wa Dimna*'s dialogic form, participating practitioners and organisations explored the chapter collectively in research-led workshops; the *hakawatis* then read and reflected on the 'Tale of the Four Friends' individually or within their own respective communities. Through these conversations – with the text and with each other – they formulated creative responses that translated the tale into new forms to be 'read' anew by contemporary audiences. Like medieval and early modern commentators before them, the artworks of the *hakawatis* glossed the fable; the intralinear comments, amendments, marginalia and textual commentary of their predecessors replaced by new material forms of interpretation. These new creative responses featured animation (Dalloul and Nachawi), calligraffiti and sculpture (DemaOne), collage and blackout poetry (Morris), digital illustration (Elnayal), miniature oil painting (Prazmari), music, soundscapes, sketches and painting (Play for Progress), oral history (ELTA) and textiles (ELTA; Kettle and 'Anna').[25] Some of the artists engaged directly with medieval artistic forms and genres – calligraphy (DemaOne), cartography (Elnayal), manuscript illumination and illustration (Prazmari, DemaOne) and oral storytelling (Dalloul and Nachawi; ELTA) – while others did so indirectly. Many referenced different material and visual traditions, including Islamic arabesque geometry (DemaOne; ELTA; Kettle and 'Anna'), Syrian textile patterns (Kettle and 'Anna'), Indian and Persian miniature traditions and Chinese oil painting (Prazmari). Mirroring the plurality of perspectives and truths contained in *Kalila wa Dimna*'s labyrinthine structure, each piece represented one of many simultaneous dialogues with these ancient fables that, when brought together, created a powerful whole.

What emerged out of this creative engagement with the book illustrates the fruitfulness of the sorts of collaborations set out by Lees and Overing, Hilevaara and Orley, and Benjamin and Corser. The artworks produced for the exhibition are a compelling example of the rich potential of earlier literatures to serve as 'conversation-starters', engendering discussions about contemporary issues while also highlighting the historical continuities of these topics. Feedback received from visitors to the exhibition demonstrates the effectiveness of this type of interdisciplinary approach for developing public understanding of an ancient literary text. *Ancient Tales for Troubled Times* sought to encourage audiences to reflect on who we are as a society and how we live alongside those who appear to be different, and to highlight the importance of non-European literatures at a time of cultural, social and political division. Visitors acknowledged that they were 'unfamiliar about the topics discussed and exhibited [beforehand] but [felt] very informed' afterwards; that they 'left with a lot to digest and think about'. In response to artworks that examined the important role that stories can play in community building and in finding one's way in the world through different languages (ELTA; Kettle and 'Anna'; Play for Progress), one visitor remarked that the exhibition 'made me think about the connections between friendship and community defence in a deeply historical way. It also helped me think about storytelling as a genre that helps to root/build identity without centering an individual self'; another commented that, 'It was interesting that the exhibition brought out the themes of diversity, tolerance, combatting ignorance/misapprehension of the "other" – how the story can be used as a "bridge" to bring people of different backgrounds together.' The mobility and movement that characterises the 'Tale of the Four Friends' also defines the lived experiences of many people globally today: some of the artists addressed this by playing with perspective and subject position, evoking feelings of dislocation, uncertainty and fear (DemaOne; Elnayal; Play for Progress; Prazmari); others explored the pain of forced displacement as a result of poverty (Morris). This topic significantly impacted exhibition visitors, who recognised 'the importance and relevance of stories like *Kalila wa Dimna* for issues around migration and belonging' and remarked that they 'would have probably not realised its ability to explore migration issues with such depth'. Other *hakawatis* foreground the symbolic associations between the weaving of stories and the weaving of threads, positioning textile art as a form of collaborative working that exemplifies the moral of the tale (Kettle and 'Anna'; ELTA). This approach also resonated with the exhibition's audience, with one visitor remarking that, 'There was something very striking about the consistent sight of weaving that came together with translation and retelling quite movingly.'

The impact of this type of interdisciplinary approach to literature and culture is also evident in the experiences of the collaborating organisations. At Play for Progress, young people seeking asylum explored the 'Tale of the Four Friends' with artists and musicians in weekly, after-school creative programmes. The charity's founder Alyson Frazier remarked that, 'The themes of cooperation and community and storytelling more generally always feature in our work but were more explicitly explored this project.

One line of the story that really struck home with us was "in your anxiety to escape, do not forget to help one another."'[26] The process of engaging with these ancient tales facilitated the group's relationship-building, their exchange of ideas, stories and experiences, and their practice of self-expression.[27] This was the first time that young people from Play for Progress had been part of an exhibition in a central London gallery, and they expressed great pride, joy, and even disbelief upon seeing their work publicly displayed. Frazier also remarked that 'being placed within a larger global context felt right' for the charity, and that this type of collaborative exhibition – on a larger scale than they were typically part of – offered 'a great opportunity' to publicise their work.[28]

Similar sentiments were expressed by Year 6 pupils and teachers at Sir John Heron Primary School in Newham who took part in workshops in October 2021, co-developed with artist Sonia Tuttiett from ELTA. The workshops sought to engage students with literature and the visual arts in a fun way, and to highlight the creative potential of storytelling (visual, textual and oral) to explore important issues such as identity, community, home and migration. These issues speak to the PSHE (personal, social, health and economic) curriculum as well as to the lived experiences of many schoolchildren in London, including some of the students in this class, whose families had experienced migration or forced displacement. The activities sought to encourage multiliteracy in the visual arts and literature, drawing on home and heritage material cultures and languages (many of the children spoke a language other than English and had learned English after coming to the UK). Finally, the workshops aimed to give students an opportunity to explore their creativity by making artworks that would be shown in the exhibition at the P21 Gallery. This was an important aspect of the project: Newham has some of the lowest levels of cultural engagement in London, and children in this multicultural and multilingual borough have fewer opportunities to participate in or benefit from creative practices.[29]

In response to group discussions about the importance of stories and storytelling, the history of *Kalila wa Dimna*, the 'Tale of the Four Friends' and the themes of the project, the Year 6 pupils produced calligrams, poems and short prose pieces. Many were profoundly moving.[30] The children also created visual artworks in response to the fable, decorating cloth figures that were sewn together in a chain, like textile 'paper dolls', to symbolise how individuals, societies and cultures are connected and interdependent. Pupils drew inspiration from textiles, decorative arts and symbols from across the world, as well as illustrations depicting *Kalila wa Dimna* in medieval manuscripts. Many pupils looked to their own heritages for inspiration, for example, borrowing from Pakistani truck art or Latvian textile patterns; others incorporated keywords relating to the themes of home, identity, community and friendship in languages they spoke at home (Urdu, Pashto, Bengali) or were learning (German, Korean, Japanese). When visiting the P21 Gallery with their teachers, the children were visibly proud to see their work exhibited publicly alongside that of professional artists, and many were excited to see themselves and their families' experiences, languages and cultures represented. Visitor feedback foregrounded the children's artwork as a particular highlight of the exhibition. Pupils likewise described the workshops as 'fun', 'creative' and 'joyful', and commented that working with literature in this way had encouraged them to explore more stories and art forms from around the world and made them think differently about how to be creative with languages. Teachers at the school also recognised the educational potential of using the visual arts in conjunction with literature to support multiple areas of the curriculum and as a way of engaging students from diverse backgrounds: one teacher commented that the workshops were 'Such a powerful way to engage children in all aspects of teaching' that they 'might use this to plan similar projects in school'. The work produced by the children was displayed in Sir John Heron Primary's corridors for other members of the community to view as part of the school's drive to promote cross-cultural understanding and learning through literature, history and the arts, and to inculcate in pupils a sense of community and pride both personally and in their academic work.

Also based in Newham, East London Textile Arts works with diverse groups of all abilities and backgrounds in the local community. The use of a literary text as the starting point for their creative practice was a new way of working for ELTA, which the group's leaders have since incorporated into subsequent projects.[31] In a blog post about their experience of working with *Kalila wa Dimna*, Sonia Tuttiett, co-founder and lead textile artist, wrote that engaging directly with a literary text had added depth to their creative work: 'we had some lively discussions that engaged people's interest before we started trying to bring the story to life through our stitching'.[32] For some members of the collective, *Kalila wa Dimna* held personal significance: in some cases, it resonated with personal experiences of migration; others recalled reading the book in school or hearing its stories read aloud when young. The pieces created by members of ELTA for the exhibition both reflected and reached out to communities in Newham: in one, embroiderers from the group produced costumes of the four animal characters and the hunter, which were worn during a performance of the fable by a local drama group for adults with learning disabilities; another, a fifteen-minute film titled *Migration Tales*, featured accounts of lived experiences of migration told by members of the group. These testimonies provided glimpses of the human reality behind statistics of migration, individualising those who are so often perceived as an impersonal multitude. The artworks produced by ELTA's members create a space in which local stories intersect with global literatures and cultures. To ensure that they reached communities in Newham who were unlikely to travel into central London to visit the exhibition at the P21 Gallery, ELTA exhibited their work in Stratford Library in Autumn 2022, engaging a local audience with *Kalila wa Dimna* and the issues explored by the project, and promoting local community-based creative practice.

Even more poignantly, in her blog post Sonia describes how working with the fables provided a shared experience of community and joy during the COVID-19 pandemic – a period of fear, instability, isolation and, for some, very real danger, that echoed the struggles faced by characters in the 'Tale of the Four Friends':

> As I reflect back on the experience of running East London Textiles Arts throughout the pandemic, I realise that we were not only considering how to illustrate the 'Tale of the Four Friends' through embroidery, but at a much deeper level these stories of co-operation, loyalty and ingenuity related in such a significant way to our collective experience of living through the uncertainty and fear around COVID and the restrictions on freedom it brought with it. [. . .] As we worked away at the embroideries, unable to meet in person during lockdown, we found new ways in which to connect, communicate, work together, and encourage one another, centred around our work on the fables. [. . .] Coming out of this time, we all have a new story to tell of how we have been affected by the pandemic and its consequences. The embroidery group became very important as a virtual social space through Zoom and WhatsApp at a time when we weren't

> able to meet in person. The personal stories of coping, of loss, of family and friends, as well as the embroidery, became the thread that bound us all together. Without the embroidery and knitting, I think that our conversations would have petered out fairly quickly. It's the *Kalila* stories, the creating and making, the discussion and debate, the positivity of a project to focus on that kept our group alive and able to weather those difficult times together.

Sonia's reflection on ELTA's work for *Ancient Tales for Troubled Times* communicates the contemplative, meditative aspect of engaging with literature, of sharing stories, listening, inviting conversation; a process that has ancient roots.[33] Alice Kettle, another of the project's *hakawatis*, describes the creativity of craft 'as a common language' that 'extends to become a multi-cultural, totally inclusive connecting force which can affect change'.[34] Sonia's description of storytelling as a means of creating and sustaining community – as being 'the thread that bound us all together' – echoes the message of the 'Tale of the Four Friends': that conversation lies at the heart of the animals' ability to see beyond their differences and find peace and companionship. Most relevant, perhaps, for the discussions in this chapter, her words offer a powerful statement about literature's potential for real-world impact.

These types of 'critical conversations' that bring into dialogue past and present, literature and the visual arts, and research and creative practice can be highly beneficial for scholars of ancient literatures, offering different and even unexpected perspectives and bringing to light comparisons and connections that may not be so evident when texts are approached solely through an academic lens. Creative responses to literary works can furthermore provide a fruitful way of thinking about how and why literatures travel and evolve, about the global circulation and reception of works like *Kalila wa Dimna* that have undergone complex histories of transmission and taken on a cultural life of their own.[35] Creating conversations between the visual arts and literary research serves as a reminder that the texts we study cannot be separated from the material conditions of their production and transmission, that there is more to literature than the words on the page and that words live through the bodies and groups that speak and perform them in their everyday creative interactions and encounters with past and present worlds.

Notes

1 The Barbican, *The Mirror for Princes – Kalila wa Dimna*, 10–27 May 2006. Written and directed by Sulayman Al-Bassam and commissioned by Sheikha Hussa Sabah Al-Salem Al-Sabah. Co-produced by Dar al-Athar al-Islamiyyah (Kuwait), Tokyo International Arts Festival and barbicanbite06.

2 https://web.archive.org/web/20160609193009/http://www.sabab.org/the-mirror-for-princes-kalila-wa-dimna/ [page archived 9 January 2016; retrieved 9 January 2025].

3 BBC Radio 3, Nightwaves, interview by Gabriel Gbadamosi (9 May 2006), https://web.archive.org/web/20140206222622/http://www.sabab.org/wp-content/uploads/2012/03/BBCRadio3_NightWaves.pdf [page archived 9 January 2016; retrieved 9 January 2025].

4 Oxford English Dictionary, s.v. 'objectify (v.), sense 1,' December 2023, doi:10.1093/OED/8688003935.

5 For details of Adwan's opera: https://festival-aix.com/en/programmation/opera/kalila-wa-dimna [accessed 17 June 2026]. The production can be viewed on YouTube: https://www.youtube.com/watch?v=SsdQotHWP8o [accessed 17 June 2026]. The *Fables Across Time* exhibition ran April–October 2015 in Manama, Bahrain, and March–June 2016 at the Children's Museum of Indianapolis; Al Khemir's animations in both English and Arabic can be found on YouTube, along with other animations aimed at children, which are still popular today in the Arabic speaking world.

6 Clare Lees and Gillian R. Overing, *The Contemporary Medieval in Practice* (UCL Press, 2019), p. 1.

7 Lees and Overing, *The Contemporary Medieval*, p. 44.

8 Lees and Overing, *The Contemporary Medieval*, p. 45.

9 The concept of scholarship as a conversation is not new; Kenneth Burke used the metaphor in what has come to be known as the 'Burkean Parlour Model'. Kenneth Burke, *The Philosophy of Literary Form: Studies in Symbolic Action* 3rd ed. (University of California Press, 1973).

10 Jonathan Bate ed., *The Public Value of the Humanities* (Bloomsbury, 2011).

11 Rick Rylance, *Literature and the Public Good* (Oxford University Press, 2016), pp. 5–7.

12 See, for example, the case studies submitted by University of Central Lancashire, 'Stories By, With, and For Disadvantaged Young People: Collaborative Literacies For Social and Personal Change', https://results2021.ref.ac.uk/impact/03b0d35b-150f-4d3d-8147-97ef20817d64 [accessed 26 March 2026]; University of Central Lancashire, 'Poetry, Grief and Healing', https://results2021.ref.ac.uk/impact/5059a81d-f89f-47d9-8934-695f347fac42 [accessed 26 March 2026]; University of Leeds, 'Applying a New Model of Bibliotherapy to Improve the Mental Well-being of Asylum Seekers and Refugees', https://impact.ref.ac.uk/casestudies/CaseStudy.aspx?Id=6382

[accessed 26 March 2026]; University of Leeds, 'Representing Autism: Using Cultural Narrative to Change Medical Practice, Creative and Artistic Production, and Inform and Stimulate Public Debate of the Condition', https://impact.ref.ac.uk/casestudies/CaseStudy.aspx?Id=6380 [accessed 26 March 2026].

13 For example, the case studies submitted by Bath Spa University, 'Changing Practice: Bringing Arts and Humanities Perspectives on Nature, Wellbeing and Environmental Crisis Into New Spaces', https://results2021.ref.ac.uk/impact/1916e50e-4af7-47fc-b5f9-ca5b80a3861a [accessed 26 March 2026]; Newman University, 'Contemporary Literature and Discourses of Race and Identity', https://impact.ref.ac.uk/casestudies/CaseStudy.aspx?Id=29888 [accessed 26 March 2026]; University of Exeter, 'Exeter Centre for Literatures of Identity, Place, and Sustainability: Informing and Influencing Public Debates on Regional and National Identity', https://impact.ref.ac.uk/casestudies/CaseStudy.aspx?Id=39780 [accessed 26 March 2026]; and University of Warwick, 'Representing Islam: Challenging Preconceptions, Strengthening Empathy, Empowering Voices', https://results2021.ref.ac.uk/impact/0a932893-f160-4c28-8543-aedd523df6e4 [accessed 26 March 2026].

14 See, for example, the case studies submitted by University of Bristol, 'African Print Activism: Making the Work and Heritage of African Literary Enterprises Visible and Sustainable', https://results2021.ref.ac.uk/impact/70fa1336-cd2f-4a32-8f33-577957c958f7 [accessed 26 March 2026]; Nottingham Trent University, 'The Changing Wor(l)ds Partnership: Enabling Cultural Self-Representation for Marginalised Communities', https://results2021.ref.ac.uk/impact/ca885587-d3c0-4b90-a17d-35bc5053c3ac [accessed 26 March 2026]; Teesside University, 'Muslims Writing Britain', https://impact.ref.ac.uk/casestudies/CaseStudy.aspx?Id=30192 [accessed 26 March 2026]; University of Nottingham, 'Improved Mediation Outcomes Through an Enhanced Understanding of the Cultural Aspects of Translation and Interpretation', https://impact.ref.ac.uk/casestudies/CaseStudy.aspx?Id=39940 [accessed 26 March 2026].

15 Bate, *The Public Value*, p. 1.

16 *Ancient Tales for Troubled Times* was funded principally by Arts Council England and *Language Acts and Worldmaking* (https://languageacts.org/) [accessed 5 June 2026]. Individual activities were also supported with further funding from the University Council for Modern Languages (UCML) and Centre for Visual Cultures at Royal Holloway, University of London. East London Textile Arts was funded by the De Laszlo Foundation, John Cutforth Charitable Foundation, Arts Council England, The National Lottery Fund and Art Workers' Guild.

17 For information about the project's events, see: https://www.kalilawadimnaexhibit.com/exhibition-events [accessed 17 June 2026]. Recordings of the talks can be accessed online: https://www.kalilawadimnaexhibit.com/online-events [accessed 26 March 2026].

18 François De Blois, *Burzoy's Voyage and the Origin of the Book of* Kalilah wa Dimnah (Royal Asiatic Society, 1990), p. iii. I have addressed this elsewhere – see Rachel Scott, 'Framing Intercultural Encounters in Three Iberian Translations of *Kalila wa-Dimna*', in *The Routledge Companion to Medieval Iberia: Unity in Diversity*, ed. by E. Michael Gerli and Ryan D. Giles (Routledge, 2021), pp. 508–27;

'Translating an Oriental Frame Tale and its Translator in Hapsburg Spain: The Prefaces to the *Espejo político y moral*' (1654, 1659), *Bulletin of Hispanic Studies*, 97.7 (2020), pp. 699–714.

19 On the Arabic, Persian and Turkish illustrative traditions, see Bernard O'Kane, *Early Persian Painting:* Kalila and Dimna *Manuscripts of the Late-Fourteenth Century* (I. B. Tauris, 2003); '*Kalila wa Dimna* iii. Illustrations', *Encyclopædia Iranica*, Vol. XV, Fasc. 4 (2010), pp. 395–7, https://www.iranicaonline.org/articles/kalila-wa-demna-iii/ [accessed 30 April 2025]. The fables even acquired a material life quite separate from the written text, appearing in statues, frescos and staircases, on which see Simona Cohen and Housni Alkhateeb Shehada, 'From the *Panchatantra* to La Fontaine: Migrations of Didactic Animal Illustrations from India to the West', *Artibus Asiae*, 77.1 (2017), pp. 5–68.

20 Louis Cheiko cited in Anna Contadini, 'Intertextual Animals: Illustrated *Kalīla wa-Dimna* Manuscripts in Context', in *Les périples de Kalila et Dimna: Quand les fables voyagent dans la littérature et les arts du monde islamique* (Brill, 2022), pp. 95–129 (p. 104).

21 Katja Hilevaara and Emily Orley (eds), *The Creative Critic: Writing as/about Practice* (Routledge, 2018), pp. 9–10.

22 Elizabeth Benjamin and Sophie Corser, 'Literature and Art: Conversations and Collaborations', *MHRA Working Papers in the Humanities*, 9 (2014), pp. 1–8 (p. 2).

23 Benjamin and Corser, 'Literature and Art', p. 3. The advantages of bringing together the study of languages and literatures with the visual arts, for example, in primary and secondary education, have also been established by Marilyn Fryer, *Creative Teaching and Learning* (Chapman, 1996); *Creativity and Cultural Diversity* (Creativity Centre Educational Trust, 2004); Nancy Lampert, 'Enhancing Critical Thinking with Aesthetic, Critical, and Creative Inquiry', *Art Education*, 59.5 (2006), pp. 46–50; Lynn C. Hartle, Patricia Pinciotti, and Rebecca L. Gorton, 'ArtsIN: Arts Integration and Infusion Framework', *Early Childhood Education Journal*, 43 (2015), pp. 289–98; and the 1999 *All Our Futures* report by the National Advisory Committee on Creative and Cultural Education.

24 Lees and Overing, *The Contemporary Medieval*, p. 98.

25 For details of the artists and their work, see: https://www.kalilawadimnaexhibit.com/all-artists-contributors [accessed 17 June 2026].

26 Personal correspondence.

27 For details of the work produced by young people with Play for Progress, see: https://www.kalilawadimnaexhibit.com/play-for-progress [accessed 17 June 2026].

28 Personal correspondence.

29 According to Creative Newham, an independent alliance of arts, cultural, educational, social and voluntary organisations committed to growing and strengthening cultural mobility in all its forms in Newham, 'Cultural investment in the borough is amongst the lowest in London and as a consequence Newham has the second lowest level of cultural engagement of all the London boroughs at 36.6%' (https://www.creativenewham.com/about [accessed 30 April 2025]). The borough was identified as a priority area for arts investment by Arts Council England in 2021: https://www.newham.gov.uk/news/article/695/newham-identified-as-a-priority-area-for-arts-investment-by-arts-council-england [accessed 17 June 2026].

30 The Sir John Heron pupils who took part in the workshop were Sulaiman, Liyana, Saffiyah, Khizar, Fairin, Jamilah, Imtiaz, Tahmid, Zubair, Zainab, Lakhbir, Mobinal, Eliza, Tanzila and Megy. A report on the workshop can be found online: https://www.kalilawadimnaexhibit.com/the-arts-of-storytelling [accessed 17 June 2026].

31 Personal correspondence.

32 To read the entire blogpost see: https://www.kalilawadimnaexhibit.com/stitching-in-a-pandemic-kalila-wa-dimna-in-the-community. For details of the work produced by East London Textile Arts, see: https://www.kalilawadimnaexhibit.com/elta [accessed 17 June 2026].

33 See Lees and Overing, *The Contemporary Medieval*, p. 45, who note: 'Practices of contemplation, meditation and conversation are shared by the medieval and modern, contemporary worlds.'

34 Alice Kettle, 'Creativity', in *Transnational Modern Languages: A Handbook*, ed. by Jennifer Burns and Derek Duncan (Liverpool University Press, 2022), pp. 77–86 (p. 78).

35 Another work of world literature with a similar 'afterlife', inspiring countless artistic and literary responses, is *The Arabian Nights*; on which see Wen-Chin Ouyang, 'Metamorphoses of Scheherazade in Literature and Film', *Bulletin of SOAS*, 66.3 (2003), pp. 402–18; and Sandra Naddaf, '*The Thousand and One Nights* As World Literature (Part IV): The Geographical Dimension', in *The Routledge Companion to World Literature*, ed. by Theo D'haen, David Damrosch, and Djelal Kadir (Routledge, 2011), pp. 487–96.

References

Atil, Esin, *Kalila wa Dimna: Fables from a Fourteenth Century Arabic Manuscript* (Smithsonian Institution Press, 1989)

Bate, Jonathan, (ed.), *The Public Value of the Humanities* (Bloomsbury, 2011)

Bath Spa University, 'Changing Practice: Bringing Arts and Humanities Perspectives on Nature, Wellbeing and Environmental Crisis into New Spaces' (2021), https://results2021.ref.ac.uk/impact/1916e50e-4af7-47fc-b5f9-ca5b80a3861a [accessed 26 March 2026]

Benjamin, Elizabeth, and Sophie Corser, 'Literature and Art: Conversations and Collaborations', *MHRA Working Papers in the Humanities*, 9 (2014), pp. 1–8

Burke, Kenneth, *The Philosophy of Literary Form: Studies in Symbolic Action* 3rd ed. (University of California Press, 1973)

Cheiko, Louis, *La version arabe de Kalīlah et Dimnah d'aprés le plus ancien manuscrit árabe daté* (Imprimerie Catholique, 1905)

Cohen, Simona, and Housni Alkhateeb Shehada, 'From the *Panchatantra* to La Fontaine: Migrations of Didactic Animal Illustrations from India to the West', *Artibus Asiae*, 77.1 (2017), pp. 5–68

Contadini, Anna, 'Intertextual Animals: Illustrated *Kalīla wa-Dimna* Manuscripts in Context', in *Les périples de Kalila et Dimna: Quand les fables voyagent dans la littérature et les arts du monde islamique* (Brill, 2022), pp. 95–129

De Blois, François, *Burzoy's Voyage and the Origin of the Book of Kalilah wa Dimnah* (Royal Asiatic Society, 1990)

Fryer, Marilyn, *Creative Teaching and Learning* (Chapman, 1996)

Fryer, Marilyn, *Creativity and Cultural Diversity* (Creativity Centre Educational Trust, 2004)

Hartle, Lynn C., Patricia Pinciotti, and Rebecca L. Gorton, 'ArtsIN: Arts Integration and Infusion Framework', *Early Childhood Education Journal*, 43 (2015), pp. 289–98, doi:10.1007/s10643-014-0636-7

Hilevaara, Katja, and Emily Orley eds, *The Creative Critic: Writing as/about Practice* (Routledge, 2018)

Kettle, Alice, 'Creativity', in *Transnational Modern Languages: A Handbook*, ed. by Jennifer Burns and Derek Duncan (Liverpool University Press, 2022), pp. 77–86

Lampert, Nancy, 'Enhancing Critical Thinking with Aesthetic, Critical, and Creative Inquiry', *Art Education*, 59.5 (2006), pp. 46–50, doi:10.1080/00043125.2005.11651611

Lees, Clare and Gillian R. Overing, *The Contemporary Medieval in Practice* (UCL Press, 2019), doi:10.14324/111.9781787354654

Naddaf, Sandra, '*The Thousand and One Nights as World Literature* (Part IV): The Geographical Dimension', in *The Routledge Companion to World Literature*, ed. by Theo D'haen, David Damrosch, and Djelal Kadir (Routledge, 2011), pp. 487–96

National Advisory Committee on Creative and Cultural Education (NACCCE), *All Our Futures: Creativity, Culture and Education* report (1999)

Newman University, 'Contemporary Literature and Discourses of Race and Identity' (2014), https://impact.ref.ac.uk/casestudies/CaseStudy.aspx?Id=29888 [accessed 26 March 2026]

Nottingham Trent University, 'The Changing Wor(l)ds Partnership: Enabling Cultural Self-Representation for Marginalised Communities' (2021), https://results2021.ref.ac.uk/impact/ca885587-d3c0-4b90-a17d-35bc5053c3ac [accessed 26 March 2026]

O'Kane, Bernard, *Early Persian Painting:* Kalila and Dimna *Manuscripts of the Late-Fourteenth Century* (I. B. Tauris, 2003)

O'Kane, Bernard, '*Kalila wa Dimna* iii. Illustrations', *Encyclopædia Iranica*, Vol. XV, Fasc. 4 (2010), pp. 395–7, https://www.iranicaonline.org/articles/kalila-wa-demna-iii/ [accessed 30 April 2025]

Ouyang, Wen-Chin, 'Metamorphoses of Scheherazade in Literature and Film', *Bulletin of SOAS*, 66.3 (2003), pp. 402–18

Rylance, Rick, *Literature and the Public Good* (Oxford University Press, 2016)

Scott, Rachel, 'Framing Intercultural Encounters in Three Iberian Translations of *Kalila wa-Dimna*', in *The Routledge Companion to Medieval Iberia: Unity in Diversity*, ed. by E. Michael Gerli and Ryan D. Giles (Routledge, 2021), pp. 508–27

Scott, Rachel, 'Translating an Oriental Frame Tale and its Translator in Hapsburg Spain: The Prefaces to the *Espejo político y moral*' (1654, 1659), *Bulletin of Hispanic Studies*, 97.7 (2020), pp. 699–714

Teesside University, 'Muslims Writing Britain' (2014), https://impact.ref.ac.uk/casestudies/CaseStudy.aspx?Id=30192 [accessed 26 March 2026]

University of Bristol, 'African Print Activism: Making the Work and Heritage of African Literary Enterprises Visible and Sustainable' (2021), https://results2021.ref.ac.uk/impact/70fa1336-cd2f-4a32-8f33-577957c958f7 [accessed 26 March 2026]

University of Central Lancashire, 'Poetry, Grief and Healing' (2021a), https://results2021.ref.ac.uk/impact/5059a81d-f89f-47d9-8934-695f347fac42 [accessed 26 March 2026]

University of Central Lancashire, 'Stories By, With, and For Disadvantaged Young People: Collaborative Literacies for Social and Personal Change' (2021b), https://results2021.ref.ac.uk/impact/03b0d35b-150f-4d3d-8147-97ef20817d64 [accessed 26 March 2026]

University of Exeter, 'Exeter Centre for Literatures of Identity, Place, and Sustainability: Informing and Influencing Public Debates on Regional and National Identity' (2014), https://impact.ref.ac.uk/casestudies/CaseStudy.aspx?Id=39780 [accessed 26 March 2026]

University of Leeds, 'Applying a New Model of Bibliotherapy to Improve the Mental Well-being of Asylum Seekers and Refugees' (2014), https://impact.ref.ac.uk/casestudies/CaseStudy.aspx?Id=6382 [accessed 26 March 2026]

University of Leeds, 'Representing Autism: Using Cultural Narrative to Change Medical Practice, Creative and Artistic Production, and Inform and Stimulate Public Debate of the Condition' (2014), https://impact.ref.ac.uk/casestudies/CaseStudy.aspx?Id=6380 [accessed 26 March 2026]

University of Nottingham, 'Improved Mediation Outcomes Through an Enhanced Understanding of the Cultural Aspects of Translation and Interpretation' (2014), https://impact.ref.ac.uk/casestudies/CaseStudy.aspx?Id=39940 [accessed 26 March 2026]

University of Warwick, 'Representing Islam: Challenging Preconceptions, Strengthening Empathy, Empowering Voices' (2021), https://results2021.ref.ac.uk/impact/0a932893-f160-4c28-8543-aedd523df6e4 [accessed 26 March 2026]

Chapter 10

Fox tales, community concerns: why collaborative storytelling matters

Anja Rekeszus

Introduction

This chapter tells a story of unexpected findings, and of how remaining open to what creative critical work has to tell us can lead us down exciting new pathways. Between October 2024 and March 2025, the project 'Retelling the Urban Fox: A Collaborative Fairy Tale' set out to explore the power of fairy tales to impact humans' relationships with urban biodiversity – more specifically with urban foxes. Foxes have played a central role in historical and contemporary fairy tales across different media: we find foxes in popular medieval narratives such as *Reynard the Fox* (twelfth century), in the character of Mr Tod in Beatrix Potter's stories (1912), all the way to Wes Anderson's well-known, contemporary film *Fantastic Mr Fox* (2009), based on Roald Dahl's book of the same name (1970). In these tales, foxes are depicted to incorporate a multitude of different attributes, such as cunning and intelligence, but also bravery and insightfulness.

Such nuance is rarely found in public discourse on urban foxes. Despite an increase in research that acknowledges these animals as an integral part of biodiverse urban ecosystems,[1] many city-dwelling humans continue to view them as invasive and threatening 'pests'.[2] The perception of urban foxes in London poses a particularly potent example for these negative associations; media discourses of recent years have reinforced one-sided narratives of urban foxes, accusing them, for instance, of carrying rabies and other dangerous diseases.[3] An especially prominent assault on the reputation of urban foxes was a series of reports of alleged 'baby-snatching' incidents according to which these animals had broken into homes to attack babies and small children. For the most part, these claims were shown to be either unfounded or blown out of proportion;[4] however, a study undertaken by the *Daily Telegraph* in reaction to one specific fox attack in 2010 suggested that it left a negative impact on city-dwellers' perceptions of foxes, and wildlife in general.[5]

'Retelling the Urban Fox' sought to explore the extent to which these negative depictions were reflected in the views of the project's participant base, and whether writing fairy tales about urban foxes, given these animals' long-standing tradition as story protagonists, would impact these views. In literary studies, fairy tales are often attributed an 'explanatory and utopian core' that enables those telling or writing them to envision possible and desirable futures[6] – a phenomenon that Marek Oziewicz terms the 'anticipatory imagination' evoked by folk and fairy tales.[7] In fairy tales, an 'intentional synthesis of magic with the concretely mundane' takes place to tell stories that speak to contemporary concerns such as food and financial scarcity or poor family relations.[8] In his article 'The Meaning of Fairy Tale within the Evolution of Culture', Jack Zipes draws on a broad range of cultural historians such as Walter Burkert to show how 'tales can be related to basic human needs, rituals, customs, and the resolution of problems in human adaptation to changing environments'.[9]

The fairy tale's enduring relevance in human culture – evident in a constant stream of newly produced films, video games and written fairy tales – is, to a large degree, due to its adaptability.[10] In her article 'Why Fairy Tales Matter: The Performative and the Transformative', Maria Tatar points out how 'the stories themselves function as shape-shifters, morphing into new versions of themselves as they are retold and as they migrate into other media'.[11] This quality, in turn, is rooted in its accessibility as a genre: having been traded orally and across different media for centuries, fairy tales share a set of narrative elements such as characters, tropes and types of plot progression that are recognisable even across cultural spheres,[12] making them easy to discuss and adapt in groups of people from different backgrounds. These qualities of the fairy tale have made it a popular genre for use in creative, community-based and action research. Vivian Labrie, for instance, found that using folk tales in her research gave rise to 'fresh frames of reference that allowed collective thinking outside the box and long-lasting appropriations of specific issues'.[13]

This focus on specific issues has been applied successfully to environmental topics and issues. Both Rachel Harcourt and others, as well as Else Talgorn and Helle Ullerup, undertook studies in which participants explored desirable environmental futures by telling stories about climate adaptation from the planet's perspective, thus encouraging empathy for non-human actors.[14] In an energy research context, Sea Rotmann explored the uses of a fairy tale 'story spine' for the co-design of more effective behavioural interventions,[15] while researchers at the University of Lancaster mobilised fairy tale characters as metaphors for existing research around renewables, cars and plastics in order to communicate energy research and facilitate adaptation processes.[16]

My use of fairy tales for 'Retelling the Urban Fox' was also based on my own research, which showcases how fairy tales were used by nineteenth-century women to engage with contemporary discourses on gender and national identity.[17] As a literary scholar and cultural historian by training, I was keen to employ my skills of literary and narrative analysis within the context of creative data gathering, and to make use of the accessibility of the fairy tale – and the fox's long-standing role within it – to examine if and how creating literature can impact community members' views on the urban biodiversity surrounding them.

However, as the project unfolded, it became clear to me that there were broader implications emerging from it that spoke to the potential of literature, and literary research, for social and societal change. Apart from providing insights into participants' perceptions of urban foxes, the project also provided insight into the value of literary production in the form of collaborative storytelling. As this chapter will show, the genre of the fairy tale and the ways in which participants interacted with it were central to the creative processes that emerged from the storytelling activities. This chapter will use critical reflection as well as narrative analysis on the qualitative data collected to showcase two important creative processes that emerged throughout the workshop: exploring community needs and navigating difficult conversations. In so doing, the chapter discusses the value of literature and literary research within the context of creative data collection using storytelling.

Project setup and participant base

'Retelling the Urban Fox' consisted of three stages. Stages one and three involved surveys, one to be completed before the storytelling workshop and one after, which asked participants to respond to a series of questions and prompts. The surveys drew on mixed methods taken from the social sciences and anthropology, as well as creative approaches to data collection. They included, for example, Likert scales which asked participants to respond to statements on urban foxes, such as 'I am worried that urban foxes will harm people, animals or objects I care about', indicating the extent of their agreement with the prompt on a scale from 1 to 7. A large portion of the surveys used methods of creative and poetic inquiry; for instance, participants were asked to describe an imagined situation involving an urban fox, based on an image they were provided with.[18] In addition to the surveys, a fairy tale writing workshop, held in February 2025, formed the centrepiece and stage two of the project. Here, artist and storyteller Elizabeth Dearnley provided insight into the history and roles of foxes in folk and fairy tales since the Middle Ages.[19] Workshop participants were then invited to compose individual vignettes on urban foxes using prompts provided by rolls of a dice. Groups of participants were then formed and collaboratively wrote their own fairy tales on urban foxes, some of which will be cited in this chapter. By combining quantitative methods with creative ones in this way, I sought to retain 'complexity, ambiguity and openness', which Cate Watson names as the prime benefits resulting from creative methods such as poetic enquiry.[20]

This project's participant base was located in Southwark, a highly diverse borough in the south-east of London;[21] apart from being a participatory project, the storytelling workshop brought community members from different backgrounds together in the premises of the Centre for Wildlife Gardening, run by the London Wildlife Trust. In this way, participants were not only able to meet and interact with each other, but also engaged with a free-of-cost nature resource in their area which, itself, draws on community members and volunteers to ensure its continuing existence.

Participants were recruited via a range of social media channels (including the Nextdoor app and local Facebook groups), newsletters (for example, Southwark Cathedral) and physical posters placed in libraries and on public notice boards. In spite of the £100 recompensation offered in the hope of recruiting participants with a wide range of views on urban foxes, most participants (85%) arrived with an overall favourable view on these animals, according to Likert scales included in the project's first survey. For potential future iterations of this project, it would be interesting to run more targeted rounds of recruitment in order to attain a more balanced range of views and assess the impact this has on the tales created by participants.

Exploring community issues: subverting and abiding by the fairy tale form

> *We are on Rye Lane. A family of foxes goes up to the bin to have a little rummage, and finds the latest edition of Southwark News. The headline says: 'Southwark Takes a Stand on Bin Menaces', with a picture of a fox rummaging through a bin. The council wants to get rid of the bins and replace them with new ones with lids on them. The foxes are very angry, because this is where they get some of their food, and they are being portrayed as evil, and that's not who they are. So they rally foxes across London, and they have a meet at Peckham Levels and they make a really compelling speech to organise a protest. They get together and make placards, one says 'Don't bin us off', another 'The bin proposal is a load of rubbish!'. And they march together to Tooley Street where the council is, and they are chanting and gathering a lot of momentum. The councillors are all cats. They are domesticated and they don't understand wildlife, they don't understand the nature of the fox. They are quite rattled by this protest, and so they hold a cabinet meeting. The cats realise during their meeting that if they get rid of the bins the foxes will eat the mice, and no mice will be left for the cats. So they agree to negotiate, and in the end, the foxes get to keep the bins, and in return, they help keep the city clean and help with recycling.*

The above tale, transcribed from an audio recording taken of the workshop, is a striking example of how the process of creating fairy tales was used by participants to explore fictionalised issues and needs within their community, and how one might engage with these. In this tale, urban foxes take on the role of a marginalised community group within a hyperlocal setting. They are ostracised by the council for their eating habits, which are, it seems, wilfully misunderstood by the council of cats, and presented as coming from malicious intent. The foxes' final protest leads to a deal with the cats in which both parties play their part in protecting the other's priorities – food on the one hand, tidy streets on the other.

Though it may not appear this way at first sight, many common elements of the fairy tale can be observed in this story. While there isn't one exemplary definition of the 'fairy tale' genre, the most well-known stories – such as those collected and edited by Jacob and Wilhelm Grimm – often feature protagonists from disadvantaged or marginalised backgrounds.[22] These protagonists are often faced with a challenge that forces them to venture out into the world and out of their comfort zone; they tackle the challenge, often over the course of several escalating stages, until they finally overcome it at the end of the narrative. Oftentimes, a moral lesson is conveyed through the ending: in the case of our story here, the ending speaks to the value of resistance and community organisation, but also to the value of compromise to facilitate peaceful coexistence.

While these common fairy tale elements are used as a skeletal structure in our tale, certain genre paradigms have also been subverted: there are no magical processes involved – though talking and protesting animals could be seen as magical, they are clearly anthropomorphised here and are, as such, a stand-in for humans – and the generic feudal background of Grimms' fairy tales is replaced with the highly specific one of Peckham's Rye Lane. In many well-known fairy tales, the protagonist is saved or protected by a miraculous higher power – this applies to the Grimms' iteration of *Cinderella*, for example, wherein the protagonist's dead mother acts as a giver of glorious garments that enable her daughter to dance at the prince's balls. In the tale of *Iron John*, the princely protagonist is provided with a horse, armour and weapons by the mysterious Eisenhans, which assist him in overcoming all trials thrown at him, ultimately leading him to riches and a prosperous marriage. In our Peckham fox tale, the protagonists' ultimate success builds on their ability to organise and argue convincingly, rather than on external assistance. There is also no individual hero or heroine in this tale; in fact, the foxes could not have achieved success if they had not acted as a group. In this way, the story also differs from many nineteenth-century examples of the genre in which the plot follows the fate of an individual character.

In *Fairy Tales and the Art of Subversion*, Jack Zipes has shown how fairy tales across history have been used as a fundamentally subversive genre insofar as all fairy and folk tale narratives have been born out of a 'historically explicable desire to overcome oppression and change society'. However, he also rightly points out that most widely traded fairy tales ultimately affirm or only marginally improve pre-existing conditions by largely following similar story patterns, including the well-known trope of the 'happy end' in which the morally good are rewarded and the morally bad are punished.[23] The subversion of central genre paradigms of the fairy tale therefore has a role to play in drawing added attention to certain story elements that disrupt the 'status quo'.

In the above fairy tale, using urban foxes as protagonists has led participants to break the 'social contract' that is the genre of fairy tales in specific ways: the world of magic and supernatural assistance has been replaced with a contemporary, hyperlocal reality, and social struggle is explicitly depicted.[24] This is to say: we are not following the story of an individual fox who, through a mixture of wit, good morals and external help, changes their individual fate to good fortune, but we are witnessing the playing out of systemic social issues between groups in a specific urban setting.

The change in setting is relevant in that it disrupts two further key elements of the 'classic' fairy tale: the hero's departure into a different land and the 'fundamentally acartographical space' within which fairy tales so often take place.[25] Vladimir Propp has defined the hero's venturing into a 'different kingdom' as one of the functions of the fairy tale: the different kingdom is a nameless, usually generic, land in which the challenges facing the hero can take place.[26] In our example fox tale, the adventure remains within the confines of Peckham; in fact, the challenges faced by the foxes concern the imagined future of this area. We encounter buildings and landmarks that participants perceive as central to Peckham's character, such as Rye Lane – the area's main shopping street – and Peckham Levels, a converted parking garage filled with creative studios and meeting spaces. The foxes and cats grapple with the conditions within these spaces, and the nature of their challenges are far from magical: waste management, littering and recycling.

While all of these changes to the fairy tale fabric can be read as subversive, one may well ask, at the same time, why participants chose this setting and these issues for their fairy tale, as they were not prompted to do so in the workshop. Rather than using subversion to disenchant the fairy tale genre, there may be reason to suggest that Peckham and its bin issues are being enchanted by their insertion into a fairy tale. Fairy tales can reframe places and turn them into spaces where the most unlikely events – a form of magic, we might say – can happen. This has been shown by Aslıhan Şenel and Ece Yetim, for instance, in their 'Spatialized Myths' project in which myths and fairy tales were used as a medium to address individual urban experiences and resistance against Gaziantep's gentrification. This process included a rewriting of historical and contemporary myths through a shadow performance put on by participants, which enabled the apparition of 'silence' to emerge as a part of urban life – a seemingly unlikely thing to find in urban spaces.[27] In our fox tale, Peckham is shrouded in the fairy tale form in the same way to enable the protagonists to find and execute unlikely, perhaps even magical, solutions – after all, when has a single protest ever changed a council's mind? At the same time, by being written into a fairy tale narrative, the events in Peckham are endowed with a 'universal' relevance accumulated by this genre due to its longstanding existence and cross-cultural transferability.[28]

This is true especially with regards to the social struggles described in the tale. The fairy tale genre is used here by participants to outline the dynamics of a social struggle without pointing towards human parties that could correspond with the animal actors. Certain aspects of this struggle are heightened and emphasised in a comical way, such as the foxes' carrying of placards with witty puns. Other aspects, however, appear more pronounced, even absurd, when acted out by animals within a fairy tale framework. The fact that everyday citizens, represented by the urban foxes, and council members, represented by the cats, are depicted as different species gives some insight into views on political representation and participation present within this group of writers. It appears strange that a species with entirely different dietary needs and preferences would be elected to represent a community in which urban foxes form a significant part of the population. The cats are 'domesticated' and 'do not understand wildlife', meaning they are ill-equipped to understand the needs of at least one significant part of their borough's population. The conflict between foxes and cats also appears grossly imbalanced not only in terms of power structures, but also regarding their respective demands within the 'hierarchy of needs'[29] – the foxes' food source is being threatened due to what is, presumably, a need for tidiness on Peckham's streets. Viewing all of these aspects together, we can see how the fairy tale form and its fantastical elements – in this case anthropomorphised animals – were used by participants to explore aspects of social struggles present at the level of local government; at the same time, this tale provides a hopeful outlook on community action which aligns with Jeannine Blackwell's outlook on fairy tales as a fundamentally utopian medium.

This utopian drive comes not only from the positive action depicted in the tale, but from reading its creation as an empowered act of placemaking. Historically, fairy tales have played an important role in shaping the identities of 'places' as defined by Doreen Massey, who writes that as opposed to spaces, places are 'always constructed out of articulations of social relations which are not only internal but which link to elsewhere'.[30] For Massey, 'elsewhere' constitutes the global as opposed to the local, both of which contribute contesting interpretations of a landscape's past towards a 'place', a conglomerate of stories relating to a space.[31] In the particular case of the fairy tale, we may also view these stories as iterations of 'elsewhere': while not historic documents, fairy tales have nevertheless been traded as culturally 'authentic' tales that have tangibly changed the perceived identity of many places, including cities – one famous example being the German city of Hamelin, where the tale of the notorious Pied Piper is set. By drawing on and subverting the fairy tale tradition, the collaborative authors of our fox tale are thus intervening in the cultural and historical 'constitution of the present', adding a storied concept to Peckham's conglomerate of ever-developing interpretations that make up a place.[32]

Navigating difficult conversations through the fairy tale

> *In the Kingdom of Southwark, in the Hamlet of Peckham, is where our story is set. As the sun came up one morning, the geese of Goose Green decided to take Fox Kennel Hill for themselves. After a successful breeding season, they needed space for their golden eggs. They had already successfully taken Peckham Rye Park without any trouble from the poor pigeons, robins, and blue tits. The foxes had always lived peacefully on Fox Kennel Hill, though these days they were free not to live in kennels. Clever and handsome, they spent their days reading and beautifying, generally being kind to their community and helping the less fortunate. Geese on the other hand were greedy and kept to themselves, wanting land for their golden eggs. The foxes come up with a plan to capture the geese as they try to take Fox Kennel Hill. They wonder whether to eat them, but instead, a council meeting of all the animals is held, presided over by the owl. The decision is made that the foxes keep Fox Kennel Hill, the geese get Goose Green, and any excess eggs get divided out.*

In this section, I will focus on fairy tales as a means of facilitating collaborative engagement with difficult and controversial subjects. The above tale carries significant social subtext: the geese of Peckham are rapidly expanding their territory with the help of their golden eggs, displacing smaller local species such as robins, pigeons and blue tits. The foxes, threatened with a similar fate, resort to capturing the geese and are faced with the decision of whether to eradicate them by eating them. The resolution is not dissimilar to that of the previous tale: a council meeting is held, and an agreement is reached which involves the assignment of specific plots of land to different species and what is, in essence, the destruction of 'excess' goose eggs to curb the uncontrolled spread of these birds.

In this tale, we may read the events taking place as signifying a variety of themes and issues. Within the south-east London context of the story, the geese may stand for the societal forces of gentrification, foreign investment or, in a more problematic reading, members of a specific ethnic group. The geese's targeted spreading of eggs may remind us of the 'Great Replacement' conspiracy theory proliferated by far-right groups across Europe and the US which, in confluence with the 'Eurabia' conspiracy theory, predicts an Islamic takeover of Europe through, among other things, the purchase of property and high birth rates.[33] Indeed, all of these aspects, including the aforementioned conspiracy theories, were discussed as part of the group's writing process, as I was able to glean from my workshop observations and recordings.

Although 'Retelling the Urban Fox' did not include plans for a wider publication of the tales beyond an academic context, I found myself feeling alarmed at the emergence and likely inclusion of potentially discriminating narratives in the fairy tales produced during the project. Over the course of history, fairy tales have been used as means of conveying and masking political messaging in equal measure. For example, the Nazi regime in Germany used fairy tales and mythology liberally to indoctrinate both children and adults with national socialist propaganda,[34] and the Soviet Union spread communist propaganda in the same way.[35] This form of fairy tale usage is not confined to the past; Ashton Kingdon, in her recently published work *The World White Web*, shows how contemporary propaganda shares structural similarities with historical representations of oppressed groups and describes how the far right have co-opted normative culture, including fairy and folk tales, to conceal racialised messages.[36] Fairy tales lend themselves to such appropriation due to a variety of factors, including their alleged familiarity and simplicity, and the adaptability of the symbolism used in these stories. In essence, the usage of fairy tales for ideological means is so historically engrained and widespread that participants may not have been consciously producing a tale along such lines, but merely reproducing or imitating stories they had read before.

However, as I overheard this group during their work and later listened to workshop recordings, a much more nuanced understanding of their process presented itself. The group members actively – and sometimes quite heatedly – discussed, for example, the notion of allegedly high Muslim birth rates indirectly through their storytelling process by disagreeing on whether or not the element of the golden eggs should be included. The representation of the foxes in the story was another source of difference across the group, as participants disagreed on which activities should mark them as the positively depicted protagonists of the story. Some felt that 'reading' and 'beautifying' shouldn't be seen as markers of positive behaviour and were, in fact, quite 'middle-class' behaviours. In this way, the discussions had between group members gestured towards differing views not only on diversity within the local community, but also on gentrification and to what extent the middle class should be depicted as positive.

Both the 'product' and the process surrounding this fairy tale raise several important points for reflection. On the one hand, this anecdote may lead us to think about the potential of collaborative storytelling for addressing and discussing sensitive topics such as race and class, specifically in groups wherein participants may have differing opinions. When the group presented its fairy tale at the end of the workshop, participants, despite having previously been involved in a somewhat heated discussion, remained relaxed around and supportive of each other; this could be seen in their body language as well as in the way they recounted their experience of the workshop afterwards. On the other hand, some participant reflections suggested that writing in the fairy tale genre may have drawn out and encouraged a binary 'good versus evil' narrative such as the one produced by the group:

> [. . .] had we been asked to write about humans, I think you would have got much more specific and therefore less revealing stories. For example, I cannot imagine a participant so boldly telling a story about humans having too many babies and forcing out the local indigenous population, even though this was absolutely the moral of the aforementioned golden eggs story. This psychological displacement onto the fox, along with the childhood connection with

> fairytales perhaps encouraging a feeling of play and whimsy that would otherwise have been absent/inappropriate, and the simple (simplistic?) good-vs-evil requirements of the fairytale genre encouraging broad sweeping narratives, led to a subconscious spillage on our parts that was very interesting to witness.

Did the 'feeling of play and whimsy' and 'psychological displacement' mentioned here facilitate a productive, cross-ideological discussion, or did the fairy tale form merely function as a well-known vehicle that encourages, perhaps even strengthens, pre-existing binary worldviews? The participant's statement that the fairy tale itself encourages 'broad sweeping narratives' should be questioned, given the genre's subversive potential, as explored by participants in the previous tale. Nevertheless, perhaps it should be seen as worrying that some participants so easily and readily latched on to such a simplistic iteration of the fairy tale.

These questions feed into wider discourses of process and product, the relationship between the two, and whether we deem one or the other more important within the context of creative participatory research. The heated discussions within the group in question and their collaborative creative process produced 'emergent knowing' in participants: lasting personal knowledge regarding how their respective voices relate to each other as well as embodied and affective knowledge. In this way, arts-based research such as this project contributes to 'the negotiation of knowledge across voices, and thus carries the promise of radically destabilising traditional knowledge hierarchies', as Louise Phillips, Maria Bee Christensen-Strynø and Lisbeth Frølunde have stated.[37] Inger Lise Oelrich writes on these qualities of storytelling in particular within the context of cross-ideological conversations:

> Storytelling is an eminent way of bringing hidden stories, often difficult stories, into the light of day. [. . .] Storywork exercises strengthen the experience of human connection, creating a common ground between people who normally do not sit together and listen to each other. Storywork addresses the growing erosion of social cohesion and sense of belonging that are at the roots of much personal suffering, conflict and violence today.[38]

While Phillips, Christensen-Strynø and Frølunde discuss 'traditional knowledge hierarchies' with a view towards academic knowledge and impact, we might use their thinking as a lens that helps us read Oelrich's writing as a call to destabilise social knowledge hierarchies: to replace the hierarchies of who 'sits together' with the emergent knowings that result from connection. There are no guaranteed or necessarily tangible 'outputs' from this knowing. Applying outcome-oriented research methods to measure the 'impact' of the conversations between participants on their respective ideologies would mean funnelling emergent knowing into a system interested only in pre-determined criteria of success. Particularly when faced with sensitive or controversial issues, this uncontrollable quality of emergent knowing can be very unsettling for researchers and participants alike. Nevertheless, the importance of creating spaces in which emergent knowing can arise is becoming increasingly evident in times of ever-deepening digital silos, societal divides and radicalisation. Emergent knowing can foster empathy and bridge divides specifically *because* it creates awareness and experiential knowledge without demanding pre-determined actions as a result. The specifics of the fairy tale – or lack thereof, narratologically speaking – make this genre an especially valuable one for creating this kind of knowledge. I have already addressed how fairy tale symbolism can liberate stories from the constraints of realism and, at the same time, enchant realist locations and events, imbuing them with a universal relevance. These attributes of the genre can be useful when bringing people together who 'do not normally sit together', as they temporarily remove those specifics from stories which so often – as we see in news and social media landscapes – are used as part of narratives of otherness and separation. Therefore, exploring more deeply the potential of the fairy tale in engaging humans with different viewpoints that may be uncomfortable to them could prove a valuable future angle for research, both from a fairy tale studies and a social sciences perspective.

Having said this, I must also admit that I did not foresee the emergence of sensitive topics such as conspiracy theories in the workshop, given its intended focus on participants' views on urban foxes. I was, therefore, not ideally prepared to account for the potential harmful consequences of the collaborative process or product of this group. There is no doubt that the tale presented by these participants carries symbolisms that may have caused upset to certain groups, including some of the participants involved in this research project. For potential future iterations of this project, I would set up the workshop explicitly for cross-ideological dialogue through fairy tales; this would involve implementing more rigorous safeguards against discriminatory use of language and symbolism, and explicit invitations to participants to reflect on the binary of 'good' and 'evil' that some fairy tales can establish.

Conclusion and outlook: fairy tales, literature and the potential for change

'Retelling the Urban Fox' initially set out to explore the impact of collaborative storytelling on participants' perceptions of urban foxes. While some insights on this were gained that have not been addressed here, it was even more interesting to observe how the creative methods used toppled my more positivist, linear research framing and encouraged me to showcase instead the creative processes participants developed during the workshop. While proponents of creative research methods, such as Patricia Leavy, have been arguing for years that these approaches can foster more diverse, unexpected and ethical research insights,[39] it is still worth reflecting on the specifics that led to this transformation in focus. For one thing, participatory research requires an ever-open and flexible mindset if one is to honour the emergent knowledge produced by participants during a creative process. In this case, participant engagement with the writing process was lively, engaged, sometimes divisive – in short, it exposed fairy tales as a source of emergent knowing which would have been foolish to ignore.

In addition, I believe that being a literary researcher by training allowed me to assess the fairy tales produced by participants as texts in their own right, rather than merely as vehicles for potential attitudinal change. The process of close reading is itself, in many ways, an open-ended and creative process which, in conjunction with my observational data, led me beyond the boundaries of pre-determined outcomes. Having little previous training in social science methods was, in this context, quite liberating, as it felt possible to shift my focus in this way without feeling like I was 'doing it wrong'. It was interesting to see how, in line with the focus of the project, my internal stance also changed: from seeing myself as a literary researcher struggling to be a social scientist, to seeing the value literary research had to add to social sciences methods. Having a shifting research framework and question comes with its challenges, particularly with regards to preparedness in situations like those that arose in the context of the second tale presented here. Despite these difficulties, for the reasons outlined in this chapter I can only recommend approaching a creative research project from a place of curiosity, rather than absolute preparedness.

Having thus shifted in its focus of inquiry, this chapter has explored how collaborative storytelling – creating fairy tales, in this case on urban foxes – can evoke reflective and exploratory creative processes in participant groups which find expression in their literary creations. I have demonstrated how participants played with central elements of the fairy tale genre by abiding by and subverting them to explore issues of social struggle within Peckham, while at the same time upholding the genre's utopian function. The fairy tale was used by participants to engage with sensitive topics such as gentrification and conspiracy theories; here, I highlighted how collaborative storytelling can act as a process-oriented space for inter-ideological exchange, though care needs to be taken as to how to safeguard such spaces appropriately.

This project can serve as a rich point of departure into further research regarding the potential role of collaborative fairy tale creation for change. Much research involving fairy tale creation is focused on children and their development; while this avenue is, of course, important, 'Retelling the Urban Fox' has shown the many possible uses of fairy tales in creative research with adults.[40] The analysis and reflections here encourage us to perform further studies in which participants reflect more deeply on their relationships with the fairy tale genre and its connection to place: what does it mean to write a fairy tale based in a specific neighbourhood, a specific city? How does this change how we think about the genre, and how does the genre change how we think about the space? There may also be rich potential for larger-scale studies with adults in which participants with differing political viewpoints are brought together with the aim of co-creating fairy tales. In our current divisive and divided times, exploring the fairy tale as a resource for social healing would seem particularly pertinent. While collaborative processes are never as simple as creating empathy or changing viewpoints overnight, it would be interesting to see the changes in participants' attitudes over time, perhaps over a series of workshops. As outlined previously, such a project would also need to encourage participants to think more critically about how fairy tales can entrench dichotomic thinking and perhaps explore specifically subversive modes of fairy tale production.

Notes

1 Richard Inger, and others, 'Ecological Role of Vertebrate Scavengers in Urban Ecosystems in the UK', *Ecology and Evolution*, 6.19 (2016), pp. 7015–23; Ian Douglas and David Goode, 'Urban Natural Histories to Urban Ecologies: The Growth of the Study of Urban Nature', in *The Routledge Handbook of Urban Ecology*, ed. by Ian Douglas and others (Routledge, 2010), pp. 74–83.

2 Sandra E. Baker, and others, 'Not in My Backyard: Public Perceptions of Wildlife and "Pest Control" in and Around UK Homes, and Local Authority "Pest Control"', *Animals*, 10.2 (2020), p. 222.

3 'Deadly Urban Fox Disease Spreading to Dogs', *Daily Mail*, 6 April 2011; 'Urban Foxes Are a Health Hazard, and We Should Not Be Told to Feed Them', *Daily Telegraph*, 8 October 2013.

4 Peter Crowden, 'If These Disease-Ridden Vermin KILL a Child Next Time, Blame the Fools Who Think They're Cuddly', *Daily Mail*, 11 February 2013; Kate Stewart and Matthew Cole, 'The Creation of a Killer Species: Cultural Rupture in Representations of "Urban Foxes" in UK Newspapers', in *Critical Animal and Media Studies: Communication for Nonhuman Animal Advocacy*, ed. by Núria Almiron, Matthew Cole, and Carrie P. Freeman (Routledge, 2015), pp. 124–7; Angela Cassidy and Brett Mills, '"Fox Tots Attack Shock": Urban Foxes, Mass Media and Spatial Boundaries', *Environmental Communication*, 6.4 (2012), pp. 494–511.

5 'Fox Attack Leaves 1 in 5 Afraid of Wildlife', *Daily Telegraph*, 2 September 2010.

6 Jeannine Blackwell, 'Fractured Fairy Tales: German Women Authors and the Grimm Tradition', *The Germanic Review*, 62.4 (1987), pp. 162–74 (p. 163).

7 Marek Oziewicz, 'Introduction: The Choice We Have in the Stories We Tell . . .', in *Fantasy and Myth in the Anthropocene: Imagining Futures and Dreaming Hope in Literature and Media*, ed. by Marek Oziewicz, Brian Attebery, and Tereza Dědinová (Bloomsbury Publishing, 2022), pp. 1–12 (p. 4).

8 Blackwell, 'Fractured Fairy Tales', p. 163; Dorothy Noyes, 'Fairy-Tale Economics: Scarcity, Risk, Choice', *Narrative Culture*, 2.1 (2015), pp. 1–26 (pp. 2–3).

9 Jack Zipes, 'The Meaning of Fairy Tale within the Evolution of Culture', *Marvels & Tales*, 25.2 (2011), pp. 221–43 (p. 238).

10 See, for instance, Disney's recent remake of *Snow White* (2025), the fairy tales videogames *Cinders* (2014) and *The Wolf Among Us* (2013), or Ry Herman's *This Princess Kills Monsters* (2025).

11 Maria Tatar, 'Why Fairy Tales Matter: The Performative and the Transformative', *Western Folklore*, 69.1 (2010), pp. 55–64 (p. 56).

12 Jack Zipes, *The Irresistible Fairy Tale: The Cultural and Social History of a Genre* (Princeton University Press, 2012), pp. 25–8.

13 Vivian Labrie, 'Activism', in *The Routledge Companion of Media and Fairy-Tale Studies*, ed. by Pauline Greenhill and others (Routledge, 2018), pp. 93–102 (p. 93).

14 Rachel Harcourt, and others, 'Envisioning Climate Change Adaptation Futures Using Storytelling Workshops', *Sustainability*, 13.12 (2021), p. 6630; Elise Talgorn and Helle Ullerup, 'Invoking "Empathy for the Planet" through Participatory Ecological Storytelling: From Human-Centered to Planet-Centered Design', *Sustainability*, 15.10 (2023), p. 7794.

15 Sea Rotmann, '"Once Upon a Time . . ." Eliciting Energy and Behaviour Change Stories Using a Fairy Tale Story Spine', *Energy Research & Social Science*, 31 (2017), pp. 303–10.

16 Carolynne Lord, Katherine Ellsworth-Krebs, and Torik Holmes, '"Telling Tales": Communicating UK Energy Research Through Fairy Tale Characters', *Energy Research & Social Science*, 101 (2023), p. 103100.

17 Anja Rekeszus, *German Women Writers' Fairy Tales of the 19th Century: Transcultural Tales, Political Agendas* (De Gruyter, forthcoming 2026).

18 Cate Watson, 'Staking a Small Claim for Fictional Narratives in Social and Educational Research', *Qualitative Research*, 11.4 (2011), pp. 395–408 (p. 399).

19 For information on Elizabeth's art installations, projects and publications, please consult her website, https://elizabethdearnley.co.uk [accessed 17 June 2026].

20 Watson, 'Staking a Small Claim', p. 399.

21 'Retelling the Urban Fox' was executed during my time as an Inclusion, Participation and Engagement (IPE) Fellow at the School of Advanced Study. Concentrating the project within a single borough fulfilled the scheme's aim and ethos to increase community participation in and engagement with research.

22 Marina Warner, *Once Upon a Time: A Short History of Fairy Tale* (Oxford University Press, 2014), p. 76.

23 Jack Zipes, *Fairy Tales and the Art of Subversion* (Routledge, 2012), p. 8.

24 Fredric Jameson, *The Political Unconscious: Narrative as a Socially Symbolic Act* (Cornell University Press, 1981), p. 106.

25 W. F. H. Nicolaisen, 'The Past as Place: Names, Stories, and the Remembered Self', *Folklore*, 102.1 (1991), pp. 3–15 (p. 5).

26 Vladimir Propp, *The Morphology of the Folktale*, trans. by Laurence Scott and ed. by Louis A. Wagner (University of Texas Press, 2003), p. 50.

27 Aslıhan Şenel and Ece Yetim, 'Shadowing Silence: A Spatial Rewriting of Myths and Fairytales', *The February Journal*, 1.2 (2023), pp. 139–60.

28 Jack Zipes, *Why Fairy Tales Stick: The Evolution and Relevance of a Genre* (Routledge, 2006), pp. 41–2.

29 A. H. Maslow, 'A Theory of Human Motivation', *Psychological Review*, 50.4 (1943), pp. 370–96.

30 Doreen Massey, 'Places and Their Pasts', *History Workshop Journal*, 39 (1995), pp. 182–92 (p. 186).

31 Doreen Massey, *For Space* (Sage Publications, 2005), p. 265.

32 Massey, 'Places', p. 190.

33 Eirikur Bergmann, *Conspiracy & Populism* (Palgrave Macmillan, 2018), pp. 123–49.

34 See, for instance, Christa Kamenetsky, *Children's Literature in Hitler's Germany: The Cultural Policy of National Socialism* (Ohio University Press, 1984), pp. 91–104; Judith K. Proud 'Occupying the Imagination: Fairy Stories and Propaganda in Vichy France', *The Lion and the Unicorn*, 22.1 (1998), pp. 18–43.

35 Maria Nikolajeva, 'Fairy Tales in Society's Service', *Marvels & Tales*, 16.2 (2002), pp. 171–87.

36 Ashton Kingdon, *The World White Web: Uncovering the Hidden Meanings of Online Far-Right Propaganda* (Palgrave Macmillan, 2024), pp. 143–75.

37 Louise Phillips, Maria Bee Christensen-Strynø, and Lisbeth Frølunde, 'Arts-Based Co-Production in Participatory Research: Harnessing Creativity in the Tension Between Process and Product', *Evidence & Policy*, 18.2 (2022), pp. 391–411 (pp. 407–8).

38 Inger Lise Oelrich, 'Seeking a Common Ground: Storytelling and Social Healing', in *Routledge International Handbook of Therapeutic Stories and Storytelling*, ed. by Clive Holmwood, Sue Jennings, and Sharon Jacksties (Routledge, 2022), pp. 204–12 (p. 204).

39 Patricia Leavy, *Method Meets Arts: Arts-Based Research Practice* (Guilford Press, 2020), pp. 10–13; see also Sophie Woodward, Harriet Shortt, and Su-Ming Khoo, 'Cultivating Connections, Disrupting Boundaries: Introducing the Journal of Creative Research Methods', *Journal of Creative Research Methods*, 1.1 (2025), pp. 2–17 (pp. 2–5).

40 See, for instance, Eliot Schrefer, 'Where is the Place for Seagrass and Weevils in Children's Literature?', in *Fantasy and Myth in the Anthropocene: Imagining Futures and Dreaming Hope in Literature and Media*, ed. by Marek Oziewicz, Brian Attebery, and Tereza Dědinová (Bloomsbury Publishing, 2022), p. 88; Kristin Wardetzky, 'The Structure and Interpretation of Fairy Tales Composed by Children', *The Journal of American Folklore*, 103.408 (1990), pp. 157–76; María Palmira Massi and Adriana Marcela Benvenuto, 'Using Fairy Tales to Develop Reading and Writing Skills', *The CATESOL Journal*, 13.1 (2001), pp. 161–72.

References

Baker, Sandra E., and others, 'Not in My Backyard: Public Perceptions of Wildlife and "Pest Control" in and Around UK Homes, and Local Authority "Pest Control"', *Animals*, 10.2 (2020), p. 222

Bergmann, Eirikur, *Conspiracy & Populism* (Palgrave Macmillan, 2018)

Blackwell, Jeannine, 'Fractured Fairy Tales: German Women Authors and the Grimm Tradition', *The Germanic Review*, 62.4 (1987), pp. 162–74

Cassidy, Angela, and Brett Mills, '"Fox Tots Attack Shock": Urban Foxes, Mass Media and Spatial Boundaries', *Environmental Communication*, 6.4 (2012), pp. 494–511

Crowden, Peter, 'If These Disease-Ridden Vermin KILL a Child Next Time, Blame the Fools Who Think They're Cuddly', *Daily Mail*, 11 February 2013

Daily Mail, 'Deadly Urban Fox Disease Spreading to Dogs', 6 April 2011

Daily Telegraph, 'Urban Foxes Are a Health Hazard, and We Should Not Be Told to Feed Them', 8 October 2013

Douglas, Ian, and David Goode, 'Urban Natural Histories to Urban Ecologies: The Growth of the Study of Urban Nature', in *The Routledge Handbook of Urban Ecology*, ed. by Ian Douglas and others (Routledge, 2010), pp. 74–83

Gray, Louise, 'Fox Attack Leaves 1 in 5 Afraid of Wildlife', *Daily Telegraph*, 2 September 2010

Harcourt, Rachel, and others, 'Envisioning Climate Change Adaptation Futures Using Storytelling Workshops', *Sustainability*, 13.12 (2021), p. 6630

Inger, Richard, and others, 'Ecological Role of Vertebrate Scavengers in Urban Ecosystems in the UK', *Ecology and Evolution*, 6.19 (2016), pp. 7015–23

Jameson, Fredric, *The Political Unconscious: Narrative as a Socially Symbolic Act* (Cornell University Press, 1981)

Kamenetsky, Christa, *Children's Literature in Hitler's Germany: The Cultural Policy of National Socialism* (Ohio University Press, 1984)

Kingdon, Ashton, *The World White Web: Uncovering the Hidden Meanings of Online Far-Right Propaganda* (Palgrave Macmillan, 2024)

Labrie, Vivian, 'Activism', in *The Routledge Companion of Media and Fairy-Tale Studies*, ed. by Pauline Greenhill and others (Routledge, 2018), pp. 93–102

Leavy, Patricia, *Method Meets Arts: Arts-Based Research Practice* (Guilford Press, 2020)

Lord, Carolynne, Katherine Ellsworth-Krebs, and Torik Holmes, '"Telling Tales": Communicating UK Energy Research Through Fairy Tale Characters', *Energy Research & Social Science*, 101 (2023), p. 103100

Maslow, A. H., 'A Theory of Human Motivation', *Psychological Review*, 50.4 (1943), pp. 370–96

Massey, Doreen, *For Space* (Sage Publications, 2005)

Massey, Doreen, 'Places and Their Pasts', *History Workshop Journal*, 39 (1995), pp. 182–92

Massi, María Palmira, and Adriana Marcela Benvenuto, 'Using Fairy Tales to Develop Reading and Writing Skills', *The CATESOL Journal*, 13.1 (2001), pp. 161–72

Nicolaisen, W. F. H., 'The Past as Place: Names, Stories, and the Remembered Self', *Folklore*, 102.1 (1991), pp. 3–15

Nikolajeva, Maria, 'Fairy Tales in Society's Service', *Marvels & Tales*, 16.2 (2002), pp. 171–87

Noyes, Dorothy, 'Fairy-Tale Economics: Scarcity, Risk, Choice', *Narrative Culture*, 2.1 (2015), pp. 1–26

Oelrich, Inger Lise, 'Seeking a Common Ground: Storytelling and Social Healing', in *Routledge International Handbook of Therapeutic Stories and Storytelling*, ed. by Clive Holmwood, Sue Jennings, and Sharon Jacksties (Routledge, 2022), pp. 204–12

Oziewicz, Marek, 'Introduction: The Choice We Have in the Stories We Tell . . .', in *Fantasy and Myth in the Anthropocene: Imagining Futures and Dreaming Hope in Literature and Media*, ed. by Marek Oziewicz, Brian Atterby, and Tereza Dědinová (Bloomsbury Publishing, 2022), pp. 1–12

Phillips, Louise, Maria Bee Christensen-Strynø, and Lisbeth Frølunde, 'Arts-Based Co-Production in Participatory Research: Harnessing Creativity in the Tension Between Process and Product', *Evidence & Policy*, 18.2 (2022), pp. 391–411

Propp, Vladimir, *The Morphology of the Folktale*, trans. by Laurence Scott and ed. by Louis A. Wagner (University of Texas Press, 2003)

Proud, Judith K., 'Occupying the Imagination: Fairy Stories and Propaganda in Vichy France', *The Lion and the Unicorn*, 22.1 (1998), pp. 18–43

Rekeszus, Anja, *German Women Writers' Fairy Tales of the 19th Century: Transcultural Tales, Political Agendas* (De Gruyter, forthcoming 2026)

Rotmann, Sea, '"Once Upon a Time . . ." Eliciting Energy and Behaviour Change Stories Using a Fairy Tale Story Spine', *Energy Research & Social Science*, 31 (2017), pp. 303–10

Schrefer, Eliot, 'Where is the Place for Seagrass and Weevils in Children's Literature?', in *Fantasy and Myth in the Anthropocene*, ed. by Oziewicz, Attebery and Dědinová (Bloomsbury, 2022), p. 88

Şenel, Aslıhan, and Ece Yetim, 'Shadowing Silence: A Spatial Rewriting of Myths and Fairytales', *The February Journal*, 1.2 (2023), pp. 139–60

Stewart, Kate, and Matthew Cole, 'The Creation of a Killer Species: Cultural Rupture in Representations of "Urban Foxes" in UK Newspapers', in *Critical Animal and Media Studies: Communication for Nonhuman Animal Advocacy*, ed. by Núria Almiron, Matthew Cole, and Carrie P. Freeman (Routledge, 2015), pp. 124–7

Talgorn, Elise, and Helle Ullerup, 'Invoking "Empathy for the Planet" through Participatory Ecological Storytelling: From Human-Centered to Planet-Centered Design', *Sustainability*, 15.10 (2023), p. 7794

Tatar, Maria, 'Why Fairy Tales Matter: The Performative and the Transformative', *Western Folklore*, 69.1 (2010), pp. 55–64

Wardetzky, Kristin, 'The Structure and Interpretation of Fairy Tales Composed by Children', *The Journal of American Folklore*, 103.408 (1990), pp. 157–76

Warner, Marina, *Once Upon a Time: A Short History of Fairy Tale* (Oxford University Press, 2014)

Watson, Cate, 'Staking a Small Claim for Fictional Narratives in Social and Educational Research', *Qualitative Research*, 11.4 (2011), pp. 395–408

Woodward, Sophie, Harriet Shortt, and Su-Ming Khoo, 'Cultivating Connections, Disrupting Boundaries: Introducing the Journal of Creative Research Methods', *Journal of Creative Research Methods*, 1.1 (2025), pp. 2–17

Zipes, Jack, *Fairy Tales and the Art of Subversion* (Routledge, 2012)

Zipes, Jack, *The Irresistible Fairy Tale: The Cultural and Social History of a Genre* (Princeton University Press, 2012)

Zipes, Jack, 'The Meaning of Fairy Tale within the Evolution of Culture', *Marvels & Tales*, 25.2 (2011), pp. 221–43

Zipes, Jack, *Why Fairy Tales Stick: The Evolution and Relevance of a Genre* (Routledge, 2006)

Index

Names commencing 'Mc' appear in the index as if spelt 'Mac'.

www.ingramcontent.com/pod-product-compliance
Lightning Source LLC
LaVergne TN
LVHW050610260926
848792LV00010B/53
* 9 7 8 1 9 1 1 5 0 7 7 9 6 *